TH

D0285725

Every intelligent citizen should have some understanding of English Law, and the main purpose of this book is to introduce the man or woman with no legal training to its fundamental principles. Among the topics discussed are the history of English Law, constitutional law, torts, contract, wills and trusts, matrimonial causes, criminal law, evidence and civil procedure, juries, judges and legal aid. Although not intended as a work of reference, it is hoped that, as a bird's-eye view of English Law, this book will be useful to law students just beginning their studies.

TEACH YOURSELF BOOKS

THE LAW

J. Leigh Mellor, LL.B.
of the Inner Temple, Barrister-at-Law

assisted in the preparation of
the fourth edition by

Jill M. Gibson, B.A. (HONS.) (BRISTOL)
of the Middle Temple, Barrister-at-Law

TEACH YOURSELF BOOKS
Hodder and Stoughton

First printed 1955
Fourth edition 1974
Third impression 1976

Copyright © 1966
Hodder and Stoughton Ltd
Copyright © 1974 *edition*
J. Leigh Mellor

ISBN 0 340 18262 8

Printed and bound in England
for Hodder and Stoughton Paperbacks, a division of Hodder
and Stoughton Ltd, Mill Road, Dunton Green, Sevenoaks, Kent
by Richard Clay (The Chaucer Press) Ltd, Bungay, Suffolk

Foreword

The main purpose of this book is to introduce the man or woman without legal learning to the fundamental principles of English Law. No intelligent citizen should be without this basic knowledge. Not only will it enable him to understand more of what is taking place about him (a surprisingly high proportion of space in newspapers is taken up with reports of court proceedings), but it may help him to avoid some of the thorny thickets of the law that await the unwary. It is not meant as a work of reference, however, and still less as a substitute for a solicitor.

The lawyer, it is to be feared, will find imperfections in this work. So much has had to be omitted in the interests of space. I hope, however, that law students just commencing their studies may find it useful as a bird's-eye view. With this in mind, I have added a table of cases and statutes.

Abbreviations have been avoided as much as possible. A short table of these is printed on page viii.

The law stated in the fourth edition of this book is that in force on the July 31st, 1973, generally speaking.

I am grateful to my friends in the legal profession for their advice and encouragement. In particular I am deeply indebted to Miss J. M. Gibson for the very valuable help she has given in preparing the fourth edition. Here I must repeat my expression of gratitude to Mr. Mark Cursham for the work he did on the third edition. Thanks are also due to the publishers. Finally, I am happy to acknowledge the invaluable help of my wife. She has devoted great time and trouble to the preparation of the MS. and made many helpful suggestions.

J. Leigh Mellor

Contents

List of Abbreviations

A.E.A.   Administration of Estates Act
L.P.A.   Law of Property Act
Q.B.D.   Queen's Bench Division

Law Reports

All E.R.   All England Reports
W.L.R.   Weekly Law Reports
L.J.   *Law Journal* Reports
T.L.R.   *Times* Law Reports
L.T.   *Law Times* Reports
And see page 23.

Table of Cases

Table of Statutes

1 History

What is meant by law? There are several meanings to the word. There are natural laws, such as the law of gravity. Certain causes produce certain effects in given circumstances. The apple that fell in Newton's garden had no option, however; it obeyed the law of gravity because it was powerless to do otherwise. Obviously these are not the laws we are concerned with here; they are the province of scientists, not lawyers. Moral laws are nearer to the point. If we choose to disobey them, we may have to answer for it hereafter, and we may incur the disapproval of the righteous. Unless the moral laws are also part of the laws of the country, however, we shall suffer no temporal sanctions. If I fail to honour my father and mother, I have broken the fifth commandment, but I have not broken the law. If, however, I break the eighth commandment and steal, I can be prosecuted in a criminal court and sued in a civil court. If I break the seventh commandment, I can be proceeded against under the matrimonial law of the country.

There is a great deal more to the law than the application of principles of morality. Convenience, custom and political thought all play their part in its formation. The finished product has to be comprehensive yet certain, firm yet fair. In trying to achieve these aims, it becomes complex.

Having seen what the law is not, let us attempt to define what it is. Roughly the law is a collection of rules, binding on specified persons, made and altered only by certain institutions, and enforced by the machinery of the State.

We are concerned to examine a few of the more important of those rules. Our business, let it be made clear at once, is to study the rules as they are, *not* as they might be. If a lawyer is asked why such a result follows in law from a given action, his answer is: Because a particular Statute or Regulation or decision of the Courts says so.

Let us then examine the law as it is. First, however, its history must be touched upon, as it will make the law of today much clearer.

In the Western world today there are countless systems of law, but, broadly speaking, they spring from either of two roots: the

Roman Law or the English Common Law. Our Common Law is a hardy native plant that has germinated and sprung forth abundantly in the United States, in Australia, New Zealand and most of Canada, whereas Scotland, the Continent and South Africa have all absorbed strong doses of Roman Law. It is very curious that the Romans should have left their trace so indelibly on our language and our landscape, yet, for the most part, failed to affect our law. Though the Latin language was, until 1731 even, used in pleadings, and to-day legal text-books are liberally strewn with Latin maxims, the Roman Law exerted only slight influence on English Law, and then via the Canon Law or law of the Church and Admiralty and Mercantile Law. In these, Continental influence was greater, as may be imagined.

The next influence on English Law was the formidable William the Conqueror. Here, though, the changes were not so much substantive as in administration. The Normans were, above all, excellent Civil Servants. The greatest example of Norman method is the Domesday Book, compiled for tax purposes. It listed every parcel of land in the country, with details of its ownership. This helped William in one of his aims—more centralised control of the Government. For an essential part of government was the feudal pyramid. It meant that, directly or indirectly, every landowner held his land from the King. In feudal times this was of great importance, and has had considerable affect on the present land law.

Henry II was the first great lawyer among the English kings. To him we owe the Assizes and the jury system as a regular mode of trial. His reign opened, however, with a bitter dispute over the rights of the Church Courts and the King's Courts. A compromise was reached in the Constitutions of Clarendon, in 1164, which restricted the Church Courts' power in many ways; for example, an appeal to Rome from the Church Courts was not possible without the King's permission.[1]

Benefit of Clergy was a source of great contention between the King's and the Church Courts. (This was the right of anyone in Holy Orders, and accused of a crime, to be tried by the Church Courts.) As most felonies were punishable with death in the King's Courts and only by very mild penalties in the Church Courts, it was a great advantage to be a clerk.[2] Henry proposed that the convicted

[1] Appeal to Rome was abolished altogether in the reign of Henry VIII.
[2] 'Clerk'—clergyman.

'Criminous clerks' should be remitted to the King's Courts for punishment, but he had to give way on this point after the murder of Becket. Benefit of Clergy became a most peculiar institution. Anyone who could read or even repeat parrotwise a verse in the 51st Psalm (known aptly as the Neck Verse) could claim the benefit of clergy. In theory it could be claimed only once, and in 1490 this was ensured by branding on the first offence. Its importance was diminished by statutes making the important felonies non-clergiable, but it survived in theory until 1827.

'Assizes' comes from the French *s'asseoir*, 'to sit'. Up to the beginning of 1972, when it was abolished in the Courts Act, 1971, it meant the court at which judges of the High Court on circuit tried civil and criminal cases. But it also meant a legislative enactment, e.g. the Assize of Clarendon, or a form of action.

The system of sending the judge round the country to take the assizes was preceded by the General Eyre. Several judges and magnates were commissioned to tour the country and enquire into all administrative matters in each district. As they went, they tried all the cases in the district. These Eyres became very unpopular, as they were used for oppressive tax-gathering. It is recorded that once the inhabitants of Cornwall fled to the woods to avoid the examination of the Eyre. It gradually fell into disuse because it was unpopular and cumbersome, and the system grew up of sending itinerant justices to try the civil actions set up by Henry II, known as Assizes, and to hear and determine criminal causes and try the suspected persons in gaol. Until the Courts Act, 1971, took effect the Commissions of Assize judges were of 'oyer and terminer'[1] and general gaol delivery. At first, these travelling justices were often laymen, but soon the Assizes were taken only by the King's justices or commissioners, who were lawyers.

The title to land was originally tried by battle, It took place between champions, who made a profession of it in many cases. Some of them had standing retainers for large landowners. This somewhat unsatisfactory procedure was attacked by Henry II, who allowed trial by jury instead, if the defendant wished. In 1166 he introduced new forms of action, called the Petty Assizes, also involving jury trial. These are the origins of the civil jury. The criminal jury had a more tortuous career. The Grand Juries, finally abolished in 1948, were the first criminal juries. They had to present the criminals in

[1] 'to hear and determine'.

their district to the itinerant justices for trial. In the early Middle Ages the actual mode of proof of the offence might take one of three forms: battle, compurgation or ordeal.

Battle, in criminal cases, was a fight to the death between accuser and accused in person, not the relatively polite encounter between champions found in civil matters. It was not abolished until 1819, and then hurriedly, as a man accused of murder had dramatically flung down his glove and called on his accuser to fight (*Ashford* v. *Thornton*).[1]

Compurgation, or wager of law, occurred when the accused swore on oath he was not guilty and found twelve men who would swear he was telling the truth. In that event he was acquitted.

The ordeal was originally performed under ecclesiastical supervision. Ordeal by fire consisted of carrying a hot iron a certain distance. The accused's hand was then bound, and if not healthily healing within three days he was guilty. Or he might have to pick a stone from a vessel of boiling water and his guilt depended on whether his hand healed. Perhaps the most unfortunate ordeal was where the accused was bound and lowered into a tank of water. If he sank he was innocent, but if he floated, guilty! The ordeal was condemned by Pope Innocent III in 1215 and soon fell into disuse.

Another method of trial became essential, and gradually jurors to try the accused were chosen from among those presenting them. At first, they merely tried whether the accusation was made through hate and spite, and it was a short step from this to the trial of the offence itself. In its early days the jury would try the offender, taking its personal knowledge of the facts into account. Jurors took some time to settle down to twelve, at first varying greatly in number.

In the early days of the jury an accused could choose 'to put himself on his country', as jury trial was called, or be tried by ordeal. As the jury system became more firmly established, trial by jury became compulsory, and prisoners who refused to accept it were tortured by weights being placed on them until they capitulated—the '*peine forte et dure*'. One man was crushed to death rather than submit to jury trial.

If juries gave an irresponsible verdict, they were tried by a larger jury. If the second jury found the first guilty, they were severely punished. Such a process was called attaint.

In Stuart times jurors were sometimes fined for bringing a verdict

[1] B. & Ald. 405.

of which the judge disapproved. This was finally stopped by the decision in *Bushell's*[1] case in 1670. A tablet in the Central Criminal Court (the Old Bailey) commemorates this celebrated trial:

'Near this Site

> William Penn and William Mead
> were tried in 1670
> for preaching to the unlawful assembly
> in Grace Church Street.
> This tablet commemorates

The courage and endurance of the Jury, Thos Vere, Edward Bushell and ten others who refused to give a verdict against them although locked up without food for two nights and were fined for their final verdict of Not Guilty.

The case of these Jurymen was reviewed on a writ of Habeas Corpus, and Chief Justice Vaughan delivered the opinion of the Court which established the Right of Juries to give their Verdict according to their convictions.'

Jurymen were formerly always locked up without 'meate or drinke, fire or candle' while they considered their verdict. In Bushell's case, it is said they were denied even the elementary necessity of a chamber pot. Jurymen who tried to stay the pangs of hunger by covertly taking food with them when they retired, were fined in one case: 'After the Jurors had been locked up together some time, the officer who attended them, being surprized at their delay in agreeing a Verdict, searched them and found Figs in the Pockets of three of them and Pippins in the Pockets of two others. This being represented to the Judge, the three—who confessed the having eaten of the Figs—were fined four Pounds each, and the other two—notwithstanding they declared on Oath that they had not eaten of the Pippins—were fined forty shillings each; but the Verdict was upon a Conference with the Judges of the other Courts holden to be good.'

Gradually the rigours of the Common Law rules were relaxed. In 1870[2] a statute was passed which allowed juries fire and refreshment. The modern law as to juries is discussed in a later chapter.

We have seen that King Henry II was a great law-giver. He was succeeded by the martial Richard I in 1189. He was followed by the

---

[1] 6 St. Tr. 999.   [2] Juries Act, 1870.

unhappy John and the enormous reign of Henry III, so it was not until 1272 that England again had a great lawyer upon the throne. Then came Edward I, and with him much important legislation. He has been called the English Justinian, after the Roman Emperor of that name who produced a monumental code. Besides tidying and arranging, he built to last, for several of his enactments are even today important parts of our law. Like his predecessor, Henry II, he was determined that the King's Courts were to be the dominant tribunals of the land. The Statute of Gloucester of 1278, as interpreted, dealt a lethal blow at the local courts by providing that actions involving 40s. or over were to be taken to the King's Courts. As will be seen later, the resulting inconvenience of over-centralisation was checked by the Statute of Westminster II, but though actions might be tried far from Westminster it was the King's justices that tried them.

The statute ranging widest over the law was the Statute of Westminster II.[1] One of its provisions greatly affected the growth of the Court of Chancery. The Chancellor was at first the King's secretary and his importance grew rapidly. From his department writs issued. For each cause of action there was a separate writ. Obviously the person who issued writs would have power to alter the law itself if he could invent new writs. This was forbidden by the Provisions of Oxford in 1258, as the barons recognised this great power of the Chancellor and feared it. No writ was to be issued of a type which had not been issued before. This provision would have hopelessly stunted the growth of the Common Law. Edward I saw this, and the clause '*In Consimili Casu*' (in like case) modified the law. In future the Chancellor could issue writs for cases not merely identical with but similar to those for which writs had obtained before.

Another important clause, '*nisi prius*', did much to aid the civil litigant. By 1285 the local courts were in a state of decline and the King's Courts had settled at Westminster. To avoid the hazards and expense of a journey to the King's Courts it was provided that civil cases in the different counties through which the Assize judges travelled should be heard at Westminster only 'unless before' (*nisi prius*) the Justices of Assize should not arrive to try it locally. Assizes were to be held three times a year, and the circuits of the judges were fixed.

[1] In early times legislative enactments frequently were known by the name of the place at which they were made.

The right of appeal is now universally recognised as necessary. In early English Law, however, it was a clumsy and technical process. Proceedings could be reviewed in a higher court only by alleging an error on the face of the record. This would not occur often. The Statute of Westminster II therefore provided that a party might raise a point of law at the trial, and if the judge decided it against him he could compel the judge to seal a writing containing the 'exception'. This document was called a 'Bill of Exceptions' and could be reviewed even though not on the record.

Nowadays, the right to appeal is provided and regulated by Statute and Rules of Court.

Another important statute was the Statute of Wales. Passed in 1284 after the Welsh conquest, it began the assimilation of the law of Wales to that of England.

Edward I's grandson, Edward III, has won more martial glory than legal renown, but in his reign there came into existence in their modern form the justices of the peace. At first their duties were more those of policemen than magistrates. They were to keep the King's peace, to apprehend malefactors and hold them for the King's justices. In 1361 they were given power to try felonies. Sessions of the justices with juries to do this were held four times a year—hence the name Quarter Sessions. Quarter Sessions have now been abolished by the Courts Act, 1971. But as time went on, Parliament created many minor offences—relating to weights and measures, for example—for which jury trial was unnecessary. Hence the statutes creating these offences provided that the justices could try them on their own in a summary way. This is the origin of Petty Sessions. So the justices assumed important judicial powers. In Mary Tudor's reign, statutes provided that they were to examine accused persons with a view to their committal for trial to a higher court. At first it is probable that the justices acted as inquisitors on behalf of the Crown, but this preliminary investigation has changed its character in the course of years. Today the justices hold the scales between the Crown and accused in exactly the same way, when deciding whether an accused should be committed for trial, as they do when trying a case at Petty Sessions.

So much for the judicial part of the justices' work. They have always had many executive tasks as well.

In 1349 the terrible plague, the Black Death, destroyed over a third of England's population. The scarcity of labour produced great unrest in the country and higher wages were demanded. Justices were given power to fix wages. Since then the administrative tasks of the justices have grown enormously. For example, the Poor Law was under their control. In the last hundred years the tide has turned the other way, however, and much of their work has been transferred to the shoulders of such institutions as the County Councils. Perhaps the most important quasi-administrative function of the justices today is licensing.

But what the justices have lost on the administrative swings they have gained on the judicial roundabouts. Various statutes, beginning in the nineteenth century, empower them to try not only crimes but also matrimonial cases, affiliation cases and small civil matters—for example, a local authority may sue for its rates before the justices.

Magistrates (with the exception of stipendiaries, first introduced in London in 1792) have no legal training and are unpaid. In the early days they were paid a small salary.

Having considered the humblest courts in the land, let us now consider the highest. Parliament, the Privy Council and the superior courts of justice all sprang from the same origins. In mediaeval times there was none of the specialisation that is found today. The King would surround himself with a group of large landowners, ecclesiastics and household officials, and these, his councillors, would advise him when he wished and perform such tasks as he delegated. This council would act as a court in the modern sense, a Cabinet and a Parliament. This supreme body was known in Saxon times as the *Witamagemont*, or council of wise men. When the Normans came, the system was much the same. The deliberative assembly was called the *Curia Regis*, or Great Council. As time progressed, so many notabilities were summoned that it became too unwieldy for everyday business and was split into two. The larger, summoned for extraordinary purposes, became Parliament. The smaller became the King's Council, later the Privy Council. For convenience, the group of officials about the King began to split up, each assuming a specialist function. In 1178 Henry II appointed five men to hear cases between subject and subject. This is the origin of the Court of Common Pleas. Cases involving the King and breaches of the King's peace were not heard by the Common Pleas but by the great men about the King. Frequently the Sovereign would be there in person. This is the origin of the Court of King's Bench.

The third Common Law Court started as a Government department. The earliest branch of the *Curia Regis* was the Exchequer, so called from the checked cloth on the table used for counting money. In the course of collecting the revenues, legal disputes would frequently arise and it was natural that the Exchequer should establish its own court to deal with such matters. The judges of the Court of Exchequer were known as barons.

No sooner had the three Common Law Courts separated than a fierce rivalry developed between them. As the incomes of the judges and officials depended on the fees received, litigants were eagerly wooed, and each court tried to steal jurisdiction from the other two by means of legal fictions. (A legal fiction consisted of the assumption by the Court of facts which were not necessarily true but which the parties were not allowed to deny.) Legal fictions were the most daring and unashamed way of creating new law, and were in great vogue in the Middle Ages. To increase its jurisdiction the King's Bench invented the device of Bill of Middlesex and Writ of Latitat. The King's Bench had jurisdiction over anyone in the custody of the Sheriff of Middlesex. If to the issue of the Bill the sheriff replied that the defendant was not in the county, a writ would issue for his apprehension. The writ alleged that the defendant 'lurks and runs about' (*latitat et discurrit*).

By this device the King's Bench was enabled to try some actions properly the province of the Common Pleas. The latter court retaliated by using a fiction of its own. At the same time, the Court of Exchequer filched jurisdiction by a third fiction.

These fictions lasted until 1832. The jurisdictions of the three Courts overlapped widely. In addition to its civil jurisdiction, the King's Bench always possessed a limited criminal jurisdiction and a general supervisory power over inferior courts and officials, exercised through prerogative writs, dealt with later.

The hierarchy of courts hearing Common Law appeals was illogical and confused until 1830, when it was provided that appeals from the three Common Law Courts were to be heard by a court called the Court of Exchequer Chamber, and appeals from it were to lie to the House of Lords.

While the Common Law Courts were quarrelling among themselves, a new court, and along with it a new system of law, was stealthily and steadily growing up beside them. This was the Court of Chancery. Whereas the three Courts just mentioned administered

Common Law, the Chancery Court dealt in a very different com-
modity—Equity. At first this was what the name suggests, but later
it became as rigid as the Common Law. There became two laws of
the land, alongside one another.

As we have seen, the Common Law was governed by the writ
system. And despite the slight loosening by the enactment *'in
consimili casu'*, the Common Law was excessively rigid and technical.
Some institutions it refused to recognise. One such was the use, the
ancestor of the modern trust. A would transfer the legal estate in
land to B, called the feoffee to uses, to hold to the use of either A
himself or some other person. Now A, if B was holding it to A's
use, would receive the practical benefits of the land, the 'beneficial
ownership', but avoid certain disabilities which the legal ownership
involved. Thus, in the unsettled Middle Ages, a lord contemplating
a rebellion against the King would prudently assign his land to a
feoffee, so that if the rebellion was a failure his land would not be
forfeited as part of the punishment. Only the legal estate could be in
jeopardy and that was in the feoffee who had, of course, not partici-
pated in the revolt.

A more peaceful employment of uses was to make wills of land.
Land could not be devised,[1] so before death the landowner would
enfeoff a trustworthy person and direct that on his (the landowner's)
death the feoffee was to transfer the land to certain persons. These
are but two examples of the benefits of the use. Always the feoffee
to uses had the legal estate, whereas the *cestui que use*[2] was said to
have the 'equitable estate'.

Now it will be noticed immediately how dependent this system
was on the honesty of the feoffee to uses. For the Common Law
Courts refused to recognise equitable estates and uses. A *cestui que use*
who complained that his feoffee to uses had defaulted was told that
the legal estate was in the feoffee, and there was an end of the matter.

This was but one example of hiatuses in the Common Law. Frequently, justice would be denied to a poor ignorant suitor by a
court or jury overshadowed by a local lord. All these persons to
whom right had been denied would turn to the 'fountain of justice',
the King, petitioning for relief. The King would refer the petitions
to his Council. In time, the Council, because of pressure of work,
would delegate the cases to the Chancellor.[3] He already had a staff

---

[1] Passed by will.   [2] The beneficial owner.
[3] Derived from the Latin *'Cancellarius'*, a secretary.

of clerks to issue writs, and his office was well suited to dealing with these petitions. So the Chancellor grew in status and dignity. At first a mere secretary, he became a great officer of state, and in time the highest judge in the land. Many of the early Chancellors were ecclesiastics, the best-known being Cardinal Wolsey. They were the 'keepers of the King's conscience'. As can be imagined, Equity was a flexible system, in each case righting the wrongs the Common Law permitted, according to conscience.

The Chancellor sat without a jury. The procedure of the Court was different from that of the Common Law Courts. The staff of clerks attached to the Court was invaluable when dealing with a case involving accounts. The Court of Chancery, too, had its own remedies. Instead of awarding damages it would act '*in personam*' and compel a defendant against whom judgment had been given to perform obligations (specific performance) or forbid him to break equitable rules (injunction). It acted *in personam* to compel the defendant to attend under a penalty (*subpoena*). The *subpoena*, unlike a Common Law writ, did not state the cause of action. Unlike the Common Law writ, too, it did not admit of endless delays in appearance.

It should be noted that Equity did not at first claim to overrule the Common Law but merely, by filling in its gaps, to aid it. In fact, Equity is not, and never has been, entirely independent of the Common Law. It is a patchwork imposed on it, and from its very nature is dependent on the pre-existence of the Common Law.

The Court of Chancery dealt purely with civil matters. Another court developed from the Council, which was its criminal counterpart. This became known as the Court of Star Chamber, from the room in which it sat.[1] It was originally a method of doing swift and effective justice in cases where the Common Law had no remedy, or where an offender was so powerful that local juries were afraid to convict. The Star Chamber was responsible for the creation of several new offences, such as libel, perjury and riot. As was to be expected, the offences it sought to stop were chiefly of a public character, affecting the administration of justice or the King's Peace. At first the Court was useful and welcome. But it was used oppressively under the later Tudors and Stuarts, and became hated. There was no jury, torture was sometimes used, procedure and sentences

[1] The ceiling was covered with stars.

were alike arbitrary and unpredictable. The Common Lawyers de-
tested it and it was abolished in 1641.

The relations between Common Law and Chancery Courts grew
steadily worse. The Court of Chancery would set aside judgments of
the Common Law Courts and imprison the successful party at law,
if he would not obey the Chancery decree. The Common Law
Judges retaliated by releasing the prisoner on a *habeas corpus*.[1] The
quarrel was exacerbated by the growing enmity between the King's
supporters and the Parliamentary party. For the Court of Chancery
was a prerogative court and the idea of such an institution overruling the sacred Common Law outraged the Common Lawyers.
Their leader was Chief Justice Coke, a man of massive erudition,
whose doctrine might be stated simply—the King is subject to the
Common Law. Implicit in that, of course, is the superiority of the
Common Law Courts to Chancery. At length the dispute became so
bitter that the Lord Chancellor, Lord Ellesmere, appealed to James I.
James was advised by his Attorney-General, Francis Bacon, the
arch-supporter of the royal prerogative and Coke's deadly rival. On
his opinion, Chancery triumphed. But the prerogative's victory was
short-lived, for the Parliamentary ascendancy and subsequent civil
war swept away all the prerogative courts save Chancery, and that
was allowed to remain only after much hesitation.

At first, Equity was said to vary with the length of the Chancellor's foot. But the work of three great Chancellors, helped by the
doctrine of binding precedent and the introduction of law reports,
aided its crystallisation into a fixed body of law. The first of these
Chancellors was Lord Nottingham (1675–1682). He aptly described
the change in Equity's character by saying that the Chancellor's
conscience, when appealed to to correct injustices, must be not a
private but a legal and public one.

Lord Hardwicke (1737–1756) was a lawyer of great learning, and
his judgments must have been of an interest unique in the law, for
it is recorded that crowds would flock to his court to hear his judgments as they would to a theatre. Though the law developed under
his guidance, procedure in the Court was allowed to remain un-
altered.

The third great Chancellor was Lord Eldon (1801–1806, 1807–
1827). After a runaway marriage, he made a name at the Bar sud-
denly by his brilliant argument in the case of *Ackroyd* v. *Smithson*.

[1] See page 27.

When he attained the Chancellorship he was extremely painstaking —too much so—and suits would drag on for years. As with Hardwicke, the law was developed and interpreted with great learning, but the court machinery grew more and more ponderous and archaic.

When he died, the situation in the Court of Chancery was truly depicted by Dickens in *Bleak House*. The Court was burdened with huge numbers of superfluous officials. An unnecessary number of documents was required. The procedure was fantastically cumbrous, and interminable delays resulted from the fact that there was only one judge, the Lord Chancellor,[1] whose time was limited by all his other pressing duties of state. The Master of the Rolls could hear cases, but his decisions could be upset by the Chancellor on appeal. A Royal Commission sat in 1827. Once more the Court of Chancery's life was in jeopardy. Slowly, however, reforms were effected, more judges appointed, sinecures abolished and a way cut through the lush jungle of paper for justice to proceed. In 1851 an appeal court, the Court of Appeal in Chancery, was established.

The Court of Chancery was not the only court Coke fought. He engaged the Court of Admiralty in battle to try to filch its mercantile jurisdiction. During the Middle Ages many local courts, called courts of 'pie powder' (*pieds poudres*—from the dusty feet of the travellers who resorted to them), had provided a speedy and effective mercantile jurisdiction. These had declined by Coke's time and the chief commercial court was the Admiralty. Its international character resulted in a strong Roman Law flavouring which the Common Lawyers disliked. By his onslaughts, Coke swept much of its mercantile business into the grasp of the Common Law Courts. The resultant gratification of their practitioners was not shared by the merchants, who found the Common Law a clumsy method of dealing with mercantile disputes. The customs of merchants were not recognised as part of the Common Law; they had to be proved afresh in every case as special customs. One Chief Justice did much to change this. He was Lord Mansfield (1756–1788). He was a man of wide culture and learning and had studied Roman Law. He was especially interested in the Mercantile Law and would invite prominent City merchants to dine with him and discuss the law and customs of commerce. Lord Mansfield adopted the system of requiring a merchant's custom to be proved only once. This done, it became

[1] A Vice-Chancellor had been appointed in 1813.

part of the law. In this way the Common Law absorbed the customs of merchants and became attuned to modern commercial needs.

Throughout the eighteenth century the Common Law slowly changed, adapting itself to an England undergoing the Industrial Revolution. Procedure, however, as in the Court of Chancery, was archaic and dilatory. Antiquated fictions abounded. After the Napoleonic Wars, the spirit of change could not be resisted. Such anachronisms as trial by battle and the Bill of Middlesex were abolished. A new Common Law Court of appeal, the final Court of Exchequer Chamber, was established. Various Acts made available useful methods of Chancery procedure, such as discovery,[1] while at the same time Chancery was given powers used before only in the Common Law Courts, such as the power to hear oral evidence and award damages. All this tended to one thing, the fusion of the courts. This was finally achieved by the Judicature Acts of 1873 and 1875. There was to be one Supreme Court, consisting of the Court of Appeal, replacing the Court of Appeal in Chancery and the Court of Exchequer Chamber, and the High Court, replacing the various superior courts. For convenience it was divided into five Divisions: Chancery, Queen's Bench, Common Pleas,[2] Exchequer,[2] and Probate, Divorce and Admiralty.[3] The age-old struggle between Law and Equity was put to rest by enacting that when the two conflicted the rules of Equity were to prevail.

Something should be said about the Family Division—formerly the Probate, Divorce and Admiralty Division.[3] These jurisdictions are grouped together because they are all derived from Roman or Civil Law which was practised by the Doctors of Civil Law. These were to be found in Doctors' Commons and were a race apart from the Common lawyers and Chancery practitioners. Probate law was derived from ecclesiastical law, as the Church assumed control over wills of personal property. Likewise, matrimonial relations were the particular concern of the Church. But, until 1857, the Courts alone could not give a divorce but only a judicial separation. Previously, to obtain a divorce a Common Law action, an ecclesiastical suit and a Private Act of Parliament were necessary, which meant that the chains of marriage remained unbroken for all but the most wealthy. In 1857 the Courts of Probate and Divorce were established, taking

---

[1] See page 193.   [2] Abolished in 1881.
[3] Renamed by the Administration of Justice Act, 1970.

over jurisdiction in these spheres from the ecclesiastical courts. That left the Church Courts with an obsolete jurisdiction over the morals of the population—in theory they may still punish fornicators, for example—and over the internal affairs of the Church. This jurisdiction the Church Courts still possess.

By the Administration of Justice Act, 1970, contentious probate business was assigned to the Chancery Division, and Admiralty and prize cases to the Queen's Bench Division. Cases involving minors previously heard in the Chancery Division are now assigned to the Family Division.

The highest court in the land today is the House of Lords. In theory any peer sitting in the House may take part in an appeal, even if completely unqualified legally. It is a custom, however, and has been for many years, that only those in the Lords holding, or who have held, high judicial office may do so. In the 1840s and '50s, however, the House of Lords was singularly unfit to be our highest tribunal, as there were only a tiny number of such qualified peers, and most of these were very old. It was proposed to abolish the House of Lords as an appellate court, but it was saved by a change of government. The Appellate Jurisdiction Act of 1876 provided that Law Lords were to be appointed. They were to be life peers and were lawyers of the highest experience and eminence.

Under the Administration of Justice Act 1969, in certain cases there may be a 'leapfrog' appeal direct to the House of Lords from the High Court.

Until recently, a peer accused of felony had the right to trial by the House of Lords. For this purpose all the peers assembled—not merely the Law Lords and those holding, or past holders of, high judicial office—in their robes and voted whether the accused were guilty or not. The last trial of this kind was in 1935 for manslaughter. This form of trial was abolished by the Criminal Justice Act of 1948.

When the Star Chamber disappeared, many of the new crimes it had created were incorporated into the ordinary Criminal Law. Common Law crimes were divided into two classes: felonies (the more serious) and misdemeanors (less grave). With the exception of petty larceny and mayhem, all felonies were punishable with death. The increasing lawlessness of the eighteenth century scared Parliament into creating a huge number of new capital offences. At one time there were over two hundred capital crimes. They included such ludicrous peccadilloes as damaging Westminster Bridge. Public

opinion, led by such men as Sir Samuel Romilly, cried out against
the slaughter. Juries refused to convict for minor offences, and the
law was brought into disrepute. For example, to steal an article
worth 40s. or more was capital, and the jury had to find the object's
value. It has been recorded that a jury found a verdict that a prisoner
had stolen a £10 note 'to the value of 39 shillings'. With the forces
of reform sweeping away so many Civil Law archaisms in the early
nineteenth century Criminal Law could not escape. Capital penalties
were abolished for hundreds of offences. Now it remains for only
two.[1] Other punishments were similarly mitigated. Transportation
beyond the seas gave way to penal servitude, and the treadmill to
hard labour. Penal servitude and hard labour have gone, in their
turn, under the 1948 Criminal Justice Act.

Not only punishments were reformed. Prisoners were not allowed
counsel in cases of felony (unless to argue a point of law) until 1837.
The custom of manacling prisoners in the Court was discontinued
early in the eighteenth century, owing to the humanity of Chief
Justice Holt. The *peine forte et dure* was abolished in 1772. It was not
until 1898[2] that prisoners could give evidence in their own defence.
This has proved a mixed blessing to many accused. But, as Mr.
Justice Devlin observed: 'The interests of justice are not necessarily
the same as the interests of the accused.'

Until 1907 there existed only a limited appeal[3] in criminal cases.
Following public outcry after the Adolf Beck case, in which an
innocent man was imprisoned for several years, the Court of Criminal Appeal was established by the Criminal Appeal Act, 1907. This
Court was abolished by the Criminal Appeal Act, 1966, which
established the Criminal Division of the Court of Appeal. A further
appeal from the Court of Appeal (Criminal Division) to the House
of Lords lies with the consent of either Court. The Court of Appeal
must certify that a point of law of general public importance is involved.[4]

As has been remarked, the King's Courts had fought a successful
battle with the local courts in the Middle Ages. By the nineteenth
century hardly any local civil courts remained. Endless delay was
caused by the attempts of the Courts at Westminster and the Assizes

---

[1] Piracy with attempted murder, and treason.
[2] Criminal Evidence Act, 1898.
[3] Other than offences tried at Petty Sessions.
[4] Administration of Justice Act, 1960, s. 1.

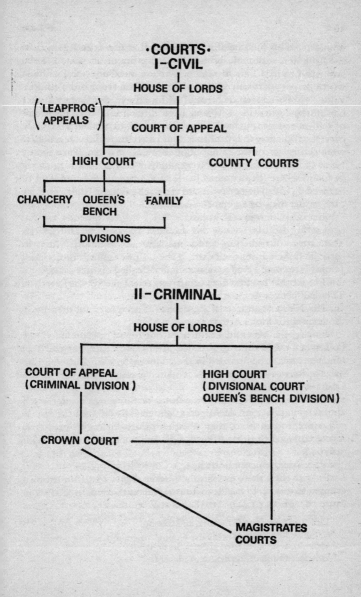

·COURTS·
I-CIVIL

HOUSE OF LORDS

'LEAPFROG'
APPEALS

COURT OF APPEAL

HIGH COURT   COUNTY COURTS

CHANCERY   QUEEN'S   FAMILY
            BENCH

DIVISIONS

II-CRIMINAL

HOUSE OF LORDS

COURT OF APPEAL   HIGH COURT
(CRIMINAL DIVISION)   (DIVISIONAL COURT
                           QUEEN'S BENCH DIVISION)

CROWN COURT

MAGISTRATES
COURTS

to cope with innumerable trifling civil matters, and justice was denied to the humble litigant by the costs of an action in the superior courts. There was a pressing need for local tribunals capable of summarily despatching small causes. Lord Brougham came to the rescue. As a result of his efforts, the County Courts[1] were established in 1846, and have thrived mightily. Their small limits of jurisdiction have been several times expanded. Today, they have jurisdiction to try most actions of contract and tort where the subject-matter of the dispute does not exceed £750. They have an Equity jurisdiction up to £5000 and may hear actions for recovery of land where the net annual value for rating of the land does not exceed £1000. They hear actions remitted from the High Court, and the parties may, by agreement, confer an unlimited financial jurisdiction on the Court in certain cases.

County Courts outside the London Bankruptcy District have bankruptcy jurisdiction, and some have an Admiralty.[2] Rent Restrictions Acts cases are heard in the County Court. Some County Courts are empowered to deal with undefended divorce cases.

The Restrictive Practices Court was established by the Restrictive Trade Practices Act, 1956.

The National Industrial Relations Court was established by the Industrial Relations Act, 1971.

Finally, the very old Coroner's Court must be mentioned. The office of Coroner was established in 1194, in order that the Royal interests might be guarded in the counties. In particular, the King was jealous of the Sheriffs, the county representatives, and desired that they be kept in check.

Nowadays, the Coroner watches the Sovereign's interests by holding inquests to decide whether valuables found hidden are Treasure Trove. If so, they are the property of the Crown. A far more common function is his duty to enquire into deaths occurring in sudden or suspicious circumstances. A Coroner nowadays must be a barrister, solicitor or doctor.

In later years there has been a great tendency to set up tribunals similar to courts, to decide matters falling within a particular scope, with or without an appeal to the courts.

Some of these tribunals, notably Rent Tribunals, have been

[1] Not to be confused with the County or Shire Courts of mediaeval times.

[2] County Courts Act, 1959.

criticised on the grounds of their procedure and membership, and the lack of appeal from their decisions. The Tribunals and Inquiries Act,[1] 1971, is designed to remedy the defects previously chiefly criticised.

[1] Previously the Tribunals and Inquiries Acts, 1958 and 1966.

2 Constitutional Law

Having briefly mentioned the history of English Law, we can now pass to the law as it is today. This presents a field of such terrifying vastness that some sort of dividing and classifying is necessary. The classification adopted for the purpose of this book is shown on the chart overleaf. Specialised subjects like Admiralty Law and Patent Law are omitted. It should be noted that much of Constitutional and Criminal Law is Common Law, and that the Common Law of Property has been much affected by Equity. The branches shown in the chart are all Substantive Law. Superimposed on them all are the laws of Civil and Criminal Procedure, called Adjective Law. In practice, they assume as great an importance as substantive rules of law. For example, if the law forbids a litigant to bring an action, from his point of view it is equivalent to denying him the existence of the rule on which his case is founded. Maine, a celebrated legal historian, has well said that the law was 'secreted in the interstices of procedure'. Also in the category of adjective law is the Law of Evidence.

One topic more remains before we can grapple with the first branch of substantive law, and that is the question of Sources. In what guises is the law to be found? Broadly speaking, in two: (1) written law, comprising statutes and enactments made under statutory power, and (2) unwritten law.

Statutes or Acts of Parliament are the supreme example of law in this country. No court can declare them invalid. A statute can only be repealed or altered by another statute, though the Courts may interpret them in a way Parliament possibly did not intend. Each statute is numbered according to the regnal year in which it is passed Thus, the Act of 15 George V, c. 23, was passed in the Session of Parliament held in the fifteenth year of the reign of George V. 'C' is short for chapter, and means it was the twenty-third statute passed. in that session. All Acts now have short titles as well. Thus, another name for 15 George V, c. 23, is the Administration of Estates Act, 1925.

With the tremendous growth of legislation in recent years, Parliament has laid much of the burden on other shoulders. An Act will provide, for example, that a Minister may make Statutory Rules and

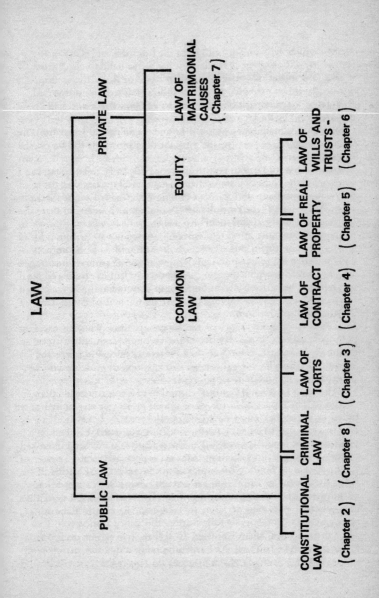

LAW

PUBLIC LAW

CONSTITUTIONAL LAW
(Chapter 2)

CRIMINAL LAW
(Chapter 8)

LAW OF TORTS
(Chapter 3)

COMMON LAW

LAW OF CONTRACT
(Chapter 4)

LAW OF REAL PROPERTY
(Chapter 5)

EQUITY

LAW OF WILLS AND TRUSTS
(Chapter 6)

PRIVATE LAW

LAW OF MATRIMONIAL CAUSES
(Chapter 7)

Orders which, when made, will have the full force and effect of the statute itself. But whereas Parliament has a free hand to enact what it likes, a Minister may make only such Rules or Regulations as are within the limits provided by the enabling statute. Any purported Regulation outside such limits is said to be *'ultra vires'*[1] and will be declared void by the Courts.

Such subordinate law-making is known as delegated legislation. Other examples are the byelaws of a local authority or the British Railways Board.

England has no written constitution or code of law. The nearest approach is the codifying statute which gathers all the law on a topic into one convenient statute. An example is the Sale of Goods Act, 1893. Also, there is the consolidating statute which tidies up many old Acts and amalgamates them into one convenient whole.

Many of our most important rules of law are not to be found in any written enactment but are part of our Common Law. 'Common Law' is a chameleon-like phrase, taking its meaning from a contrast. We have already seen its meaning as opposed to Equity. In this context it means 'unwritten law' as opposed to Statute Law.

The Common Law is a living thing, changing and adapting itself imperceptibly to the altering economic and social life of the country. Its custodians are the judges of the superior courts, who, in interpreting it, make it. For every decision on a rule of law, either Common Law or Statute, is binding on an inferior court. It remains the law until Parliament should change it by statute, or a higher court overrule it. The hierarchy of courts is shown on the chart (p. 17). The House of Lords and Court of Appeal bind lower courts by their decisions. The House of Lords since 1966 is no longer bound by its previous decisions. The Court of Appeal generally binds itself in civil cases, but its Criminal Division does not if satisfied that the previous decision is clearly wrong. The lower courts do not bind themselves, though previous decisions have great persuasive authority.

The system of 'binding precedent' is not found on the Continent. It has the advantage of making for certainty, but it sometimes leads to unnecessarily fine distinctions. A High Court judge faced with a case where a previous decision, if followed, would produce injustice, seizes on a relatively unimportant difference in the two cases and 'distinguishes' them, refusing to follow the earlier decision. Hard cases make bad law. The case involving a fine distinction is

[1] Beyond his powers.

with us permanently as a precedent, creating unnecessary compli-
cation in the law.

The entry of the United Kingdom into the European Economic
Community brings about an important development in the field of
precedent. Any question as to the meaning or effect of the Treaties
or any Community instrument is to be treated as a question of law.
These questions of law are decided by the European Court, which
gives a ruling on the point which creates a precedent. If therefore a
point of Community law arises in the United Kingdom Courts, the
principle laid down by the European Court will have to be followed.
This would mean that Community law will coexist with British
national law.

Being precedents, all cases of importance are reported. Law reports in comparatively modern form date from the sixteenth century.
Some of the early ones are notoriously unreliable. It was said of one
reporter that he heard only half of what took place in Court and
wrote down the other half. Since 1865 the official series known as
the Law Reports has been issued. These reports are corrected by the
judges themselves. There are four series, known by the initials of
the Courts of whose proceedings the Reports are a record: A.C.
(Appeal Cases) for the House of Lords and Privy Council; Q.B.
(Queen's Bench); Ch. (Chancery); and Fam. (Family).[1] The three
last also report decisions of the Court of Appeal from their respec-
tive Divisions. References are abbreviated, thus: the Court of
Appeal case of *Carlill* v. *Carbolic Smoke Ball Co.*, [1893] 1 Q.B. 256, is
reported at page 256 of the first volume of Queen's Bench reports
in 1893.

Text-books are not in themselves any legal authority, save for
'works of authority'. Where the law is not settled by statute or cases,
however, the opinions of text-book writers of repute are received
with respect by the Courts.

Works of authority are certain text-books written many years ago
by eminent lawyers. Where there is no statute or case to the contrary, they are authority for what the law is when they were written,
and hence, unless it has changed, the law as it is today. Works of
authority are not often consulted because of the growth of law
reporting and the changes in the law, but sometimes they are found
to be of great value even today, hundreds of years after they were
written.

[1] Formerly P. (Probate, Divorce and Admiralty).

The first work of authority is known by the name of its author, Glanvil, and was published at the end of the twelfth century. An improvement, also known by its author's name, Bracton, was published in the thirteenth century. Littleton on Tenures, described by Coke as the most perfect work in any human science, followed about two hundred years later.

Sir Edward Coke compiled his famous *Institutes* in four parts, basing the first part on Littleton's work. Perhaps this is the most famous legal text-book ever written. Coke wrote at the beginning of the seventeenth century. A noteworthy publication towards the century's end was a treatise on Criminal Law by a great Chief Justice, Sir Matthew Hale, entitled: *Pleas of the Crown*.

Written in beautiful English, Blackstone's *Commentaries* appeared in 1765. Sir William Blackstone was the first professor of English Law at Oxford[1] and later a judge.

Constitutional Law

This is the branch of law which regulates how the government of the country is to be carried on. Further, it governs the relationship between the different members of the Commonwealth. Though it has been mentioned that England has no written constitution, that is not to say it has no constitutional law. The constitutional law of this country is nothing more or less than the Common Law buttressed by Constitutional Conventions and fortified by a few statutes of constitutional importance, such as the Bill of Rights, 1688.

Many implications flow from this. To start with, any part of the law may be altered by simple Act of Parliament. In Australia, for example, a referendum (a national poll) is necessary to make fundamental changes in the Federal Constitution. In the United States, the Supreme Court may declare that an enactment of the legislature is repugnant to the constitution and therefore of no effect. Here, Parliament, consisting of the Queen, Lords and Commons, is supreme. Its supremacy or sovereignty is twofold: (1) there is nothing Parliament cannot do; (2) it has no rivals.

It has been said Parliament can do everything except make a man a woman and a woman a man. But it could, in law! If such an enactment were passed, the legal status of men and women would be interchanged. Such an inconvenient statute is unlikely to be passed,

[1] Before this date, English Law was not taught at the Universities but only by the Inns of Court.

however. The dominant force in Parliament, the House of Commons, has to answer to the electorate every five years. And there are many checks on Parliament's *effective* sovereignty, even if they are of no legal force, such as the Press, the Trade Unions and various forms of organised public opinion. Parliament cannot be bound by a previous enactment, and this carries as its converse the only restriction on Parliament's legal sovereignty—it cannot bind future Parliaments. An example is *Vauxhall Estates Ltd.* v. *Liverpool Corporation.*[1] There it was held that the words of an Act passed in 1919 could not prevent its repeal by an Act of 1925.

There has been much recent discussion as to the effect of Britain's entry into the European Economic Community on the traditional concept of the Sovereignty of Parliament. An Act of Parliament was necessary for accession to the Community, but membership is intended to be permanent. An objection raised is that membership strikes a fundamental blow at Parliamentary sovereignty since future parliaments could not revoke the Act of Accession. The author's view is that a future Parliament could, as a strict matter of law, repeal it in the same way as any other Act. Such action, however, taken without the consent of the other member countries, would be a breach of international obligations.

One result of entry is that Britain is bound by the Article in the Treaty of Rome which lays down that the Member States of the Community are bound by the regulations issued by the Council of Ministers and the Commission, which may override any conflicting statute or case law.[2]

Parliament has no rivals. At one time the Sovereign could suspend the operation of statutes and dispense from them—that is, exempt certain persons from their operation. The Bill of Rights of 1688 declared the suspending power illegal, and the dispensing power 'as it hath been assumed and exercised of late' illegal. Though the Sovereign may not exempt a person from a duty, he may, through the responsible Minister, pardon a criminal offender and remit his punishment. The action of the Home Secretary in 1948 in stating that all persons convicted of murder would be automatically

[1] [1932] 1 K.B. 733.
[2] The Council of Ministers takes all the major decisions about Community policy. The European Commission carries out the decisions of the Council, puts forward proposals to the Council and safeguards the interests of the Community as a whole.

reprieved was, as Lord Goddard pointed out, probably illegal as being an improper exercise of the dispensing power.

However much the Courts dislike a statute, they cannot overrule it. And subordinate bodies authorised by Parliament to make regulations must keep strictly within their prescribed limits, as we have seen.

A resolution of either House acting alone will not alter the law (*Stockdale* v. *Hansard*).[1] The House of Commons by resolution ordered a report to be published. It contained a libel on Stockdale. It was held that a mere resolution could not make legal that which was illegal. (In consequence of this the Parliamentary Papers Act of 1840 was passed, making publishers of papers printed by resolution of either House privileged from actions for libel.)

As the law of the constitution is part of the Common Law, it is administered in the ordinary courts of the land. In France, for example, this is not so. There is a '*droit administratif*', dealing with the relations between the State and private citizens, and actions brought under it are tried in special courts. This was expressed by Dicey,[2] the great writer on constitutional law, as the second branch of the 'Rule of Law'. Writing in the late nineteenth century, he described it thus: 'Every man's legal rights or liabilities are almost invariably determined by the ordinary courts of the realm.' This is not so true now. Many tribunals have been set up for specific purposes under various Acts, which oust the jurisdiction of the Courts, though in some cases an appeal to the Supreme Court is allowed.

The third branch of Dicey's Rule of Law is: 'Each man's individual rights are far less the result of our constitution than the basis on which the constitution is founded.' Private rights enforced by the Courts are our constitution. Note, too, that the *law* regulating the constitution of the country must be supplemented by conventions not of legal force but invariably followed, otherwise government would become impossible. The oil of the conventions is necessary before the constitutional machine will run. There are many of these conventions. One is that the Government must be able to command a majority in the House of Commons. There is no law providing this. In theory there could be a Liberal or a Communist administration. But money is necessary for government, and it is unlikely that a House of Commons consisting almost entirely of Conservative and Labour supporters would grant money to continue such a Government. As the Government is prohibited *by law*

[1] 9 A. & E. 1.   [2] In his *Law of the Constitution*.

from spending money without Parliament's[1] authority, it is obvious that a breach of convention would be shortly followed by a breach of law. This is the case with most of the conventions. For example, Parliament must meet at least once every three years by the Triennial Act of 1694. But there is no legal obligation to meet oftener. However, if it does not do so, not only will the Government have no money at the close of the financial year but also, after a while, no army. A peacetime standing army is illegal in this country, and the Army (and the Air Force, but not the Navy) must be given a fresh life every year by Act of Parliament.

The first branch of the Rule of Law reads: 'In England no man can be made to suffer punishment or to pay damages for any conduct not definitely forbidden by law.'

This has been the law in England since a time when '*lettres de cachet*' flourished in France, to compare just one European country with ours.

One of the principal ways of securing this is by the Habeas Corpus Acts of 1679, 1816 and 1862. If a person is imprisoned and no lawful reason given, he, or anyone else, may apply for a writ of 'habeas corpus'.[2] This is directed to the person in whose custody the prisoner is, and he must show good cause for the detention to a High Court judge. If the custody is justified, the prisoner is sent back or given bail; if not, he is discharged. The writ runs throughout the Queen's dominions. Severe penalties await anyone sending a prisoner out of the Queen's jurisdiction, or the judge who refuses to hear an application. In fact, this sending a prisoner out of the jurisdiction is one of the two offences which the Crown *cannot* pardon.[3]

The Bill of Rights, 1688, provides that excessive bail shall not be demanded of a prisoner awaiting trial.

The executive may not take the law into their own hands. Thus 'general warrants' are illegal. A warrant was issued directing seizure of the unnamed authors, printer and publishers of No. 45 of the *North Briton* (a paper that had attacked the Government), together with their papers. Wood entered Wilkes's house without permission and removed his papers. Wilkes sued Wood for trespass and recovered heavy damages, as such a warrant which did not name the

---

[1] For all purposes, in this case, the House of Commons.
[2] Literally, 'have the body'.
[3] The other is a public nuisance unabated.

persons to be arrested was illegal (*Wilkes* v. *Wood*).[1] Two years later
it was held that a general warrant directing a search for the papers
of a named person was illegal.[2] A decision that must be regretted is
Elias v. *Pasmore*.[3] A person was arrested and the police searched the
premises where this occurred for evidence of the crime with which
he was charged. While doing so, they removed papers belonging
to another man with intent to charge him with a different crime,
and it was held that this further, quite accidental seizure was legal!

What is 'conduct according to law' is sometimes difficult to ascertain, particularly with the right of public meeting.

To start with, if three or more persons assemble to commit a
crime or a breach of the peace, or even to carry out a lawful purpose
in an unlawful manner, behaving so that a reasonable person would
fear a breach of the peace, they will be committing the crime of unlawful assembly. The violent execution of a common private purpose by three or more persons to the terror of Her Majesty's subjects
is a riot. It is lawful to use such force as is reasonable in the circumstances to suppress a riot.

Even if a meeting is quite peaceful, it may be an obstruction if in
a public place—for example, Trafalgar Square. If a public meeting
is held on private premises, the police have a right to attend if they
fear a breach of the peace may occur (*Thomas* v. *Sawkins*).[4] A lawful
public meeting does not become unlawful merely because it may
provoke unlawful disturbances on the part of others (*Beatty* v. *Gill-
banks*).[5] In that case the lawful meeting was one of the Salvation
Army. But if there is reason to fear a breach of the peace, a police
constable may forbid it, and if it is then held, those holding it will be
guilty of obstructing the constable in the execution of his duty.

The Public Order Act, 1936, gives the Home Secretary power to
sanction banning of public processions. The Act forbids the wearing of uniforms by members of political organisations and prohibits
the use of words or behaviour in a public place likely to cause a
breach of the peace.

It will be seen that freedom of public meeting enjoyed in England
is due more to the common sense of authority and the discipline of
those meeting than to any undue leniency of the law.

Subject to avoiding defamation,[6] sedition, obscenity and blas-

---

[1] (1763) 19 St. Tr. 1153.   [2] *Entick* v. *Carrington* (1765), 19 St. Tr. 1029.
[3] [1934] 2 K.B. 164.   [4] [1935] 2 K.B. 249.   [5] 9 Q.B.D. 308.
[6] Defined in Chapter 3, page 58.

phemy, a citizen may say and write what he pleases. If his speech or writings tend to excite disaffection against the Queen, Government, Parliament or the administration of the laws, or are an inducement to the people to change any institution of Church or State by unlawful means, he is guilty of sedition. Obscene matter is that which tends to deprave or corrupt those who are open to such influences. Blasphemy is a scurrilous attack on Christianity or the Bible in a manner likely to outrage the feelings of Christian people.

No system of licensing of the Press and books now exists. The Lord Chamberlain no longer censors stage plays. Local authorities may prohibit the showing of films but are guided by a voluntary organisation—the British Board of Film Censors. The B.B.C. are masters of their own destiny in this respect.

Montesquieu, the French revolutionary philosopher, was a great admirer of the English system of government and concluded that the freedom of the people was due to the Separation of Powers—that is, the Executive, Legislative and Judicial powers were exercised by different persons or bodies, in this case, the Government and Civil Service, Parliament and the Judges respectively. Though this doctrine is in full force in the United States, it is not and has never been wholly so in this country. To start with, the Queen, as well as heading the Executive, is part of Parliament and the 'fountain of justice'—for example, prosecutions are conducted in her name. However, in all these functions the Sovereign's part is more nominal than real.

The Act of Settlement, 1700, provided that holders of offices of profit under the Crown might not sit in the House of Commons. But there are many exceptions to this, otherwise government could not be carried on. The most notable is the Prime Minister. Many Ministers have a legislative power to make regulations, though only within the limits prescribed by Parliament.

The Supreme Court judges are independent of the Executive, as they hold office during good behaviour and can only be removed by Her Majesty on an address presented by both Houses of Parliament. But Circuit judges and magistrates may be removed without these preliminaries, in case of misconduct or incompetence. Supreme Court and Circuit judges may not sit in the House of Commons, and judges who are members of the House of Lords intervene in debates only on legal topics.

The House of Lords is a judicial body as well as a legislative one.

in practice, this judicial function is exercised only by the Lord Chancellor, the Law Lords and those of its members with experience of high judicial office. Both Houses assume a semi-judicial function when examining Private Bills. The Executive exercises a judicial function sometimes—for example, when the Secretary of State for the Environment hears appeals from local planning authorities.

The judges of the Supreme Court may make Rules of Court, and they thus exercise a legislative capacity.

The final example of a mixture of all three functions is the Lord Chancellor. Now invariably a peer, he presides over and takes part in the debates in the House of Lords. He is one of the heads of the Executive, with a seat in the Cabinet. And he is the head of the judges. He is now also responsible for the jury system.

We must now consider Parliament, the Executive and the Judges separately, and in more detail.

Parliament

Leaving aside consideration of the Sovereign for the moment, the Upper House is the House of Lords and consists of those summoned by the Crown to sit in it. These are divided into the Lords Spiritual and Temporal. The Lords Spiritual are the Archbishops of Canterbury and York, and twenty-four other bishops. The Lords Temporal are certain peers. Peers of the United Kingdom, Great Britain, England and Scotland are entitled to a summons. Irish peers may not sit in the House of Lords but may be elected to the House of Commons. The Law Lords have only life peerages and number nine. The Life Peerages Act, 1958, provides for the creation of life peers (who may be women) other than Law Lords, with a right to speak and vote in the House.

Under the Peerage Act, 1963, the holder of a hereditary peerage may now disclaim it for life, thus enabling him to seek election to the House of Commons should he so wish.[1] Peeresses in their own right may now sit in the Lords.[2]

Peerages are inalienable. They do not pass by virtue of ownership of land (*Berkeley Peerage Case*).[3]

The following may not sit in the House of Lords: minors, bankrupts, aliens and peers serving sentences of imprisonment.

The House of Lords has several Privileges, such as freedom of

[1] Section 1.   [2] Peerage Act, 1963, s. 6.   [3] 8 H.L.C. 21.

speech and the right to regulate its own internal affairs to the exclusion of the jurisdiction of the Courts. Through its Committee of Privileges, the House of Lords judges claims to peerages and who is entitled to sit in the House. Anyone committing a breach of the Lord's privileges may be committed to prison.

Privileges of individual peers include the right of personal access to the Sovereign and freedom from jury service.

The functionary who presides over the Lord's deliberations is the Lord Chancellor. He is one of the principal officers of State and is nowadays a distinguished lawyer. In practice, he is always a peer, but he need not be, as the Woolsack on which he sits is technically outside the House. His office is very different from that of the Speaker, who presides over the House of Commons. The Speaker does not speak in the House and is so-named because he speaks on behalf of the Commons and to the Sovereign. He renounces party politics on his election, and acts as an impartial chairman. He does not change with the Government but is re-elected each Parliament. He has the power to suspend members for misbehaviour. Contrast his position with the Lord Chancellor's. The Lord Chancellor is active in the party fray, being one of the chief spokesmen for the Government in the House of Lords. Naturally, he goes out of office with his Government. He has no authority to speak on behalf of the whole House and has no powers of discipline. These are not likely to be necessary, in any case.

The House of Commons

All members of this House are elected.

When a seat falls vacant, the returning officer for the constituency is directed by a writ to hold an election for the return of a member. Any British subject[1] resident in that constituency at a certain date, called the qualifying date, is entitled to be put on the Electoral Register.[2] If he is not, then he cannot vote. Each person has now only one vote. A returning officer who refuses to register the vote of a person entitled to vote is liable to prosecution. Persons disqualified from a vote are minors, persons of unsound mind, peers, and persons convicted of certain offences. Persons convicted of certain corrupt or illegal practices at elections may be deprived of

---

[1] Or Irish citizen.　　　[2] If not disqualified.

their vote for a time. Certain electors, such as Servicemen, may vote by proxy, or by post. Otherwise, voting is in person by secret ballot.

Various classes are disqualified from membership, such as minors, peers,[1] mental patients, aliens, judges, clergy (except Nonconformist clergy), bankrupts, convicted criminals, and those guilty of corrupt practices at elections. A deposit of £150 must be paid by the candidate, who forfeits it if he obtains no more than one-eighth of the total votes.

Once elected, the member must make an oath of affirmation of his loyalty to the Throne before he may speak or vote. He will have the individual privileges of freedom of speech and freedom from civil arrest. These two privileges, together with the privileges of the House as a whole—that the Commons through their Speaker will have access to the Crown and that the Crown will put the most favourable construction on their deliberations—are claimed by the Speaker at the opening of Parliament. The privilege of freedom of speech includes the right to prohibit the public from attending the debates and the right to prevent their publication. A very important privilege, not so claimed, is the right of the House to regulate its own proceedings. This includes the right to determine disputes over elections. This right is exercised on behalf of the Commons by the High Court.

The House may suspend or expel members, though an expelled member may be re-elected by his constituents. The House may commit either its members or strangers to prison for breach of its privileges. This imprisonment ends with the Parliamentary session. In regulating its own affairs the House of Commons is not subject to control by the Courts. Thus, in *Bradlaugh* v. *Gossett*,[2] the Serjeant-at-Arms of the House of Commons had excluded the plaintiff from the House of Commons, in obedience to a resolution of that House. It was held by the Court of Queen's Bench that no action would lie against the defendant as the Court had no power to interfere in such a matter. 'What is said or done within the walls of Parliament cannot be enquired into in a court of law.'[3]

If a return to a writ of *Habeas Corpus* states merely that the prisoner is detained by order of the House, the Court may not enquire further, but if a reason is given the Court is at liberty to enquire whether it is sufficient (*Burdett* v. *Abbott*).[4]

[1] Except Irish peers.   [2] 12 Q.B.D. 271.
[3] Lord Coleridge, C. J., at page 275.   [4] 14 East 1.

Parliament and Bills

A Parliament, as we have seen, by law must be held every three years, and, in fact, every year. The duration of Parliament is five years by the Parliament Act, 1911. In practice, it ends sooner. Parliament's life is ended by the Sovereign dissolving it. It is a constitutional convention that the Queen dissolves Parliament only at the request of the Prime Minister. Similarly, the Queen issues a Proclamation to bring into being a new Parliament. The life of a Parliament is divided into Sessions, which end by prorogation. And each House may adjourn its meetings by resolution.

Bills are embryo legislation. When they have passed both Houses of Parliament and received the Royal Assent, they became Acts, and part of the law. There are four types of Bill: Public Bills, Private Bills, Hybrid Bills and Provisional Order Bills. Public Bills affect the country as a whole, whereas Private Bills deal merely with a particular district or group of persons, or even one person.

An example of a Private Bill is a Bill giving a municipal corporation power to improve streets, etc. Before 1857 Divorce Bills were fairly frequent examples of Private Bills. Hybrid Bills affect the community in general, yet one part of it much more than another. Provisional Order Bills confirm Orders made by a member of the Executive under Parliamentary authority.

The procedure followed in the last three types of Bill ensures that the private interests involved have a full opportunity of being heard, if they wish, at the Committee stage of the Bill. The Committee assumes a judicial function at this stage. A Private Member's Bill[1] is one introduced by a member of either House, independent of Government support. An outstanding example was the Matrimonial Causes Bill, 1937, introduced by the late Sir Alan Herbert.

A Bill may be introduced in either House, but it is a constitutional convention that Money Bills shall be introduced in the House of Commons first. Let us follow the progress of a Bill, assuming it is introduced in the House of Commons.

It receives a first reading. This is formal, and no discussion of the Bill is permitted. The second reading gives an opportunity for debating the general principles of the Bill. It then is referred to a Committee. This may be of the whole House or a Committee composed of a number of members representing it. If the whole House

---

[1] Do not confuse this with a *Private* Bill.

is in Committee, it is presided over by the Chairman of Committees, and not the Speaker. This is the time for detailed discussion and amendment. The Committee reports back to the House; this is known as the Report Stage, and more amendments may be moved. Finally, there is the third reading. Only formal amendments, to tidy up the language for example, may be moved.[1] When it has survived this ordeal, it undergoes the same process in the House of Lords. After that it is ready for the Royal Assent. On the day it receives this, unless otherwise provided, it becomes law. The Sovereign signifies assent by the words *'La Reine le veult'* (the Queen wishes it).[2]

The Queen might say *'La Reine s'avisera'* (the Queen will take advice) and the Bill would be rejected, but this is unlikely. The last time it happened was in 1707.

Until 1911 the Lords could reject Bills of which they disapproved. The Parliament Act of 1911, as amended by the Parliament Act of 1949, provides that Money Bills not passed by the Lords within one month and other Bills not passed by the Lords which have been passed by the Commons in two successive Sessions with a year between the Bills may be presented for the Royal Assent nevertheless. The Lords, however, may still reject outright a Bill for the prolongation of Parliament. The Parliament Act, 1911, was passed when feeling against the Lords had been stirred up by Lloyd George. The preamble referred to a future reform of the House of Lords, which has been partially attempted by the Life Peerages Act, 1958.

The Revenue

None of the country's money may be spent without Parliament's consent, and most of it could not be raised either.

Revenue may be 'ordinary', consisting of such things as Treasure Trove, or 'extraordinary', consisting of taxes and duties imposed by Parliament. One of these, the Income Tax, needs yearly reimposition. The peculiar 'ordinary' revenue was formerly the Sovereign's personal income. Since the eighteenth century ordinary revenue has been paid into the National purse in exchange for a fixed Civil List for the Royal Family's maintenance.

The estimates for the next year's expenditure by the various Government departments are presented to the House. They are considered by the Committee of Supply, a Committee of the Whole

---

[1] In the Lords, any amendment may be moved.
[2] For Private and Money Bills, different words are used.

House. The necessary grants of money are sanctioned by resolution in this Committee. But this money must be paid from the Consolidated Fund, and a resolution authorising this must be passed by another Committee of the Whole House, the Committee of Ways and Means. This Committee also studies the Budget proposals and approves them by resolution.

These resolutions are later embodied in Acts—the Appropriation Act, which allots the sums to different departments from the Consolidated Fund, and the Finance Act, which authorises any necessary taxation. If a department runs short of money, a temporary Consolidated Fund Act is passed to tide it over until the Appropriation Act is passed.

An official—the Comptroller and Auditor-General—is the watchdog of public finance. Like the Supreme Court judges, he holds office during good behaviour and may only be removed on an address presented to the Crown by both Houses of Parliament. His duty is to safeguard the proper application of the Consolidated Fund and to audit Government accounts. He submits accounts of the Consolidated Fund to the Public Accounts Committee of the Commons.

The two Revenue departments are the Inland Revenue (responsible for, e.g., income tax) and the Customs and Excise (responsible for, e.g., V.A.T.).

The Parliamentary Commissioner

The first Parliamentary Commissioner (popularly known as the 'Ombudsman', after the Danish official whose office formed the inspiration for that of Parliamentary Commissioner) was appointed in 1967. His function is to investigate complaints by individuals and bodies corporate (other than Local Authorities and public bodies) who claim to have suffered injustice as a result of governmental maladministration. The complaint must be referred to the Commissioner by an M.P. and must be in writing. If the Commissioner decides the matter warrants investigation, he has extensive powers of obtaining information and may hear evidence on oath. The Commissioner's duty is to make a report of the results of his investigation, not to take active steps himself to rectify any administrative decision. If he feels an injustice has occurred, however, he may make a special report to both Houses of Parliament.

Attainder and Impeachment

Both Houses possess a quasi-criminal jurisdiction, now practically obsolete. An Act of Attainder is an ordinary Act in effect convicting a person and imposing a punishment. The offence charged need not be a crime and the punishment need not be one imposed by the Criminal Law. The last such Act was in 1715.

Impeachment is a procedure whereby a person accused by the Commons of an offence of a public character is tried by the Lords. The last impeachment was that of Lord Melville in 1805.

The Executive

The Queen is head of the Executive. The succession to the Throne is limited to the heirs of the body of the Electress Sophia of Hanover excluding H.R.H. The Duke of Windsor and his heirs (Abdication Act, 1936). The Sovereign must be a Protestant.

The Sovereign is a corporation sole[1] and thus never dies. On the death of one Sovereign the Crown passes to his successor that instant. At one time the King's death caused widespread chaos— Parliament ended, and officers of State and the judges were automatically discharged. Nowadays, the only consequence of importance is that Ambassadors must be re-accredited.

The Monarch comes of age at eighteen. If he ascends the Throne under that age or is incapable, through insanity, his powers will be exercised by a Regent until the disability ends. The Regent is the Queen's child or grandchild over eighteen, failing which, the Duke of Edinburgh. Counsellors of State, consisting of members of the Royal Family, may exercise most of the Royal functions if the Sovereign is out of the country or partially incapacitated.

The Royal Prerogative

This consists of the powers and privileges peculiar to the Sovereign. Formerly they were much greater than now. Those that remain are practically all exercised on the advice of the Queen's Ministers.

The Queen has no power of arbitrary imprisonment. This was stated in *Magna Carta*, 1215, s. 39: 'No freeman shall be taken or imprisoned except by the lawful judgement of his peers or by the

[1] See Chapter 4, page 74.

law of the land.' This, as we have seen, is secured by the writ of *Habeas Corpus*. Neither can the Queen change the law nor legislate by Proclamation[1] in this country. But it may still be done in certain Colonies. Money may not be raised without Parliamentary Sanction. Charles I claimed to be able to do this and the *Case of Ship Money*[2] resulted. Charles had imposed a tax to pay for ships. He had no Parliamentary authority for this, and John Hampden and others refused to pay. The judiciary at that time held their offices at the King's pleasure and, whether or not this was the law, held such taxation to be legal. This was one of the causes leading to the Civil War. The Bill of Rights, 1688, declared levying of money by the Royal Prerogative to be illegal. As late as 1922 a case resulted from this (*A.-G.* v. *Wilts. United Dairies Ltd.*[3]). Under war-time Acts, the Food Controller was permitted to make regulations affecting the nation's food supply. One of these established a system of licensing. The Food Controller attempted to make charges in respect of these licences. It was held there was no authority in the Acts to do so and the charges were illegal, even though their purpose was not fiscal but that of regulating the price of milk.

The Bill of Rights, 1688, also made a standing army illegal in peacetime.

It used to be said that the King can do no wrong. As the Courts are the King's Courts, no action may be brought against him personally and he may not be prosecuted. Normally, too, a master is liable for his servant's torts committed during the course of his employment. But the King was not similarly liable for his servants' acts. Thus, a person injured by the negligence of the driver of an army lorry could not sue the Crown. Various unsatisfactory substitutes for this were allowed, but the growth of Government influence and activity in everyone's lives rendered a change necessary. The Crown Proceedings Act of 1947 allows the Crown to be sued in tort and for breach of contract in nearly every case, but the Queen may not be sued in her personal capacity.

The Queen's remaining prerogatives are subject to constitutional conventions. She must be guided by her Ministers. She must dissolve Parliament when advised by her Prime Minister and appoint the Ministers of his choice.

[1] Proclamations are usually to announce something of national importance, e.g. summoning of Parliament.
[2] 3 St. Tr. 825.　　　[3] (1922), 91 L.J. K.B. 897.

The Crown may make treaties and declare war, annex and cede territory, without Parliamentary sanction. But this is subject to the proviso that the Crown cannot change English Law and cannot raise money of its own accord.

The Queen is the fountain of justice and may establish a new court if she pleases. But the expenses of running it would need Parliamentary sanction. The Queen may sit in judgment herself, but it is a constitutional convention that she does not. The last monarch to attempt to do so was James I, and all the learning and persuasion of Chief Justice Coke were needed to prevent it.

The Crown, through its appointed officers, appoints judges and magistrates.

The Queen is head of the Armed Forces. She is also the 'Fountain of Honour'. She alone can confer titles and decorations.

We have glanced at the prerogative writ of *Habeas Corpus*. The prerogative orders of Prohibition, *Certiorari* and *Mandamus*, are also important. They afford a means whereby officials and inferior judicial institutions may be kept to the strait and narrow path of duty by an order made by the Divisional Court of the Queen's Bench Division.

An order of prohibition is issued to stop an inferior court or body which is supposed to act judicially from acting improperly, as by exceeding its jurisdiction. The order of prohibition is appropriate before the proceedings of the inferior court have commenced. If it has already concluded the hearing, an order of *Certiorari* wi'l be granted to bring the proceedings before the Queen's Bench Division for review and quash them if improper.

These two remedies have been much used against Rent Tribunals who have exceeded their jurisdiction or failed to act in accordance with natural justice, as by failing to hear both sides.

Mandamus is an order compelling an inferior court, institution or person to carry out a duty imposed on them by law, provided that no other way of obtaining justice (as by ordinary action) is available.

This order would be available against a bench of magistrates, for example, who refused to hear a case for which they had jurisdiction.

The Privy Council

As we saw in Chapter 1, the Sovereign's group of close advisers in high matters of State became known as the Privy Council. This body still exists and its members are styled Right Honourable. Its functions are mostly formal now. Orders in Council and Proclamations are made by the Privy Council, acting through three or four of its members. The Judicial Committee of the Privy Council hears appeals from Commonwealth Courts and ecclesiastical and prize appeals. In legal theory, it is not a court (it is referred to as a Board) and merely advises Her Majesty to take a certain course. In practice, it is a court. Its members are usually the Law Lords, with an occasional judge from the Commonwealth.

The Cabinet

The Cabinet originated in the reign of Charles II. As the Privy Council was a smaller, more select version of the Great Council, so the Cabinet was derived from the Privy Council. It is called the Cabinet, for at first it met in the King's cabinet. George I, however, could not speak English and rarely attended Cabinet meetings. His successors rarely did so, and no Sovereign has done so since George III.

The Cabinet consists of the Prime Minister presiding over the principal Ministers of the Government. Its meetings are, of course, secret, and all Government actions of major importance are discussed by the Cabinet. Once a certain policy has been adopted, all Cabinet Ministers must share in the responsibility for it. If a Cabinet Minister is unable to agree to a course resolved on by the rest of the Cabinet, he must resign from the Government. The Prime Minister must keep the Queen informed of what is discussed at the Cabinet meetings.

The Prime Minister is the country's leader. His power is much more real than apparent. Until recently, he was not even mentioned in any statute. His position of pre-eminence over the Ministers he owes to constitutional convention and not to the law. His salary is £20 000, which is paid to him on account of the office of Prime Minister and that of First Lord of the Treasury, invariably occupied by him. It is a constitutional convention that the Prime Minister should be the leader of the party with most of the seats in the House of Commons, and nowadays he is always a member of that House himself.[1]

Under the Prime Minister are the various Ministers and Secretaries of State, each in control of a particular Government Department.

[1] This is probably the reason Mr. Baldwin became Prime Minister in 1923 instead of Lord Curzon, who would otherwise have been the first-choice.

Each Ministry has a senior Civil Servant at its head to advise the Minister. This is an invaluable arrangement, ensuring that the Minister has someone with specialised experience to guide him and making for continuity in the policy of a Department. The Minister has the final word and takes responsibility for the doings of his Ministry.

The Office of State of most dignity and antiquity is that of Lord Chancellor. This has been described before.

In political importance, the Chancellor of the Exchequer is generally placed next to the Prime Minister. His duties are to direct the national financial policy, supervise the spending of all Government Departments and prepare the Budget, raising the necessary taxes in the best way.

The Secretary of State for Foreign and Commonwealth Affairs is entrusted with safeguarding this country's relations with foreign powers and representing Great Britain abroad. This is done to a certain extent through our Embassies abroad, but their importance has greatly declined, largely through improved communications.

The Secretary of State for Home Affairs is responsible for the maintenance of order in this country. He controls the Metropolitan Police through its Commissioner and, less directly, all other English police forces. He is responsible for prisons and the supervision of aliens.

The Secretary of State for Trade and Industry and President of the Board of Trade has in his Department the Minister for Trade, the Minister for Aerospace, the Minister for Industry and the Minister for Industrial Development. He deals with the promotion and regulation of trade and industry.

The Secretary of State for Employment is responsible for the best use of the Nation's manpower. His department is responsible for the enforcement of the Factories Act by inspection.

The Department of the Environment merges the Ministry of Housing and Local Government, the Ministry of Public Buildings and Works, and the Ministry of Transport. Under the Secretary of State for the Environment are the renamed Minister for Local Government and Development, the Minister for Housing and Construction, and the Minister for the Transport Industries. The Department has responsibility for such things as pollution control, Government policy on transport, the upkeep of trunk roads, housing policies, control of Local Authorities and the preservation of historic buildings.

The Ministry of Aviation Supply deals with the provision of materials, machinery, armaments, etc., to the Government. General responsibility for the promotion and control of atomic energy is now vested in the Department of Trade and Industry.

The Secretary of State for Defence has the duty of co-ordinating the services and so operating with other Departments as to ensure a proper supply of men and materials. The Ministry is organised into central staffs concerned with general defence policy under the Admiralty, Air Force and Army Board of the Defence Council.

All members of the Armed Services, men and women,[1] are subject to Military Law. If they offend against this, they may be tried and punished by military tribunals known as Courts Martial.[2] These are composed of a number of officers of the particular Service. Sometimes they are assisted as regards the law by an official known as the Judge Advocate. A finding of 'guilty' and sentence must be confirmed by a senior officer, known as the Confirming Officer.

Appeal lies to the Courts Martial Appeal Court, established in 1952. Courts Martial sometimes try offences against the ordinary law. An offender tried by a civil court for an offence cannot afterwards be tried by a military court for the same offence, but if tried first by a military tribunal the offender may be tried again for the same offence by a civil court, in theory, at any rate.

Orders of a superior cannot make an unlawful act lawful. A serviceman may thus be in the trying position of offending against the Civil Law if he obeys his superior officer and breaking Military Law if he disobeys. If a serviceman, acting honestly, in the course of his duty obeys an order not illegal on the face of it, he will be protected.[3]

Another Ministry of great importance is the Ministry of Health and Social Security, entrusted with the running of the National Health Service, including the hospitals. Various other Ministries exist, the titles of which are self-explanatory.

The Crown's legal advisers are the Law Officers: the Attorney-General and the Solicitor-General.[4]

The three positions of Lord President of the Council, Lord Privy Seal and Chancellor of the Duchy of Lancaster involve merely nominal duties. They afford a means whereby a man may be freed

[1] Not members of the W.R.N.S.
[2] Certain ranks and offences may be tried summarily.
[3] R. v. *Smith*, 17 Cape Supreme Ct. Rep. 561.   [4] See page 204.

from the cares of a Department so that he may undertake some special task while yet remaining a member of the Government. Alternatively, they may be refuges for those whose infirmity of mind or body makes them unfitted for great governmental responsibility, while at the same time their political careers entitle them to office of some sort.

A personage receiving a salary of £9500 from the Crown is by no means a Government supporter but the Leader of the Opposition. This unique course is taken in the belief that an effective and sensible Opposition is an aid to good government.

Local Government

Many functions of government are undertaken by the Local Authorities. These are: the County Councils, County Borough Councils, Borough Councils, Urban District Councils, Rural District Councils and Parish Councils. The local government of the London area is now undertaken by the Greater London Council and the London Borough Councils. The present arrangements derive from the London Government Act, 1963. This excludes the City of London, which is governed by its Lord Mayor and Corporation.

A County Council is composed of a Chairman, Aldermen and Councillors. The Chairman is elected annually by the Council. The Aldermen are elected by the Councillors every six years, one-half retiring every three years. The Councillors are elected every three years by the local government electors. Upon the County Council devolve the responsibilities for education, maintenance of most roads, provision of infirmaries, etc. Under the Local Government Act, 1933, it may legislate by making byelaws within the prescribed limits.

A Borough Council is composed of the Mayor (or, in some cities, the Lord Mayor), Aldermen and Councillors. The Mayor is elected annually by the council; the Aldermen are elected every six years by the Councillors, one-half retiring every three years. One-third of the Councillors are elected every year by the local government electors. Councillors retire every three years.

The composition of a County Borough is similar to that of a Borough. Both Boroughs and County Boroughs may make byelaws.

Urban and Rural District Councils consist of a Chairman (elected annually by the Council), who presides over Councillors elected by the local government electors every three years.

The functions undertaken by the four last authorities are similar, except that County Borough Councils exercise the powers of County Councils in their area, to the exclusion of the local County Council. They include public transport, street cleaning, public libraries, housing, public health, public parks, etc.

The humblest local authority is the Parish Council, which deals with parish property, such as the parish hall. It is presided over by a Chairman, elected yearly by the Councillors—who are themselves elected every three years.

Certain local government functions are discharged at Parish Meetings.

The structure of local government will be greatly altered after April 1974. England will be divided into local government areas known as Counties, each being administered by a County Council, and the Counties in turn will be divided into Districts, each being administered by a District Council. Parish Councils will remain. Wales will be divided into Counties, Districts and Communities. The Counties will either be Metropolitan Counties, e.g. Greater Manchester, or non-Metropolitan Counties, e.g. Berkshire. County Councils will have greater responsibilities than at present.[1]

The income of local authorities is derived from a tax on property in their areas, known as Rates, and by grants from the Treasury. In addition, income is often derived from trading ventures such as municipal transport.

Control of Local Authorities by the Government is mainly exercised through the Secretary of State for the Environment.

The Commonwealth

This consists of the British Islands (the United Kingdom, the Isle of Man and Channel Islands), fully independent Members of the Commonwealth and countries which are still, to a greater or lesser degree, subject to the rule of the Crown. The Queen is recognised as Head of the Commonwealth. The Crown also exercises control of Protectorates and Trust Territories, the latter under the supervision of the United Nations. These are not part of the Commonwealth.

The United Kingdom Parliament at Westminster is supreme over the British Isles, but the Isle of Man and the Channel Islands have

[1] Local Government Act, 1972.

their own legislature which are restricted in their scope. Northern Ireland has undergone profound changes. In 1972 direct rule from Westminster was imposed and the Northern Ireland Parliament, which had restricted legislative power, was prorogued. A new Northern Ireland Assembly was set up and elected in 1973, and provisions for its powers are contained in the Northern Ireland Constitution Act, 1973. When these are implemented, the temporary direct rule will expire. Northern Ireland sends members to the United Kingdom Parliament. Its Courts administer what is virtually English Law and appeal lies from their Court of Appeal to the House of Lords.

Scotland has no separate legislature but returns members of Parliament to Westminster. In practice, Scottish affairs are discussed only by the Scots Peers and M.P.s. The Secretary of State for Scotland has charge of Scottish Home Affairs, Education, Health and Agriculture. Scots Law is different from English, and the judiciary and Law Officers are separate. Appeals from the superior court of Scotland (the Court of Session) lie to the House of Lords.

Wales sends members to the United Kingdom Parliament. There is now a Secretary of State for Wales. England and Wales have the same judiciary and legal system, but the Welsh language may be used in court.

The Members are the Sovereign independent States of the Commonwealth and their dependencies. Certain older Members were formerly known as Dominions. The Queen is Head of the Commonwealth but is no longer the Queen of each member country, as most countries are republics.

The Commonwealth Secretariat, set up in 1965, assists in co-ordinating Commonwealth activities and supplies information to the Members. It has no executive powers. The statute which ensures the autonomy of the oldest Member countries, Canada, Australia and New Zealand, is the Statute of Westminster, 1931, which provides that the Dominions[1] shall not be affected by an Act of the United Kingdom Parliament unless the Act recites that the Dominion concerned has requested and consented to the passing of the Act. A Dominion may repeal any United Kingdom Act applying to it.[2]

[1] As they were then known.
[2] Save certain Acts relating to the Canadian and Australian constitutions.

The legislatures of the various Dominions differ greatly. In each the Crown is represented by a Governor-General. He must be guided by his Ministers in the same way as the Queen. The position of a Governor-General is one of enormous responsibility, for on him, to a large extent, depends the relations between the United Kingdom and his Dominion. In addition, by his tact and experience he can smooth the path of government considerably.

The difference between a Colony and a Dominion is that the former is subject to legislation by the United Kingdom Parliament, or the Crown in some cases, without the consent of the Colony.

The powers of Colonial Legislatures are laid down by the Colonial Laws Validity Act of 1865. Colonies may make laws for the peace, order and good government of the Colonies. It is doubtful whether they can pass legislation having effect outside their own territories.

If a Colonial enactment is repugnant to an English Act, Order or Regulation, the Colonial legislation will be void to the extent of the repugnancy (s. 2 of the Act). Section 5 gives Colonies with a representative legislature the power to make laws regulating the legislature's constitution, powers and procedure. The same section gives *all* Colonial legislatures the power to establish Courts of Justice.

Several former Colonies became non-dependent States in 1967 and 1969. Each state is responsible for its own internal affairs and s. 2 of the Colonial Laws Validity Act ceases to apply. Each may amend its constitution and become unilaterally independent. The British Government retains responsibility for external affairs and defence. Her Majesty's representative is the Governor.

Some of the few remaining Colonies have internal self-government, with the Governor having responsibility for external affairs, defence and internal security, while in others the Governor has legislative powers.

The Foreign and Commonwealth Office is responsible for Commonwealth and Colonial affairs. The Minister for Overseas Development has charge of its development schemes.

The Judicial Committee of the Privy Council is the supreme Court of Appeal of dependencies in the Commonwealth and also from the Courts of certain Members.

3 Torts

What is a tort? The word is derived from the French, meaning 'wrong'. The literal translation is too wide, for the legal term merely includes actionable *civil* wrongs, apart from breach of contract and breach of trust. Torts are many and various, ranging from trespass to libel, but they have this in common: that the remedy for all may be in damages, and, if so, the damages are unliquidated. 'Unliquidated' damages are those which the Court has power to fix, exercisable in its discretion, as distinct from liquidated damages, which is a fixed amount claimed by the plaintiff.

The first tort we may consider is trespass, which may be to land, to chattels or to the person. Trespass is an unjustifiable interference with possession. When anyone enters another's land without justification, he commits the tort of trespass. Note that trespass is merely a tort and not a crime.[1] The notice boards' 'trespassers will be prosecuted' are hollow threats. Trespassers to land may be asked to leave and, if they do not, they may be removed with no more force than is reasonably necessary. An action for damages lies for a mere trespass, even though no damage is caused. If you trespass, trampling heavily through a man's flowerbeds, he can recover damages; but he can still recover damages, though at a nominal figure, if you discreetly tread his asphalt drive, doing no harm to it. For you have interfered with his possession of it without excuse, and that is sufficient. As a landowner is said to own not only the surface of the land but also the earth down to the infernal regions and the air above to the heavens, it is possible to trespass by burrowing under a man's land or by hanging an illuminated sign over it, for example. It is possible to trespass on the highway, for, though the surface of a public highway is vested in the highway authority, the subsoil beneath may belong to a private owner. *Harrison* v. *Duke of Rutland*[2] is an example. Harrison stood on the highway and deliberately scared the Duke's game. It was held that this was an improper use

---

[1] Except on railway property, where it is an offence punishable with a fine, or otherwise where made an offence by statute.

[2] [1893] 1 Q.B. 142.

of the highway and a consequent trespass to the subsoil, of which the Duke was owner.

Trespass to goods or chattels is a tort. Chattels personal are movable goods, as contrasted with land and buildings and crops growing in the ground. They include animals and all inanimate objects.[1]

The third type of trespass differs from the other two in that it must be intentional—trespass to the person, known otherwise as assault. Another difference is that assault is a crime as well as a tort. An assault, strictly speaking, is conduct giving rise to apprehension of force being applied to the person. If the force actually results, it is a battery as well. Thus if A shakes his fist under B's nose, he assaults him; if A strikes B on that organ, he commits not only assault but also battery. In both cases the conduct must be an act; words *alone* are not sufficient. The least touching in anger or without justification is a battery, even though no injury is caused. A battery may be inflicted with the hands or by any instrument. But it must be direct, and the touching must be a positive act. Where a policeman stood in a doorway, preventing a person from passing, though not actively repulsing him, it was held the policeman was not committing a battery (*Innes* v. *Wylie*).[2] An assault and battery may be justified, as when an authorised person removes a trespasser using only necessary and reasonable force. Beating an otherwise inoffensive trespasser senseless would be unjustifiable, and a battery.

Detinue is the unjustifiable detention of chattels. Before the plaintiff can bring this action he must demand the return of his goods and the defendant must refuse to return them or fail to return them. The refusal must be unreasonable for the action to lie. If the finder of a gold watch was accosted by a stranger who claimed it was his, the finder would not commit the tort of detinue by keeping it while making reasonable enquiries. And the plaintiff cannot succeed unless he is entitled to the possession of the object. If a man pawns a diamond ring, he remains its owner, but he cannot sue the pawnbroker for detaining the ring until he has paid what he owes him, for until then the pawnbroker, not he, is entitled to possession.

Conversion is the implied or actual wrongful denial of another's title to goods. It may take place by an outright denial or by acts inconsistent with the other person's title. There must be more than mere interference with possession; title must be called in question.

---

[1] Chattels real are leaseholds.   [2] 1 C. & K. 257.

Thus where the owner of a ferry-boat had put the horses of X ashore after an argument between X and him, his act was held not to be conversion. X's ownership of his goods had not been interfered with, merely his possession.

Conversion cannot be involuntary. A man cannot convert something the existence of which he is unaware. And he cannot be made liable for goods thrust uninvited upon him. If an author sends his unsolicited manuscript to a publisher and that publisher negligently loses it, it may be that a masterpiece is lost to posterity, but no action for conversion lies. It would lie, however, if the publisher, perhaps in a fit of exasperation, threw the book in the fire. The position of a person who is thus entrusted with goods without previous invitation or consent on his part is difficult, for he must retain the goods until the person with a right to their possession collects them or authorises him to deal with them in any way.

The next tort to consider is the all-embracing one of negligence. This includes the negligent hairdresser whose customer's hair falls out, the doctor who diagnoses wrongly, the reckless motorist, the factory-owner whose machines are not properly fenced, a person giving negligent advice to someone who suffers financial loss as a result—all may be liable to those who have suffered damage. It will be seen what a wide field is covered. But not all negligent acts are torts. There are three necessities:

(1) The defendant must owe a duty of care to the plaintiff.
(2) The defendant must have been in breach of that duty.
(3) The plaintiff must have suffered damage as a result of such negligence.

Let us examine the careless motorist case further. Suppose a cyclist to be peacefully proceeding along the road, keeping to his left. As he rounds a corner, a motorist careers round it, without warning, going at excessive speed on the wrong side of the road. He hits the cyclist and breaks his leg. Here, plainly, the three requisites for an action for negligence are present. But not many cases are as plain as that, and each element must now be considered carefully.

The classic case is that of *Donoghue* v. *Stevenson*.[1] A girl bought a bottle of ginger-beer from a retail shop for her friend. The manufacturer had bottled the substance in opaque bottles and nothing wrong was observed when the first glass was poured. But the second

[1] [1932] A.C. 562.

contained the horrid remains of a snail. The girl was ill in consequence and sued the manufacturer for damages in tort. Lord Atkin
stated the law as follows: 'You must take reasonable care to avoid
acts or omissions which you can reasonably foresee would be likely
to injure your neighbour. Who, then, in law, is my neighbour? The
answer seems to be—persons who are so closely and directly affected
by my act that I ought reasonably to have them in contemplation as
being so affected when I am directing my mind to the acts or omissions which are called in question.'

A peculiar illustration of a person being outside this duty occurred in *Bourhill* v. *Young*.[1] A fishwife was alighting from a tramcar. As
she did so, a motor-cyclist was, owing to his own negligence, killed
by a car nearby. The fishwife did not see the collision, but heard it and
saw the blood on the ground. As a consequence she suffered severe
shock and a miscarriage. She sued the motor-cyclist's personal
representative for the motor-cyclist's negligence, and failed. The
motor-cyclist, assuming he directed his mind to the acts and omissions causing the accident, could not reasonably be expected to
contemplate this particular effect of his negligence. Pregnant women
do not normally miscarry because they *hear* accidents. Had the
motor-cyclist collided with the fishwife owing to his negligence, she
could have recovered damages, for he should have realised as a
reasonable person that negligent driving in a crowded street is likely
to affect persons in that he might knock them down.

An instance of a duty of care is the duty of an employer to provide
his workmen with safe plant, competent fellow-employees and a
safe system of working. This is a Common Law duty additional to
that laid on employers by such legislation as the Factories Acts.

An interesting recent example of the establishment of a duty of
care is *Dutton* v. *Bognor Regis United Building Co. Ltd*.[2] A Local Authority made byelaws regulating the construction of building works,
pursuant to statutory duties imposed by the Public Health Act,
1936, which also conferred power to enforce byelaws. The byelaws
made provision for the proper construction of foundations and
provided for the appointment of surveyors to see that the byelaws
were complied with. A building inspector negligently failed to
detect that a builder had failed to provide secure foundations and,
as a result, the plaintiff, who purchased the completed house from the
builder, found herself in possession of a home which subsequently

[1] [1943] A.C. 92.   [2] [1972] 1 All E.R. 462.

suffered severe damage from subsidence. It was held that the Local Authority, through the building inspector, owed a duty of care to the plaintiff to ensure that the inspection of the foundations was properly carried out and that the foundations were adequate. The Court of Appeal also said that the vendor builder was himself under a duty of care to the plaintiff, thus overruling an earlier case which had held, by analogy with the law of real property, that no legal duty arose in tort (as opposed to contract), between the builder of a house, who was also the vendor, and a purchaser.[1]

The reader will notice the word 'reasonably' occurring in Lord Atkin's definition. The doctrine of 'reasonableness' is a golden thread running through this branch of the law. The duty of care is gauged not by extraordinary prescience, or an abnormal lack of it, but by the standard of the average reasonable person.

The second element of the tort is judged by this standard of reasonableness as well. Negligence is acting other than as a reasonable man would do in the circumstances. The test is an objective one. The 'reasonable man' has been described as the man on the Clapham omnibus (by Lord Bowen), which is perhaps more helpful than Sir Alan Herbert's description of him as a 'repellent figment of the jurists' imagination'. He is the epitome of ordinariness, never reckless or absent-minded, yet not endowed with exceptional courage, foresight or skill. But note that if the reasonable man is a solicitor or a railway signalman, for example, he must possess the skill of those occupations and a correspondingly higher duty is laid on him.

The third requirement is that the plaintiff must suffer damage. The damage must not be too remote. Though in all torts of which damage is an ingredient this is so, the problem chiefly arises in connection with negligence, and it is convenient to deal with it here. It is obvious that in a sense every action that happens is just a part in an eternal chain. It is caused by, and causes, other happenings. Which are the consequences the law takes into account? It has now been decided[2] that the test is that of foreseeability. If the consequences are such that the reasonable man could not have foreseen them, then they are too remote.

When considering liability, carefully distinguish duty of care from

[1] See now the Defective Premises Act, 1972, which comes into force 1st January, 1974.

[2] *Overseas Tankship (U.K.) Ltd.* v. *Morts Dock & Engineering Co. Ltd. (The Wagon Mound)*, [1961] A.C. 388.

remoteness of liability. The fact that a person is of abnormal sensitivity—for example, has very brittle bones or a weak heart—may put him outside the duty of care. Once a duty of care is owed, however, to such a person, then the extra damage suffered by him will not be too remote.

It may be that the plaintiff has contributed to his damage by his own negligence. Since the Law Reform (Contributory Negligence) Act, 1945, the plaintiff may still recover damages, but they shall be reduced to such an extent as the Court thinks just and equitable, having regard to the claimant's share in the responsibility for the damage.

For the purposes of contributory negligence, negligence means simply lack of care. There need be no duty owed by the plaintiff to the defendant.

One more topic must be mentioned in connection with negligence—the doctrine of '*res ipsa loquitur*'.[1] This is a matter of proof. Where an operation is under the control of the defendant[2] and an accident occurs, which accident does not usually occur if the defendant takes proper care, it lies upon the defendant either positively to prove he has not been negligent or to produce a reasonable explanation of how the accident could have occurred without his negligence. In this latter case, the plaintiff will have to prove negligence, if he can. The classic case is *Scott* v. *London & St.Katherine Docks Co.*,[3] where bags of sugar fell from a warehouse, occupied by the defendants, on to a passer-by. The defendants were called on to explain how it came about that the bags so fell, because 'the thing' which caused the accident was entirely under their control.

With respect to the liability of the manufacturer or transferor of chattels, the view has been expressed that there was a higher duty of care owed when the chattels in question were dangerous in themselves than when the chattels were not inherently dangerous but might become so if handled or treated in a certain way. The former would be things like gelignite or jars of acid, the latter a glass container or an oil can. However, the better view seems to be that there is one duty of care which varies according to the circumstances of the case. The classic exposition of the manufacturer's duty was expressed by Lord Atkin in *Donoghue* v. *Stevenson*. A manufacturer

---

[1] The matter speaks for itself.
[2] Or his servants, in each case.
[3] (1865) 3 H. & C. 596.

who sells goods, in the form in which they will reach the ultimate consumer, with no reasonable possibility of intermediate examination and with knowledge that lack of reasonable care on his part will result in injury to the consumer's life or property, owes a duty to the consumer to take that reasonable care.

In *Donoghue* v. *Stevenson* a chattel (the bottle of ginger beer) was dangerous because of a defect (the dead snail). The bottle reached the consumer via the retailer from the manufacturer without any reasonable prospect of intermediate examination (as the bottle was opaque).

The concept of the manufacturer has been extended to include the repairer, packer and assembler of chattels. The duty of care may be discharged by care in the goods' preparation and packing, or, if the product is inherently dangerous, by a warning.

If a person carries on an operation involving danger to another's premises if proper care is not taken, he must take that care. The duty is higher than that in negligence, for in 'dangerous operations' cases the defendant is responsible for the damage caused by an independent contractor,[1] whereas in negligence he is not. An example of a dangerous operation is searching for a gas leak with a naked light.[2]

Where premises are dangerous through the negligence of the person in whose control they are, the duty of care is now laid down by the Occupiers' Liability Act, 1957. 'Premises' includes not only buildings but also land, vehicles and other structures.

Section 2 provides that an occupier owes the same duty of care ('the common duty of care') to all his visitors (except trespassers) except where such duty is modified (where possible) by agreement or otherwise. The distinction made by the Common Law between 'invitees' and 'licensees' is abolished.[3] The duty of care is to take such care as in all the circumstances of the case is reasonable to see that the visitor will be reasonably safe in using the premises for the purposes for which he is invited or permitted by the occupier to be there. The circumstances relevant include the degree of care, and of

[1] An independent contractor differs from a servant in that the way in which the independent contractor does his task is under his control and at his discretion.

[2] *Brooke* v. *Bool* [1928] 2 Q.B. 578.

[3] An invitee is a person who goes to the premises of another in pursuance of some common material interest. A licensee is a person who the occupier permits to come on his premises but who is not there for a material interest of the occupier.

want of care, which would ordinarily be looked for in such a visitor, so that (for example) in proper cases:

(*a*) an occupier must be prepared for children to be less careful than adults (see below); and

(*b*) an occupier may expect that a person, in the exercise of his calling will appreciate and guard against any special risks ordinarily incident to it, so far as the occupier leaves him free to do so.

In determining whether the occupier of premises has discharged the duty of care, regard is to be had to all the circumstances, so that (for example):

(*a*) where damage is caused to a visitor by a danger of which he had been warned by the occupier, the warning is not to be treated, without more, as absolving the occupier from liability, unless in all the circumstances it was enough to enable the visitor to be reasonably safe; and

(*b*) where damage is caused to a visitor by a danger due to the faulty work of an independent contractor employed by the occupier, the occupier is not to be treated, without more, as answerable for the danger if in all the circumstances he had acted reasonably in entrusting the work to an independent contractor and had taken such steps (if any) as he reasonably ought in order to satisfy himself that the contractor was competent and that the work had been properly done.

An occupier who is bound by contract or by a condition of a tenancy to permit third parties to enter the premises owes them the common duty of care (s. 3).

Where premises are occupied by any person under a tenancy which puts on the landlord an obligation to that person to repair the premises, the landlord owes to all persons who or whose goods may be lawfully on the premises, the common duty of care, in respect of dangers arising from any default in his obligation to repair (s. 4).

The duty owed by an occupier to persons entering, or sending goods to premises, under a contractual right is the common duty of care, unless the contract expressly provides otherwise (s. 5).

One who is upon another's premises without any legal right or express or implied permission is a trespasser. A trespasser until recently had no redress in law if he suffered damage from the defective state of the premises, since the occupier was under no duty of care towards him. However, in *British Railways Board* v. *Herrington*[1] the House of Lords held that if the occupier knows that there are trespassers on his land or knows that their presence is likely, and also knows of a danger on his land, he is under a duty to take steps to enable the trespasser to avoid that danger. The duty only arises if by ordinary standards of common sense and humanity he would be culpable if he failed to take such steps. In the above case a small boy was injured when he got through the appellant's defective fence and trespassed on their electrified line. The Board was held liable to the child trespasser since they had on their land a danger—the electric rail—and though they knew that children played in the field next to the line they failed to take reasonable steps to maintain the fence. Of course, the occupier must not deliberately injure the trespasser or, while the trespasser is on the premises, change their condition, thus creating a new danger, without warning. An illustration is *Mourton* v. *Poulter*,[2] where a person was cutting down a tree. Some trespassers were watching him and he ordered them off the land. He gave no warning as the tree was about to fall, and in falling it injured a trespasser who had returned. He was held liable to the trespasser.

Special considerations arise when dealing with children on dangerous premises. To start with, a child may be too young to comprehend a warning notice. Secondly, the danger may be caused by an attractive object, which is dangerous, on the land. A child might well be allured by such an object to play with it and yet be unable to understand the dangers involved in doing so. In *Glasgow Corporation* v. *Taylor*[3] the Corporation were occupiers of a public park in which were poisonous berries which, however, looked very good to eat. A child licensee ate some and died. It was held that the Corporation were liable since they knew the berries were poisonous and should have given adequate warning of this, as the berries were an allurement to children by reason of their attractive appearance.

Nuisance

Nuisances are of two types: public and private. The first range from keeping a gaming-house to failing to repair a highway. They consist of cases where the public as a whole suffers more than an individual. They are crimes and not torts. Private nuisance is a tort and consists of unlawful interference with land or any right connected with land

[1] [1972] 1 All E.R. 749.   [2] [1930] 2 K.B. 183.   [3] [1922] 1 A.C. 44.

where a particular individual is affected. Normally, nuisance is actionable without proof of damage, except for nuisances on the highway or nuisances affecting land. But the interference must affect the plaintiff's comfort or health, or his property.

Common forms of nuisance are noise, smells, falling objects, smoke, etc. What may be a nuisance in one place may not be in another. 'Time, locality and all the circumstances are to be taken into consideration.' An iron foundry that would be a nuisance in Berkeley Square would probably not be so in an industrial quarter of Birmingham. And tender plants, whether of the human or horticultural kind, must put up with occurrences that would not amount to a nuisance to persons or things of normal susceptibility. An act may be a nuisance whatever the motive that prompts it, but a spiteful motive may turn an otherwise reasonable set of circumstances into an unreasonable one and hence a nuisance. An example is *Christie* v. *Davey*.[1] The plaintiff and the defendant were neighbours. The plaintiff taught music in his house. The defendant disliked this and deliberately created a loud noise to annoy the plaintiff. It was held that the defendant's improper motive made his conduct a nuisance.

Where the damage has been caused by the defective state of a highway, the highway authority is liable unless they can prove that they took reasonable care in all the circumstances to ensure that the highway was not dangerous.

To bring an action for nuisance the plaintiff must occupy the land in question, unless the nuisance is on the highway, in which case he must be a user of the highway in question. The person creating the nuisance is normally the person to be sued, but a person may tolerate the continuance of a nuisance emanating from his land which originated with the previous owner or a trespasser, in which case he will be liable. And a landlord may be liable for a tenant's nuisances in certain circumstances. A person is responsible for nuisances created by his independent contractors unless the nuisances arise from circumstances outside the scope of the task for which they were engaged.

Two defences peculiar to the law of nuisance may be noted. The first is that if an occupation is a nuisance it is no defence to an action to plead that the plaintiff came to the scene of his own accord and that the defendant had been carrying on the nuisance for many years

---

[1] [1893] 1 Ch. 316.

before. Such was the case in *Bliss* v. *Hall*,[1] where the plaintiff went to live near the defendant's tallow factory which emitted a disagreeable smell. It would have been different had the defendant's factory been situated in an industrial region, for there tallow making is a reasonable occupation, not a nuisance, and the plaintiff would have only himself to blame.

The right to commit a private nuisance will be earned by prescription if it has been carried on without protest by the plaintiff for twenty years from the time he learnt of its existence.

The remedies for nuisance are damages, injunction and, in some cases, abatement.

The next tort to be examined is known by the name of the case in which the rule was laid down—'*Rylands* v. *Fletcher*'.[2] Like nuisance, it arises from the use of land, the *defendant's* land, but the duty it imposes on the defendant is much stricter, being well-nigh absolute. The rule is: 'The person who for his own purposes brings on his lands and collects and keeps there anything likely to do mischief if it escapes, must keep it in at his peril and if he does not do so is *prima facie* answerable for all the damage which is the natural consequence of its escape.' Rylands had employed independent contractors to construct a reservoir on his land which adjoined that of Fletcher. Owing to the contractors' negligence, old mine shafts leading from Rylands's land to Fletcher's were not blocked, with the result that the water flooded Fletcher's mines. Rylands was held liable in damages. The rule has been held to include the escape of many different things, such as poisonous vegetation, electricity, fumes and even 'noxious persons'.

The first requirement for the rule to apply is that there should be an escape from the defendant's land to a place outside his occupation or control. Thus an explosion taking place *inside* the defendant's premises cannot bring *Rylands* v. *Fletcher* into operation.

The second requirement is that the user of the land must be non-natural, considering all the circumstances.

If the thing escaping is something not normally dangerous which it is natural to have on land, e.g. a tree, there is no liability. Thus it was held in *Pontardawe R.D.C.* v. *Moore-Gwyn*[3] that rocks naturally on land which fell of their own accord were outside the rule.

If the thing escaping is kept for the common benefit of plaintiff and defendant, the rule does not apply. Supposing Fletcher's reser-

[1] 4 Bing. N.C. 183.   [2] L.R. 3 H.L. 330.   [3] [1929] 1 Ch. 656.

voir had been constructed for the use of Rylands as well, there would have been no liability.

'Act of God' is a defence but not inevitable accident.[1] 'Act of God' is an extraordinary act of nature of such an unexpected character that no human foresight could provide against it, and of which human prudence is not bound to recognise the possibility.

If the occurrence takes place through the plaintiff's own fault or that of a third person, the defendant will not be liable.

The ordinary defences of statutory authority and *volenti non fit injuria*[2] are open to the defendant.

Animals

A tort may be committed by means of an animal. Thus a dog trailing a lead was held to be a nuisance on the highway[3] (*Pitcher* v. *Martin*). But apart from ordinary torts in which the animal has been a passive instrument, strict liability for animals in certain circumstances is now laid down by the Animals Act, 1971, which supersedes the Common Law.

The Act provides that the keeper of a dog, which causes damage by killing or injuring livestock, is liable for the damage. However, there is no liability if the livestock strayed onto the land and were there killed or injured by a dog belonging to the owner of the land, or authorised by him to be there.

The provisions of the Act also replace the old Common Law tort of cattle trespass. Where A's livestock stray onto B's land and there cause damage to the land or any property on it, A is liable for the damage or expense. This applies even if A has not been negligent. Livestock includes cattle, pigs, horses, poultry and tame deer, but not dogs and cats. Someone who has an interest in land, such as a landlord, may not complain if his neighbour's cattle trespass on his land owing to defective fencing, provided that the landlord was under a duty to fence.

If damage is done by cattle straying from the highway, there is no liability if their presence was a lawful use of the highway. Thus if an ox is being taken to market with all due care and it escapes into a china shop, the animals' owner will not be liable for the result.

At Common Law the duty of an owner to prevent his cattle from straying onto the highway was very limited. However, the Act now

---

[1] See page 64.   [2] See page 64.   [3] [1937] 3 All E.R. 918.

provides that in this situation, with exceptions relating to common land, the owner must discharge the common duty of care towards the users of the highway.

Where an animal is known to belong to a dangerous species, any person who is the keeper of the animal is liable for any damage caused by it. Damage includes injury to person and property. A dangerous species is one which is not commonly domesticated in the British Isles, and fully grown members of which have such characteristics that they are liable, unless restrained, to cause severe damage, for example a tiger.

Where the damage is caused by an animal not of a dangerous species (e.g. a cat), the keeper is liable if the damage is of a kind which the animal unless restrained was liable to cause, or which, if caused by the animal, was likely to be severe. The likelihood of damage, or of its being severe, must arise from characteristics of the particular animal which are known to the keeper and which are not usually found in animals of that species.

Defamation

This may be defined as the publication of a statement which brings a person into hatred, contempt or ridicule of reasonable persons, or makes such persons shun or avoid that person. It may be libel or slander. Libel is permanent—e.g. an effigy or writing—slander is impermanent—e.g. speech or gestures.[1] Libel may be a crime as well as a tort; slander is only a tort. But the main distinction is that no special damage need be proved in an action for libel, whereas it must in slander. For example, if you write on a wall: 'Mr. Jones is an adulterer', he may sue you for that alone, but if you merely shout it to passers-by, his action for slander would not succeed unless he could show some special damage flowing from the defamation—e.g. he had been dismissed from his employment.

Four kinds of slander, however, are regarded by the law as so heinous that no proof of special damage is necessary: statements that a woman has been unchaste; that a person has committed a crime punishable with imprisonment; that a person is suffering from a contagious or infectious disease; or statements calculated to disparage the plaintiff in any office, profession, calling, trade or business. As regards the last kind of slander, the statement is actionable

[1] Speech on the wireless is libel (Defamation Act, 1952, s. 1).

per se[1] whether it is made of him personally[2] or in his professional capacity.

What is defamatory? The statement's effect on reasonable people is the guide. As a matter of law the judge must decide whether it is capable of being defamatory, and the jury must then decide whether it is so or not.

The statement may be defamatory on its face, or the meaning may be concealed or ironic ('Brutus is an honourable man'). The plaintiff must then show by an 'innuendo' that the statement is capable of being, and was, or might be, understood by reasonable persons as being defamatory. Thus in *Cassidy* v. *Daily Mirror Newspapers Ltd.*[3] a newspaper published a picture with the caption 'Mr Cassidy with Miss X. whose engagement has been announced.' Mr. Cassidy was, in fact, married at the time. Mrs. Cassidy sued the newspaper for libel. It was held that the caption conveyed that Mrs. Cassidy was not the wife of Cassidy but merely immorally cohabited with him, and she was awarded damages.[4]

The words must refer to the plaintiff. Where a defamatory statement is made of a class of persons including the plaintiff, he must show that it was reasonably capable of referring to him in particular and that reasonable persons thought it referred to him in particular.

If an author invents a name which happens to be that of a real person, he may be liable for defamation. In *E. Hulton & Co.* v. *Jones*[5] the amorous adventures of an imaginary churchwarden from Peckham, named Artemus Jones, had been described in a newspaper. There was a real Artemus Jones, a barrister, and he recovered damages. And in *Newstead* v. *London Express Ltd.*[6] a newspaper described how Harold Newstead, a Camberwell man, had been jailed for bigamy. There were two Camberwell men of that name and the guiltless one brought a successful action for libel even though the newspaper had never known of his existence.

The Defamation Act, 1952, has eased this burden, however. A person who has innocently (not merely carelessly) defamed another may make an offer of amends. This may entail making a suitable apology, and notifying persons to whom the defamatory statement

---

[1] i.e. without proof of special damage.

[2] Since the Defamation Act, 1952.   [3] [1929] 2 K.B. 331.

[4] As publication was unintentional, the newspaper could now make an 'offer of amends'.

[5] [1910] A.C. 20.   [6] [1940] 1 K.B. 377.

has been communicated of its falsity. If the offer of amends is accepted, well and good; if not, it will be a good defence, provided that it was made as soon as practicable.

For a statement to be defamatory it must be 'published'. 'Publication' entails the communication of the statement to a person other than the person about whom it is made. But if the person making the statement is the husband or wife of the person who sees or hears it, there is no publication. But communication by a third person to one spouse of matter defamatory of the other is publication. In some cases publication will be presumed; for example, a writing on a postcard is presumed to be published by passing through the post. The publisher of defamatory statements may be sued as well as their originator. As regards printed matter, however, a mere distributor, such as a newsagent (or library), may escape liability by showing that he did not know of the libellous statement and his lack of knowledge was not due to his negligence. Permission by the plaintiff to publish will prevent a statement from being defamatory.

There are four defences to an action for defamation: truth or justification, fair comment, absolute privilege and qualified privilege.

If the words complained of are true, this is a complete defence. But the truth must be complete and an answer to the whole defamation. If the defamation is divisible, it may be possible to justify one part though not another.

Fair comment on a matter of public interest is a defence. The criticism must be comment and not a statement of fact. Though it may be violent, it must be honest and free from malice. In cases of literary criticism, for example, it must be borne in mind that a book cannot sue for defamation and that criticism can only be defamatory if it passes beyond the author's works and, directly or indirectly, attacks the author himself.

The need to speak or write freely on certain occasions is judged by the law to be of such importance that it gives absolute privilege to defamatory statements made in those cases, even if the statements were made maliciously. This privilege applies to speeches in Parliament and reports published by order of either House. It applies to proceedings in Court and fair and accurate contemporaneous newspaper reports of public Court proceedings.[1] Communications be-

---

[1] Note the Judicial Proceedings (Regulation of Reports) Act, 1926, which makes it a crime to publish certain details of matrimonial cases and indecent details arising in judicial proceedings.

tween Officers of State in the course of their duties are also protected.

Qualified privilege can only exist where there has been no malice on the defendant's part. In this connection malice means absence of right motive. Fair and accurate newspaper reports of public meetings are examples of this class. Other examples are statements made under a duty to another (such as giving a 'character' of a former employee to a prospective employer) and complaints to a competent authority, concerning a matter of public interest, against a public official.

Statements made in legitimate protection of one's interests are given qualified privilege. Finally, communications between a person and his legal advisers are privileged, but it is uncertain whether this privilege is qualified or absolute.

Interference with Contract

It is a tort to induce a person to break his contract with another. Gye was the manager of a theatre. He induced an opera singer, Wagner, to break her contract with one Lumley and sing at his (Gye's) theatre. He was held liable in damages.[1] It is similarly a tort to induce a person by unlawful means not to enter into a contract with another. 'Unlawful means' may be fraud, violence or the threat to do something unlawful. Many cases have arisen from trading associations. In *Thorne* v. *Motor Trading Association*[2] it was held that a threat by the Association to place a member on its Stop List (whereby he would be prevented from contracting with other members) unless he paid a fine to the Association for breach of its rules was lawful if it was merely to protect the members' trading interests and not for the purpose of spitefully injuring the member.

It was held in the case of *Rookes* v. *Barnard*[3] that intimidation was an established tort. The ingredients are:

(1) A coercive threat to use unlawful means (which include tort and breach of contract) to compel a person to do something which he is unwilling to do.
(2) Compliance by the party threatened.
(3) Damage suffered by the plaintiff as the result of this compliance.

[1] *Lumley* v. *Gye*, 2 E. & B. 216.   [2] [1937] A.C. 797.
[3] [1964] 2 W.L.R. 269.

These torts are now excluded from trade disputes by statute.

Section 132(1) of the Industrial Relations Act, 1971, provides that an act done by a person in contemplation or furtherance of a trade dispute shall not be actionable in tort on the ground that it induces another person to break a contract to which that other person is a party or prevents another person from performing such a contract.

The tort of Conspiracy is considered under the heading of Criminal Law.[1] The last two torts we shall consider often arise together from the same set of circumstances but are logically distinct. They are Malicious Prosecution and False Imprisonment. False imprisonment is a crime as well as a tort.

There are four essentials for the plaintiff to prove in malicious prosecution. For this reason the action rarely succeeds. The first requirement is that the defendant must have been 'actively instrumental' in setting the prosecution in motion. For example, merely relating facts to a policeman, who draws a certain inference and arrests a certain person, is not sufficient.

The charge must be of a crime involving either moral stigma or the possibility of imprisonment. Such a crime would be 'bilking the railway' as distinct from pulling a train's communication cord without excuse.

Secondly, the plaintiff must have been found not guilty of the charge.

Thirdly, the prosecution must have been brought without reasonable or probable cause.

Fourthly, it must have been brought maliciously. In this connection malice does not necessarily involve personal spite. A prosecution is brought maliciously if brought for an improper motive.

False imprisonment is easier of proof. If A 'imprisons' B, he must then prove he had adequate reason for doing so or he will be liable to B in tort.

'Imprisonment' may be any restriction of liberty to a certain place. It may take place in any room or in the open as well as in an actual prison cell. But merely preventing a person leaving a place by one way when he is free to go by another is not an imprisonment.

A private citizen, as well as a policeman, has powers of arrest, though they are less extensive. For example, it is lawful for a private person, when a crime has been committed, to arrest a person on actual and reasonable suspicion that he has committed that crime.

[1] See page 152.

Where a person originally causes the arrest of someone by giving information, he will not be liable for false imprisonment if between the original information and the imprisonment a person exercising a judicial discretion orders the imprisonment. Thus if a magistrate hears the facts of a case from a person and grants a warrant for an alleged offender's arrest, the person informing the magistrate will not be liable for false imprisonment, though he may be for malicious prosecution if the other requisites are satisfied.

We must now consider some general topics affecting the whole of the law of tort. The first is death. Suppose that, owing to the tort of A, B is injured. He will have a cause of action. But if B is killed instead of being injured, is there any cause of action? Since the Fatal Accidents Act, 1846 (Lord Campbell's Act), if a person is killed through the act of another, then, if the act would have enabled the deceased to sue in tort if death had not resulted, his personal representatives may sue for the benefit of the deceased's spouse and certain close relatives. The damages recoverable will be assessed according to a reasonable expectation of pecuniary benefit from the continuation of the life. Thus if a son was supporting his parents, damages would lie for the deprivation of this financial assistance.

The Law Reform (Miscellaneous Provisions) Act, 1934, dealt with the effect of death in a different way. It provides that if a person dies all causes of action in tort (with a few exceptions), both against him and vested in him, shall continue. The action is brought by the deceased's personal representatives for the benefit of the deceased's estate. They may recover damages for the deceased's loss of expectation of life (which will be moderate) and a sum for funeral expenses, but not exemplary damages. Moneys awarded under insurance policies are not taken into account.

The remedies for tort are various. Damages are the most important. These will be unliquidated, meaning that the amount is in the discretion of the Court. Normally, damages are substantial; this is an attempt to quantify the actual damage suffered in terms of money. In cases where the plaintiff has suffered a merely nominal interference with his right, nominal damages of up to £2 will be awarded.

If the defendant has by his conduct aggravated the tort, this may be reflected in aggravated damages. Exemplary damages, in excess of substantial damages, however, are different, in that their purpose is punitive. Apart from where permitted by statute they may be awarded only:

(1) where there has been oppressive, arbitrary or unconstitutional conduct on the part of government servants; or

(2) where the defendant's conduct was calculated by him to make a profit for himself which might well exceed compensation.[1]

Finally, there are contemptuous damages of a nominal amount, sometimes awarded where the plaintiff is right in law but morally wrong and the action ought not to have been brought.

Instead of damages, the return of a specific chattel may be ordered.

An injunction will be given where damages would be an inadequate redress for the plaintiff's grievances; for example, in many cases of nuisance. They may be *ex parte*, interlocutory or permanent. *Ex parte* injunctions are temporary and are given on the application of the plaintiff alone where the matter is too urgent to notify the defendant. Interlocutory injunctions are temporary until the matter can be fully examined.

Self-help is still permitted in some cases. Thus a man falsely imprisoned may, if he can, escape from his confinement.

Defences to particular torts have already been mentioned. There are some defences which are generally applicable, however.

If the plaintiff with knowledge of the risks involved in an operation nevertheless freely assents to them, he cannot complain of damage suffered. This is expressed in the maxim '*volenti non fit injuria*'. Mere knowledge of a risk is not the same as acceptance of it (*Smith* v. *Baker*).[2] A workman worked in his employer's quarry. A crane swung heavy stones above his head. He knew there was a danger of these falling, but his employers did not warn him when the crane was working and a stone fell and injured him. It was held that the workman could recover damages, as he did not assent to the defendant's negligence, although he knew of it.

Inevitable accident is a defence to torts other than *Rylands* v. *Fletcher*. It is an occurrence not avoidable by a reasonable man exercising ordinary care and skill.[3] An example is *Stanley* v. *Powell*.[4] The defendant was shooting, and shot a beater because the pellet ricocheted off a tree. There had been no negligence on the defendant's part.

Necessity is a similar defence save that it is deliberate, though

---

[1] *Rookes* v. *Barnard*.   [2] [1891] A.C. 325.
[3] Compare with Act of God, page 57.
[4] [1891] 1 Q.B. 86.

unavoidable if further harm is to be prevented. An example is pulling down a house to prevent a fire spreading.

Statutory authority may excuse the commission of a tort. What exactly is permitted depends on the terms of the statute, but the law presumes that private rights are not taken away without compensation.

Private defence is dealt with under Criminal Law.

Vicarious Liability

The master is answerable for the servant's torts committed during the course of his employment. A servant is a person who works under the control and direction of another. He must be distinguished from an independent contractor who undertakes to produce a certain result but is not under the direction of the person contracting with him as to how that result is to be achieved. Though the servant himself remains liable as well, he is rarely sued, as the master is better able to pay damages and costs. An act occurs 'during the course of his employment' if it occurs during what it is the servant's business to do. Thus if a servant knocks down a person while driving his master's lorry on his master's business, the master will be liable. But if the servant disappears off his normal route in order to do something entirely unconnected with his employment and there injures someone, the master will not be liable.

If the negligent acts are incidental to the scope of the employment, then the master will be liable, even if he has forbidden the acts. Thus in *Limpus* v. *L.G.O.C.*[1] the defendant's servant was an omnibus driver and had been instructed not to race other 'buses. He disobeyed this order and an accident was caused. The defendant was held liable.

Capacity

Heads of foreign states and foreign diplomats cannot be sued in our courts, unless they consent.

Minors can sue and be sued for tort, but not if the effect is to enforce an unenforceable contract. In *Jennings* v. *Rundall*[2] a minor hired a horse which he injured by overriding. Held, an action in tort would not lie, as it would be enforcing the contract. But in

[1] 1 H. & C. 526.   [2] (1799) 8 T.R. 335.

Burnard v. *Haggis*[1] a minor hired a horse for riding and was particularly ordered not to jump it. A friend jumped it and the horse was
killed. The minor's tortious act was outside the contract and the
minor was liable.

A parent is not liable for his infant's torts unless he expressly
authorises them or impliedly does so by his lack of control. If parent
and child are master and servant, the usual liability results.

Each of the parties to a marriage may now sue the other in tort as
if they were not married. The Court may, however, stay an action
brought during the marriage if no substantial benefit would accrue
to either party from continuation of the proceedings—Law Reform
(Husband and Wife) Act, 1962, s. 1.

A corporation can sue or be sued for torts as a private person,
except that it cannot impliedly authorise its servants to commit
'*ultra vires*'[2] torts.

The immunity of a Trade Union against being sued in tort is
abolished by the Industrial Relations Act, 1971. Such torts in many
cases will be dealt with by the National Industrial Relations Court.

[1] 14 C.B. (N.S.) 45.
[2] Outside (its) powers. See Chapter 4.

4 Contract

It is vital to the commercial life of a country such as ours that the law of contract should be well developed and in conformity with up-to-date commercial practice. In this country we have no Commercial Code. Most of the law of contract is contained in cases, with the exception of such codifying statutes as the Sale of Goods Act, 1893.

A contract may be defined as an agreement which the law recognises as binding on the parties to it. The word 'binding' is used, for there are some contracts which are valid but are not enforceable.

Contracts may be by deed (specialty) or parol.[1] Parol contracts may be oral or written. The common fallacy that a contract does not exist unless there is 'something in writing' must be exploded at once. Certain types are, however, required to be in writing or evidenced thereby to be enforceable, and will be mentioned later.

First, what are the essentials of a binding contract? They are offer, acceptance and, in the case of parol contracts, consideration.

Dealing with the first two requirements, the rule is, that for a contract to be formed, one party, called the offeror, must make an offer and that offer must be accepted by the other party, called the offeree. As soon as that happens there is a contract. If I wish to buy your fountain-pen and I offer you £2 for it, that is an offer which you can accept, and as soon as you do so there is a binding contract. It is, however, open to me to withdraw my offer at any time before you accept it. This is so, even when I have agreed to leave the offer open for a specified time for you to consider it, unless you have given me valuable consideration for keeping the offer open. If, in the example, I had agreed to let you have a week to think the offer over in consideration for, say, 5p I could not withdraw the offer until the week was up. The reason is that the further agreement, being supported by the consideration of 5p, is a new and enforceable contract in itself.

These rules are simple when the two parties are together. What of the case where a contract is formed by post? Then, the offer becomes effective when it is delivered to the offeree. But the acceptance is complete when it is posted. And a revocation of an offer, like

---

[1] 'Parol' is sometimes used to mean 'oral', but the above use is more correct. See page 71 for the essentials of a deed.

the offer itself, takes effect only on its reaching the offeree. So if A, repenting of an offer, sends a letter of revocation and it crosses a letter by the offeree accepting, a valid contract is formed.

An offer is easily confused with many other things, such as an invitation to treat. If you see an article in a shop-window at a certain price, you cannot go into the shop and demand it as of right, for the shopkeeper may refuse to sell it to you. His price ticket is not an offer but a mere 'invitation to treat'. Your asking to purchase the article is the offer, and if the shopkeeper accepts it a contract will be formed.

At an auction, the auctioneer's cajoling 'What am I bid for this' is not the offer. The offer is the highest bid, which he accepts by the fall of his hammer. Before this fateful moment the bidder may withdraw.

An answer to an enquiry is not an offer. Harvey telegraphed: 'Will you sell us Bumper Hall Pen? Telegraph lowest cash price.' The answer received was: 'Lowest price for Bumper Hall Pen £900.' Harvey claimed to accept the reply as an offer, but it was held that it was a mere answer to a request for information (*Harvey* v. *Facey*).[1]

An offer must be communicated to the offeree. For example, A loses his dog and offers a reward of £5 to its finder. X does not know of the reward but finds the dog. A cannot be compelled to pay X the £5. There was no contract, as X was ignorant of the reward. This rule causes difficulty in connection with documents with conditions printed on them. For if the document is of such a kind that normally the person receiving it would expect to find conditions on it—for example, a railway ticket—then he may be bound by those conditions even though he does not know them. The question is, has the party issuing the document done sufficient to call attention to the terms of the proposed contract? If he has, by writing or other means, then the other party has only himself to blame if he is unaware of the conditions. Two cases will illustrate this principle. In *Henderson* v. *Stevenson*[2] Henderson took a ticket on the defendant's steamer. On the back of the ticket, with no reference to them on the front, were printed conditions stating that the defendant would not be liable for (*inter alia*) loss of passengers' luggage. Owing to the defendant's fault, Henderson lost his luggage. The defendant was not, however, able to rely on the conditions

[1] [1893] A.C. 552.   [2] L.R. 2 H.L. Sc. App. 470.

exempting him from liability as he had not brought the conditions to the plaintiff's notice or taken reasonable steps to do so.

On the other hand, in *Thompson* v. *L.M.S. Railway Co.*[1] a passenger who could not read took an excursion ticket for a journey on the defendant's railway. On the face of the ticket were the words: 'For conditions see back'. On the back, the passenger was referred to the company's timetables for the conditions. These conditions exempted the company from liability for negligence. The defendants were negligent, and the passenger was injured and sued the company. The company succeeded, as they had taken reasonable steps to bring the conditions to the notice of an intending passenger. As most passengers can read, the fact that the plaintiff could not have read the conditions herself did not deprive the company of the protection of the conditions.[2]

An offer may be accepted expressly by word of mouth or writing or by conduct. Acceptance by conduct occurred in *Carlill* v. *Carbolic Smoke Ball Co.*[3] The defendants offered £100 to anyone who should use their nostrum and yet catch influenza. The plaintiff used it but still succumbed to the disease. She sued the defendants and recovered damages. The act of using the smoke ball as prescribed was sufficient acceptance—there was no need to write a letter or otherwise inform the defendants that their offer was accepted.

The offeror, however, may indicate in which way his offer is to be accepted and, if so, purported acceptance in another way is ineffective. But the offeror must take the risk that his way may result in loss or delay. Thus in *Household Fire Insurance Co.* v. *Grant*[4] the offeror indicated that an acceptance might be made by post. The acceptance was lost in the post, but it was held that a valid contract had been formed. Remember, acceptance by post is complete at the time of posting, as distinct from revocation, which is only effective when it reaches the offeree before he has accepted.

But the offeror cannot impose on the offeree the duty of declining an offer. In *Felthouse* v. *Bindley*,[5] Felthouse wrote to the owner of a horse offering to buy it for £30 15s., saying that he would consider

[1] [1930] 1 K.B. 41.
[2] A person who is in fundamental breach of a contract, however, as by supplying something completely different from that which is contracted for, cannot rely on exempting conditions. *Suisse Atlantique, etc.* v. *N.V. Rottedansche, etc.*, [1967] 1 A.C. 361.
[3] [1893] 1 Q.B. 256.   [4] 4 Ex. D. 216.   [5] (1862) 11 C.B. (N.S.) 869.

the horse his if he heard no more about the matter. No more was heard, but it was held no contract had been made.

An acceptance can only be of the original offer. If X offers you a house at £1000, you cannot accept it at £950. If you suggest £950, this is a new offer rejecting the old one, and before a contract is formed X must accept your counter-offer of £950.[1]

Acceptance must be final and conclusive. An agreement 'subject to contract' is not a contract.

The terms of an 'agreement' may be so vague that no contract will be formed, as where a 'contract' was expressed to be on 'hire purchase terms'.[2]

All parol contracts need consideration to be effective. Consideration is a something moving from the promisee in return for the promise, and it may be a benefit given or to be given, or a detriment suffered or to be suffered by the promisee. Thus if A agrees to sell his Rolls-Royce to B for £1000, the £1000 is the consideration. It is a benefit flowing to the promisor, A, from the promisee, B. Though consideration must be present, it need not be adequate. If the price was fixed at 2p instead of £1000, the contract would still be valid.[3] If a creditor agrees to accept a smaller sum in discharge of a greater debt, unless there is a consideration for this new transaction, or it is under seal, the creditor will still be able to sue for the balance. But the compromise of an action or a forbearance to sue may be good consideration. And though the consideration is difficult to discover, a composition with creditors, each agreeing with the debtor to take a fixed proportion of their debts in final discharge of their claim, is valid and binding.

Consideration must not be past. In *Roscorla* v. *Thomas*[4] Roscorla bought a horse from Thomas. After the sale and in consideration of it, Thomas promised that the horse was not vicious. It *was* vicious and Roscorla sued Thomas. It was held that this new promise did not form a new contract, as the consideration was past.

Consideration, it need hardly be pointed out, must move from the promisee and not from some third party.[5]

[1] *Hyde* v. *Wrench* (1840), 3 Beav. 334.
[2] *Scammell* v. *Ouston*, [1941] A.C. 251.
[3] Provided the parties were of proper capacity and fraud, etc., was not present; such an unusual transaction might lead one to suspect it was!
[4] (1842) 3 Q.B. 234.
[5] *Dunlop Tyre Co. Ltd.* v. *Selfridge & Co. Ltd.*, [1915] A.C. 847.

The doctrine of consideration is not popular. Courts prefer promises to be honoured in the observance rather than in the breach, and endeavour to spell out some sort of consideration from every agreement they can. And in the case of *Central London Property Trust Ltd.* v. *High Trees House Ltd.*,[1] the rule has been expounded that where a party makes a promise intending it to be acted on and it is in fact acted on, then, even though no consideration is present and the agreement is not under seal, the promisor is bound by his promise. It gives the promisee a defence but no separate cause of action.

We have seen that a deed obviates the necessity for consideration. A deed is a document in writing 'signed, sealed and delivered' by the parties to the agreement it comprises. Sealing and delivery are formalities. The 'seal' is nowadays often a little adhesive piece of paper. Delivery means the handing of the executed document to the other party. Physical delivery is not essential if an intention to deliver is manifested. A deed-poll and an indenture are two types of deed. Formerly, a deed-poll was executed by one person and the edge was cut straight (polled), whereas an indenture was executed by several persons and each person's deed had an indented edge, so the edges fitted together. This distinction is not now of importance.

An escrow is a deed delivered subject to a condition. The deed does not take effect until the condition is fulfilled.

At Common Law a corporation aggregate[2] could only contract under seal. This rule has been so eaten into by exceptions that practically nothing remains. Companies incorporated under the Companies Acts, and any trading corporation contracting in the course of the business for which it was formed may contract through their agents by parol. And for minor contracts of everyday occurrence no seal is required. Imagine, for example, the inconvenience of executing a deed every time one travelled on a 'bus owned by a corporation. Finally, if a non-trading corporation has taken the benefit of work in furtherance of its proper objects, it must pay for it.

Certain contracts need to be in writing, thus: bills of exchange, moneylending contracts, assignments of copyright and acknowledgments of statute-barred debts. Others must be *evidenced* by writing. The Statute of Frauds, 1677, as amended by the Law Reform (Enforcement of Contracts) Act, 1954, requires the following

[1] [1947] K.B. 130.   [2] See below, page 74.

contracts to be evidenced in writing, signed by the party to be charged[1] or his agent, in order to be enforceable:

(1) Contracts of suretyship or guarantee.
(2) (Now Law of Property Act, s. 40) Any contract for the sale or other disposition of land or any interest in land.

The documentary evidence necessary must be in existence before any proceedings are commenced but need not be at the time of making the contract. Note that, as regards the Statute of Frauds, writing does not affect the existence of a contract but only its enforceability. It may be imagined that the Statute encouraged as many frauds as it prevented. So its full rigour was mitigated by Equity, which provided that in certain circumstances part performance of a contract within the Statute might be a substitute for written evidence. Thus in *Rawlinson* v. *Ames*,[2] the plaintiff orally agreed to let a flat to the defendant. This was a contract required to be in writing by the Statute. Certain work on the flat was done by the plaintiff at the defendant's request. It was held that this was sufficient evidence to render the contract enforceable.

Since the Law Reform (Enforcement of Contracts) Act, 1954, no written evidence is required for contracts for the sale of goods.

All hire-purchase contracts are required to be in writing by the Hire Purchase Act, 1965. The agreement must be signed by the hirer and, if it does not contain certain specified information such as the hire-purchase price, the amount of each instalment, etc., the contract cannot be enforced by the owner. A feature special to hire-purchase contracts is that, if the contract is not signed by the hirer at appropriate *trade* premises, the hirer has a statutory right to cancel the agreement by written notice within a specified period. This is to counter the menace of the 'door-step' salesman.

Not every class of person has full capacity to contract. The most important class under contractual disability comprises persons under eighteen, known in law as minors. The law places strict, if benevolent, limits to a minor's contractual activities and divides the class of contract he may make into four: valid, voidable, void and unenforceable. 'Voidable' means that the minor may avoid the con-

---

[1] The person to be charged is the person against whom the action is to be brought.
[2] [1925] Ch. 96.

tract or not at his option. A 'void' contract is in a sense a contradiction in terms, for it means a contract that does not exist and therefore has no legal effect.

The only contracts binding on himself which a minor may make are those for necessaries or for his benefit. Necessaries may comprise such items as food and clothing, text-books for a student, etc. Whether they are 'necessaries' will depend on the minor's station in life and whether at the time of the sale and delivery of the goods he was adequately supplied already with similar goods or not. Thus in *Nash* v. *Inman*[1] the defendant, an undergraduate and a minor, purchased, among other clothes, eleven fancy waistcoats. He was amply supplied with suitable clothes already. He refused to pay for the waistcoats, and it was held that they were not necessaries and he was not liable on the contract.

Contracts for a minor's benefit include apprenticeship contracts, contracts for his education and certain contracts of employment. Thus in *Roberts* v. *Gray*[2] a minor wished to become a professional billiard player, and a contract between him and the plaintiff, a famous player, to go with the plaintiff on a world tour playing billiards was held to be for the minor's benefit.

Contracts severely restricting a minor from competition after his employment or apprenticeship has ended will not be for his benefit. Neither will purely trading contracts. Thus an agreement for hire-purchase of a lorry to enable the minor to carry on business as a haulage contractor was held not to be for his benefit.[3]

Contracts of a continuing nature, under which a minor derives some benefit, are binding on him unless he avoids them. This he may do before and up to a reasonable time after his majority. Examples of such contracts are those to take shares where there is a liability for unpaid calls, and leases where there is an obligation to pay rent. But though the minor may avoid future liabilities, he may not recover what he has paid already unless there has been a 'total failure of consideration'—for example, if he had been allotted shares that were quite worthless.

By the Infants' Relief Act, 1874, the following minors' contracts are void: moneylending contracts, sale of goods (apart from necessaries) and accounts stated. This provision gives some scope to the infant rogue. It has been held that, even where a minor had falsely

---

[1] [1908] 2 K.B. 1.   [2] [1913] 1 K.B. 520.
[3] *Mercantile Union Guarantee Corporation Ltd.* v. *Ball*, [1937] 2 K.B. 498.

stated his age to be above majority and thereby obtained a loan, the contract was void and the money irrecoverable.[1]

A promise to perform an obligation is the fourth class. This is unenforceable if made during minority, but if the minor subsequently on attaining eighteen promises afresh to perform it and the promise is supported by fresh consideration, it is valid. An obligation does not include a debt.

Married women are now in the same position as spinsters as regards contract.[2]

Corporations

Corporations are of two kinds: corporations sole and corporations aggregate. Corporations sole are in effect offices, being legal persons apart from their holder at the time. Examples are the Sovereign and a parson. Here we are concerned with corporations aggregate.

A corporation aggregate consists of a number of persons but is a legal person on its own account, entirely different and separate from them. No matter if all its members die and are replaced, the corporation continues. Examples of corporations are limited companies and municipal corporations.

Before the European Communities Act, 1972, a company incorporated under the Companies Acts could only make contracts within the scope of its Memorandum of Association. A company incorporated by a statute could make only those contracts necessary for the fulfilment of its statutory objects. In *Ashbury Railway Carriage Co. Ltd.* v. *Riche*[3] a company was incorporated to make railway rolling stock, to carry on business as engineers and contractors, to buy and sell land and various materials, etc. The directors agreed to purchase a concession for making a railway in a foreign country. It was held that the contract was void. It was '*ultra vires*'—that is, beyond the powers contained in the Memorandum of Association. Nor had the whole body of shareholders power to ratify the contract. The positions is now modified by s. 9(1) of the European Communities Act. This operates in favour of an outsider contracting with a company. Where a person deals with a company in good faith, any transaction decided on by the directors shall be deemed to be within the capacity of the company to enter into, and the power of the directors to bind the company shall be deemed to be free of

[1] *Leslie Ltd.* v. *Shiell*, [1914] 3 K.B. 607.
[2] And see page 86.   [3] L.R. 7 H.L. 653.

any limitation under the Memorandum and Articles. Thus in a case like the above, the contract would no longer be void and the innocent outsider could enforce it. However, the contract would still be an unauthorised one and the directors would be liable for any loss incurred by the company.

The doctrine of '*ultra vires*' does not extend to companies created by Royal Charter. Such a company may contract like an ordinary person, but if it ignores limitations imposed by its charter, the charter may be rescinded.

If a person of unsound mind or a drunken person makes a contract, it is voidable at his option, provided that he was devoid of the necessary understanding to make a contract and that the party with whom he contracted knew this.

An alien has the same capacity to contract as a British subject, but he may not own a British ship or a share therein. In time of war, contracts made with enemy aliens are void. 'Enemy alien' in this connection merely means a person voluntarily living or carrying on business in enemy territory and not necessarily of the enemy nationality.

Heads of foreign states, ambassadors and their staffs are protected from actions in our Courts by diplomatic immunity. So they may make valid contracts, but if they choose to break them they cannot be sued unless they waive their privilege.[1]

Barristers and Fellows of the Royal College of Physicians cannot sue for their fees. A person not a registered medical practitioner cannot sue for fees for medical advice, attendance, surgery or medicine prescribed and supplied.

A registered trade union may be sued for breach of contract.[2]

Mistake

We have seen that offer and acceptance must be of the same thing for a contract to be formed. The parties must have *consensus ad idem* (agreement as to the same thing), otherwise there will be no agreement. One of the ways in which this consensus may be prevented is by mistake as to a fundamental of a contract. This may occur in any of three ways: mistake as to a person contracting, subject of the contract or the promise itself.

[1] *Mighell* v. *Sultan of Johore*, [1894] 1 Q.B. 149.
[2] *Bonsor* v. *Musicians' Union*, [1956] A.C. 104.

Cundy v. *Lindsay*[1] illustrates mistake as to person. A fraudulent person, Blenkarn, wrote to Lindsay from an address in Wood Street and ordered goods. In the same street was a reputable firm named Blenkiron. Blenkarn signed his name in such a way that it was indistinguishable from Blenkiron. It was held that there was no contract, and Blenkarn could not pass a good title to third parties. The reason was that Lindsay never knew of Blenkarn's existence; he intended to deal with someone else.

But in *Phillips* v. *Brooks Ltd.*[2] a contract was made, though it was voidable owing to the fraud employed to induce it. X called at the plaintiff's jewellery shop and asked to be shown some rings. He chose one and was allowed to take it away and pay by a cheque (which was later dishonoured), on his representing falsely that he was a well-known local magnate. It was held there had been no mistake to vitiate the contract, as the jeweller intended to deal with the person in the shop even though mistaken as to his identity.

Mistake as to subject-matter occurred in *Raffles* v. *Wichelhaus*.[3] Raffles agreed to sell Wichelhaus a cargo of cotton on the *Peerless*, from Bombay. There were, in fact, two ships named *Peerless* sailing from Bombay at different times. The plaintiff was thinking of one, the defendant of the other, so no contract resulted. When one party believes the other to be making a particular offer, and the other party is making a different offer and knows that the first party is mistaken, there will be no contract. For example, if a stamp-collector takes a chance in buying a particular stamp, the fact that he thinks it a rare specimen is not such a mistake as will avoid the contract, if, in fact, the stamp is not valuable. But if he thinks the dealer is *offering* it as a rare stamp, then if the dealer knows this and is not offering it as a rare stamp (in fact, he knows it is not), the mistake will prevent a contract from forming.

Another class of mistake occurs where two persons contract and, unknown to them both, the subject-matter of the contract is not in existence; an example was *Couturier* v. *Hastie*,[4] where the subject-matter of the contract, corn on a voyage, had, in fact, been unloaded and sold, owing to danger of spontaneous combustion, before the contract was made.

Misrepresentation on its own, and unaccompanied by a fundamental mistake as described above, will not make a contract void.

[1] 3 App. Cas. 459. [3] [1919] 2 K.B. 243.
[2] 2 H. & C. 906. [4] 5 H.L.C. 673.

But the party misled will be able to avoid the contract if he wishes.

Misrepresentation occurs where a party is induced to contract with another party by a misleading statement made by that second party. There must be a false statement. Merely not mentioning facts relevant to the making of a contract (except for contracts *'uberrimae fidei'*, to be discussed later) is not sufficient to avoid the contract. In sale of goods this is expressed by the maxim *'caveat emptor'*.[1] But a statement which gives only a few of the facts, not mentioning others will, if the effect is misleading, be a misrepresentation.

The statement must be one of fact. Mere opinion, high-flown promises and grandiose advertising 'puffs' are not misrepresentations. A surprising amount of latitude has sometimes been allowed; thus in *Dimmock* v. *Hallett* useless land was described as 'fertile and improvable', and this was held to be a 'mere flourishing description by an auctioneer' and not a misrepresentation.[2]

The misrepresentation must be intended to be acted on by the person to whom it is made and it must be so acted on. If the cause inducing the 'representee' to contract was something other than the misrepresentation, the contract will be valid.

There are two types of misrepresentation: fraudulent and innocent. Either will give a right to avoid the contract to the party deceived, but if the misrepresentation is fraudulent it will give rise to an action for damages as well.[3] 'Fraud is proved when it is shown that a false representation has been made, (1) knowingly, or (2) without belief in its truth, or (3) recklessly, careless whether it be true or false', Lord Herschell at page 374 of *Derry* v. *Peek*.[4]

The Misrepresentation Act, 1967, gives a statutory right to damages in cases where a misrepresentation has been made negligently but without fraud. It would be a defence to prove a belief on reasonable grounds that the facts represented were true.

Certain classes of contract known as contracts *'uberrimae fidei'* (of the utmost good faith) require not only that there be no active misrepresentation but also that the parties disclose all material facts, holding nothing back when making the contract. If a party fails in this duty, the contract will be voidable by the other. The duty is

[1] 'Let the buyer beware.'   [2] L.R. 2 Ch. App. 21 at page 27.
[3] A careless misrepresentation is actionable as a tort if the person making it assumes responsibility for its accuracy (*Hedley Byrne* v. *Heller*, [1963] 3 W.L.R. 101).
[4] 14 App. Cas. 337.

necessary because facts vitally necessary for one party to know are within the peculiar knowledge of the other. The foremost example of such a contract is that of insurance. For instance, it is necessary to disclose in applying for a policy of insurance that another company has refused to accept the risk, if that has occurred. Other examples are contracts for the sale of land (in which the vendor must disclose defects in his title) and company prospectuses.

The subject of conditions and warranties will be dealt with under 'Breach.'

Where, in the making of the contract, one party has overborne the will of another, both Common Law and Equity have recognised the consent of the overborne party to be unreal and have provided that the contract is to be voidable at his option. At Common Law such coercion was called duress. Actual or threatened violence to the person or a threat of unlawful imprisonment are examples. Equity has gone further. It provides that where 'undue influence' exists the contract is voidable. It may arise in two ways. Firstly, undue influence is presumed to arise from certain relationships—e.g. solicitor and client, parent and child, and a spiritual adviser and his charge. Undue influence is not presumed between husband and wife. Where gifts have been made to such persons, whose positions give them such scope for undue influence, it will lie upon them to prove that the gifts were made freely. The same presumption will arise where an uneducated, ignorant person has entered into a disadvantageous contract with a person in a stronger position.

Even where these presumptions do not automatically arise, undue influence may be proved wherever a stronger party obtains dominion over a weaker. For example, in *Morley* v. *Loughnan*[1] an epileptic was so much influenced by his companion that he parted with £140 000 to him. Undue influence was proved, and the money was ordered to be returned.

When the undue influence is removed, the person influenced may seek to set the bargain aside. The person exercising influence may support the transaction by showing that the person influenced had independent advice at the time. But undue influence being an equitable remedy, there must be no delay in coming to the Court to have it set aside. Delay defeats equities. In *Allcard* v. *Skinner*[2] a woman entered a religious organisation and, in accordance with its rule, surrendered her private property to it. She withdrew from it, and,

[1] [1893] 1 Ch. 736.   [2] 36 Ch. D. 145.

knowing her right to recover her property, delayed for five years before attempting to do so. It was held that she could not recover the property.

We pass now to contracts in which the parties' consent is real enough but which, for reasons of public policy, the law declares to be illegal and void. Both Statute and Common Law have been zealous in this way. The main statutory provisions relate to betting and are of hideous complexity. A wagering contract may be defined as a contract where two persons holding different views as to a certain matter agree that one of them shall pay to the other a certain stake on the discovery by them whose is the correct view, neither party having any other interest in the contract than the stake he will win or lose.[1] Gaming means the playing at a game of chance.

No action may be brought on a wager. Neither may a commission agent sue to recover a commission on a wagering contract. If a person lends money for the purpose of lawful gaming or wagering, then it is recoverable except it be accompanied by a security, when it is not. If a person lends money for the purpose of the gambler paying his lawful gaming or wagering debts, it is recoverable, but if the lender should rashly pay the debts himself, he cannot recover the money from the debtor. But if a third party is given money to make bets for another, he cannot keep any winnings he may make himself but must hand them over.

Securities given for wagering transactions on *games and pastimes* will be enforceable by a third party who does not know of its wagering origin and has given value for it. Securities given for all other wagering transactions are absolutely void, no matter into whose hands they come.

It will be seen that this branch of the law is in need of reform.

At Common Law a wide variety of contracts are illegal and thus void. Examples are contracts to commit a crime and contracts involving sexual immorality—e.g. to hire a brougham for the purpose of prostitution (*Pearce* v. *Brooks*).[2]

Contracts to introduce persons to others of the opposite sex with a view to marriage are void. Contracts to pervert justice—for example, to stifle a prosecution (but not to refrain from bringing civil proceedings for a consideration)—are void. Further examples are

[1] Adapted from the definition by Hawkins, J., in *Carlill* v. *Carbolic Smoke Ball Co.*, [1892] 2 Q.B. 484.

[2] L.R. 1 Ex. 213.

contracts for the sale of honours (*Parkinson* v. *College of Ambulance Ltd.*,[1] where the plaintiff attempted to buy a knighthood) and contracts endangering this country's relations with others (*Foster* v. *Driscoll*,[2] where the contract was to smuggle liquor to the United States, then undergoing prohibition).

Contracts in restraint of trade may be void. The law as to this was laid down in *Maxim Nordenfelt Co. Ltd.* v. *Nordenfelt*.[3] Nordenfelt was a manufacturer of guns. He sold his business to the M.N. Co. for a very large sum and covenanted that he would not for twenty-five years *anywhere* manufacture guns or ammunition or do any business in competition with the company. Certain activities were reserved to him. It was held that the general clause prohibiting any competition was too wide and was illegal. The clause about guns and ammunition was valid as it was (1) reasonable between the parties because of the large sum awarded and the world-wide nature of the business; also Nordenfelt's inventive and manufacturing abilities had an outlet in the types of business reserved to him; and (2) reasonable as regards public policy because an English company acquired assets valuable in a war. The Courts will scrutinise such contracts closely, and if they are to be upheld, considering all the circumstances, they must be reasonable as between the parties and as regards the public. A nice balance has to be preserved between stifling ability and encouraging unfair competition.

It will be noticed that the contract in *Nordenfelt's* case was severable. If the illegality in a contract has not 'tainted' the whole, and a part can stand separate from the illegal portion, the legal part only will be enforced.

Assignment

If the parties to a contract desire, they can agree to discharge their contract and form a new one. This is not assignment but novation. Assignment may be voluntary, through the act of one of the parties, or involuntary, when the law transfers the rights and liabilities of a contract irrespective of the parties' wishes. This occurs on the death of a contracting party, where (except for contracts of personal service, etc.) rights and obligations vest in his personal representatives. Another occasion is bankruptcy, which vests contractual rights and duties (with some exceptions) in the trustee in bankruptcy.

[1] [1925] 2 K.B. 1.   [2] [1929] 1 K.B. 470.   [3] [1894] A.C. 535.

Voluntary Assignment

The first point to note is that a contract may expressly provide that rights or duties under it are assignable. Subject to this, duties under a contract may not be assigned. However, in many cases they may be sub-contracted. Thus if A has contracted to repair B's railway wagons, he may perform his obligation by getting C to do the work for him. This is not an assignment, though, as A will still remain liable to B under the original contract. If the contract is one involving qualifications of a kind personal to the contracting party, he may not even sub-contract his duties. A contract to write a book would be of this kind.

The rights under a contract, provided that they are not of a peculiarly personal nature as described above, may be assigned. This is assignment in the proper sense of the term, the rights being transferred to the assignee completely, and the assignor fading from the scene. The debtor need not consent, but notice must be given to him. Two types of assignment exist, under s. 136 of the Law of Property Act, 1925, and in Equity. More formalities are required under the former, but the latter comprises a greater number of obligations. In both cases the assignee takes the assignment subject to equities. The assignor cannot give a better title than he has himself. This difficulty is overcome in the case of negotiable instruments (see page 88).

So far, we have studied the birth and life of a contract; now for its death. In what ways may a contract be discharged?

First, the parties may agree to end it. This can be done orally, even if the original contract was under seal or in writing. But if one party has performed his side of the contract, the agreement to release the other party will need a fresh consideration or must be under seal.

Secondly, the contract itself may provide that it is to end on the occurrence of certain events.

Thirdly, the contract may end by being performed as it was intended. As regards payment, a creditor may insist on legal tender.[1]

Fourthly, a contract may end by breach—that is, the failure of one

---

[1] Legal tender consists of Bank of England notes of £20, £10, £5 and £1; gold coins to any amount, cupro-nickel coins (silver) with a value up to and including 10p up to £5; 50p up to £10; and bronze up to 20p. The creditor must not be required to give change.

of the parties to perform his obligations under the contract. As *pacta sunt servanda* (agreements are to be honoured), the law provides various remedies for the aggrieved party, and these will be mentioned later.

If a party breaks a term of the contract going to its root, known as a condition, the other party will be excused from his part in the contract. But if the broken term is one collateral to the main object of the contract, known as a warranty, the innocent party will not be released from performance but must be content with damages.

An example of a condition is *Moore & Co.* v. *Landauer & Co.*[1] L contracted to buy 3000 tins of fruit from M. A term in the contract was that the tins should be packed in cases of thirty. A large number were packed in cases of twenty-four. It was held that this was a condition and that L was entitled to reject the goods. In *Bettini* v. *Gye*,[2] Gye was manager of an opera house, and Bettini, a singer, undertook to sing at Gye's opera house for about three months. A term in the contract was that Bettini should be in London for rehearsals six days before the first performance. He arrived two days before. It was held this was a mere breach of warranty.

If the injured party wishes, he may treat a breach of condition as a breach of warranty and sue for damages.

The Sale of Goods Act, 1893, has eaten into the doctrine of '*caveat emptor*' by writing various conditions into certain contracts for sale of goods. One example will suffice. . . . Section 14(3) provides:

'Where the seller sells goods in the course of a business and the buyer, expressly or by implication, makes known to the seller any particular purpose for which the goods are being bought, there is an implied condition that the goods supplied under the contract are reasonably fit for the purpose, whether or not that is a purpose for which such goods are commonly supplied, except where the circumstances show that the buyer does not rely, or that it is unreasonable for him to rely, on the seller's skill and judgment.'

Similar conditions were satisfied in *Chaproniere* v. *Mason*.[4] The plaintiff bought a bath-bun from a baker. The bun contained a stone which fractured the plaintiff's tooth when he bit it. He recovered damages from the baker.

---

[1] [1921] 2 K.B. 519.   [2] (1875), 1 Q.B.D. 183.
[3] Substituted for the original section by the Supply of Goods (Implied Terms) Act, 1973.
[4] 21 T.L.R. 633.

Breach may take the form of an express refusal. If the express refusal takes place before the time for performance (anticipatory breach), the injured party may, if he wishes, treat the contract as ended and sue at once.

An example is *Hochster* v. *De La Tour*.[1] The defendant engaged the plaintiff as guide for a foreign tour. A month before the date agreed for the tour, the defendant repudiated the agreement. It was held that the plaintiff could sue for damages at once and did not need to wait until the date agreed.

Sometimes, as in *Ogdens Ltd.* v. *Nelson*,[2] the defendant will break a contract by making it impossible for him to perform it. Ogdens Ltd. were tobacco merchants. They entered into an agreement with a tobacconist that, in consideration of his buying direct from them, they would distribute a share of the profits to him, plus a bonus. The company went into voluntary liquidation and the tobacconist sued for the money the defendants had thereby prevented him from earning. It was held that Ogdens Ltd. must pay damages for their breach of contract.

Impossibility not brought about by the act of one of the parties provides the fifth way in which a contract may be ended. The strict Common Law rule was that if parties made a bargain they must stand by it. If performance by one party *became* impossible (as distinct from being impossible at the time of contracting, which would prevent a contract from ever being formed, as in *Couturier* v. *Hastie* —see page 76), then he would have to pay damages. An illustration is *Paradine* v. *Jane*.[3] The defendant was lessee of the plaintiff's house and had covenanted to pay rent. He was rudely ejected from the house by Prince Rupert with an army of men, but he was held still liable to pay the rent. This rule might lead to unjust results. However, it was always possible for the parties *expressly* to provide in the contract that it was to end on its becoming impossible to perform. Moreover, the courts have read into many contracts such an *implied* term.

In cases where the whole basis of the contract has been dissolved by supervening impossibility, the parties have been excused further performance.

Thus in *Taylor* v. *Caldwell*[4] the plaintiff agreed to lease his music-hall to the defendant for a forthcoming performance. Before that

[1] (1853), 2 E. & B. 678.   [2] [1905] A.C. 109.   [3] Aleyn 26.
[4] (1862), 3 B. & S. 826.

happened, the building was burned. And in *Robinson* v. *Davison*[1] the
defendant had agreed to play at the plaintiff's concert and before the
date fixed became ill and was unable. Yet another example is *Metropolitan Water Board* v. *Dick, Kerr & Co. Ltd.*[1] The defendants had
agreed to construct a reservoir. Before they had done so the Government, acting in pursuance of war-time powers, forbade it. In these
three cases it was held the contracts had been frustrated. The whole
basis of their existence had vanished and the defendants were not
liable for breach of contract. A lease cannot be frustrated, as it
brings into existence rights independent of contractual ones. The
Law Reform (Frustrated Contracts) Act, 1943, provides for the
return of money paid under a frustrated contract, subject to payment
of expenses, if the Court thinks fit, and the payment of a just sum for
any valuable benefit obtained in performance of the contract by the
other party.[2]

Remedies for Breach

The normal remedy for breach of contract is damages. The aim of
the law is to place the innocent party in as far as possible the position
he would have occupied had the contract not been broken. Damages
in contract follow a principle which was laid down in *Hadley* v.
Baxendale.[3] The shaft of a mill had broken, and it was sent by the
plaintiff to the defendants, who were told the shaft must be delivered
to the makers at once. The defendants delayed delivering it, with the
result that the plaintiff's mill, which had no other shaft, could not
resume work for some while. It was held that the consequent loss of
profit could not be included in the damages. Alderson, B., laid down
the reasons: 'damages ... in respect of such breach of contract
should be such as may fairly and reasonably be considered either
arising naturally, i.e. according to the usual course of things, from
such breach of contract itself, or such as may reasonably be supposed to have been in the contemplation of the parties, at the time
they made the contract, as the probable result of the breach of it.'
Normally, such a loss would not have flowed from the breach and

---

[1] [1918] A.C. 119.   [4] (1871), L.R. 6 Ex. 269.
[2] The parties may exclude the operation of the Act from contracts and
it does not apply to certain transactions.
[3] (1854), 9 Ex. 341. The rules as to remoteness of damages for breach of
contract are now more strict than those in tort.

the plaintiff did not acquaint the defendants with the special circumstances of the case.

Where profits have been lost to the plaintiff by the fault of the defendant in delaying delivery, if the defendant should have foreseen, as a reasonable man, that such loss was liable to result he will be liable for such loss. Thus a company who had contracted with a laundry to deliver an expensive boiler by a certain date were held liable for the laundry's loss of profits when they delayed delivering the boiler.[1]

Exemplary damages are not awarded for breach of contract. Neither will the Courts enforce the payment of a 'penalty'. Contracts will frequently provide that, if broken, the damages are to be a certain amount. If the amount is a genuine attempt to quantify the actual damage suffered or to limit it to a figure below this, then the amount fixed will be recoverable. Such an amount is known as 'liquidated damages'. But if an amount is stipulated which is out of proportion to the damage estimated to be suffered in the event of breach, and intended as a punishment for the defaulting party, this is a penalty. The Courts will disregard it and assess damages in the ordinary way. The Court will scrutinise the essence of the transaction and it will be useless for the parties to describe a penalty as liquidated damages, or vice versa.

It is the duty of the party who has suffered by a breach of contract to mitigate his damage as much as he can. If a buyer of goods refuses to honour his contract and accept the goods, the seller must try to sell the goods to another and sue the original buyer for any difference that remains.

The two equitable remedies for breach of contract, specific performance and injunction, are discretionary. Specific performance is an appropriate remedy only where damages would not adequately compensate the plaintiff. Such a case would arise in a contract for the sale of land. Another would be the sale of a chattel of unique interest and value to the plaintiff, the value of which could not be gauged in money.

Specific performance will not be granted for minors' contracts, where only the minor could enforce them, as the lack of mutuality would result in unfairness. Neither will specific performance of a contract for personal service be granted, as Equity will not under-

[1] *Victoria Laundry (Windsor) Ltd.* v. *Newman Industries Ltd.*, [1949] 2 K.B. 528.

take what it cannot carry out and the performance of such a contract would require continual supervision.

An injunction will, however, be granted in a contract of this kind in some cases. In *Lumley* v. *Wagner*[1] an opera singer had contracted to sing at a certain theatre, and at no other. A rival manager persuaded her to sing at his theatre. It was held that, though the positive part of the agreement (to sing at the plaintiff's theatre) could not be enforced by a decree for specific performance, the negative part (to sing nowhere else) could be enforced by injunction. But if the effect of an injunction to refrain from doing something is, in effect, specially to enforce a contract for personal services, an injunction will not be granted. Thus a defendant had contracted to give the whole of his time to his employer's business. He gave some time to a rival concern. An injunction to stop this was refused.

Agency

Not all contracts are made personally by the contracting parties. When a person employs another to contract on his behalf, the relation between them is that of principal and agent. An agent may be appointed expressly or by conduct. If the agent is to contract under seal, he must be appointed under seal. He is then said to have a power of attorney. A person may become an agent *after* he has acted as such. If X, having no authority to act as Y's agent, or exceeding any authority he has, makes a contract with Z as Y's agent, Y may ratify the contract. But X must have had Y in contemplation as his future principal at the time, and Y must have existed. For example, if a man purports to contract on behalf of an unformed company, the company, when formed, cannot ratify the contract.

A person may become an agent of necessity. An example is where the master of a ship sells the cargo where it is in imminent danger of perishing and he is unable to communicate with its owners.

Cohabitation as man and wife (whether the parties are married or not) raises a presumption that the wife[2] is the husband's agent to purchase necessaries. This may be rebutted by the husband's showing that the wife was adequately provided with the necessaries or the money for them, that he had forbidden her to pledge his credit or that he had previously warned the tradesman in question. But if the husband has permitted his wife to make purchases with a

[1] (1852), 1 De G., M. & G. 604.   [2] Or mistress.

particular tradesman over a period, he can only escape liability by express warning to the tradesman that he has forbidden her to pledge his credit, as he will be taken to have held her out as his agent.

If an agent contracts on behalf of a named principal who has authorised him to act, the agent then drops out of the transaction, having done all he is supposed to. He is not personally liable on the contract unless it has been made by deed, or the contract has expressly made him liable.[1]

The position is different, however, if the 'agent' has contracted on behalf of a principal who does not exist. Then the agent is liable himself. But if the agent contracts on behalf of a principal who exists, but from whom he has no authority, then unless the principal ratifies the contract there will be no contract either with the principal or with the agent personally. The agent may be proceeded against for breach of warranty of authority,[2] or for fraud if he knew he had no authority and thereby deceives the third party. *Yonge* v. *Toynbee*[3] is an example. Solicitors were instructed by a principal to act for him in an action. He became insane, but the solicitors did not know of this and continued to act. They where held liable for breach of warranty of authority, as insanity ends agency.

If an agent does not disclose the name of his principal when contracting *as agent*, he is not liable personally unless the contract has been made by deed or he is expressly made liable personally. But if he does not contract as an agent, he is liable personally.

If an agent does not disclose the existence of his principal when entering into a contract, the party dealing with him, on discovering the true position, may hold either the principal or the agent liable on the contract.

There are various types of agent, such as mercantile agents, auctioneers and *del credere* agents. Such agents differ from the ordinary agent as regards rights and duties. Here we can only examine some of the normal incidents arising from the relationship of principal and agent.

A principal must pay the agent his agreed commission, and must not prevent him earning it.

He must indemnify the agent for what the agent does within his authority.

---

[1] A '*del credere*' agent guarantees payment.
[2] Not if acting under a power of attorney.   [3] [1910] 1 K.B. 215.

The agent must discharge his task to the best of his ability. He owes a high duty of faith to his principal and must not make a secret profit. In *Andrews* v. *Ramsay*[1] a principal engaged an agent to sell property for a commission. In addition to this, the agent took a secret commission from the buyer. It was held that not only did the agent have to give the buyer's commission to his principal but he forfeited the principal's commission as well.

If a person is instructed to do something as agent, he must not act as principal. Thus if an agent is appointed to sell his principal's house, he may not purchase it himself.

An agent, being himself a delegate of powers, may not delegate them further by employing an agent himself, as a rule. This is an application of the maxim *'delegatus non potest delegare'*.[2]

Agency may be ended by agreement of the parties or by the death, insanity or bankruptcy[3] of either principal or agent.

Negotiable Instruments

The chief characteristics of negotiable instruments are that a holder of a negotiable instrument, without notice of any defects in his assignor's title, takes free of those defects, provided that he has given value; secondly, notice need not be given to the debtor. The most important kinds of negotiable instruments are: promissory notes and bills of exchange, of which the commonest are cheques.

The law relating to them is mostly contained in the Bills of Exchange Act, 1882. It defines a promissory note as an unconditional promise in writing, made by one person to another, signed by the maker, engaging to pay, on demand or at a fixed or determinable future time, a sum certain in money to, or to the order of, a specified person or to bearer.

It must not be confused with an I.O.U., which is only written evidence of an account stated.

A bill of exchange is defined as an unconditional order in writing, addressed by one person to another, signed by the person giving it, requiring the person to whom it is addressed to pay on demand, or at a fixed or determinable future time, a sum certain in money to, or to the order of, a specified person or to bearer. A cheque is a bill of exchange drawn upon a banker, payable on demand, and is subject to certain special provisions.

[1] [1903] 2 K.B. 635.   [2] 'A delegate cannot delegate.'   [3] Usually.

The drawee of a bill agrees to pay the amount by 'accepting' the bill; this is done by his signing it.

The effect of the bill will then depend on how the bill is drawn. If the direction on it is to pay 'X' or bearer, it is immediately negotiable; if 'X or order' it becomes negotiable when X signs it. He may sign without further indorsement in blank or he may 'indorse it specially', indicating payment is to be made to Y. Y may indorse it to Z, and so on. Each indorser has a right to payment by the acceptor and in default by the original drawer or any previous indorser. It must be emphasised, however, that in order for the property of a bill to pass it must be delivered—i.e. possession of it must be transferred.[1]

A bill may be drawn payable to X without being accepted first. X has then a right to demand acceptance from the drawee and, if the drawee fails to accept, the holder has recourse against the drawer and previous indorsers.

A bill may be deprived of its negotiability. Crossing a cheque and marking it 'not negotiable' has this effect; it must be paid through a bank account[1] and the holder cannot pass a better title than he has himself. Thus if A steals such a cheque and passes it to B, who gives value and has no knowledge that it was stolen, B will not obtain a good title. B would, however, if the cheque were not so marked.

But if a bill be negotiable, any person holding it is presumed to be a holder in due course, i.e. to have given consideration for it and to have taken it in good faith. If, however, it is shown that some illegality attended the drawing, acceptance or transference of a bill, a

Bill of Exchange—payable on demand

£50   *London, April 1, 1973*

On demand, pay to myself or order the sum of fifty pounds for value received.

To Mr. William Grey,
400 Fleet Street,
London E.C. 4   **JOHN WHITE**

[1] Since the Cheques Act, 1957, bankers do not require the payee of an order cheque to indorse it when it is to be paid into his own account.

[2] It may not be paid over the counter unless presented by another bank.

Promissory Note—payable three months after date

> *£100*   *London, April 1, 1973*
>
> *Three months after date I promise to pay*
> *Mr. Thomas Green or order the sum of one*
> *hundred pounds for value received.*
>
> **ROBERT BLACK**

subsequent holder will have to prove that the stain on the bill's
character has been expunged by a *bona fide* transference for value
after the illegality. This may be by the holder himself or an indorsee
before him. For example, Jones is the holder of a bill, indorsed to
him by Smith. Smith is the drawer of this bill, payable to himself or
order. Brown is the drawee and acceptor.

Jones is presumed to be the holder in due course. Then he presents the bill for payment and it is refused. So he sues Brown. Brown
then raises the defence that the bill was drawn as a consideration for
blowing Lord Fitz-Nigel's safe. This will put Jones to proof that he
is a holder in due course. In this case he is lucky, as he can show he
had no knowledge of the bill's nefarious origin and had given consideration for it—he had sold his gold watch for the bill. So Jones
may sue on the bill.

Quasi-contract

Lastly, very briefly, we must note certain cases where, although the
parties have not agreed, certain obligations similar to those in contract are fixed on one of the parties to a transaction.

Where money has been received by a person under various circumstances making it unjust that he should retain it, it must be
returned. An example is money paid under a mistake of *fact*.[1] In
Kelly v. *Solari*[2] an insurance company made a mistake and paid out
money to a person whose policy had lapsed. It was held that the

[1] Not law.   [2] (1842), 9 M. & W. 54.

company could recover the money. Money is also returnable in some cases where paid under an illegal contract.

When A pays money which B owes to C, and A has been legally bound to pay the money, he may recover it from B. For example, a local authority may proceed against either the occupier or owner of premises for rates. If the owner has contracted with the occupier to pay the rates, and the occupier has paid the rates demanded of him from the local authority, he may recover the amount paid from the owner.

Similarly, where goods have been supplied or work done for a person at his request, in many cases he will be bound to pay a reasonable price therefore, even if he has not contracted to do so. This is the doctrine of '*quantum meruit*'.[1] An instance is the Sale of Goods Act, 1893, s. 2, which provides: 'Where necessaries are sold and delivered to an infant or to a person who by reason of mental incapacity or drunkenness is incompetent to contract, he must pay a reasonable price therefor.'

[1] 'So much as he has earned.'

5 Real Property

England today is chiefly dependent on industry and commerce for living, and thus we have a highly developed law of contract. In the Middle Ages this was not so. Land was the source of wealth and power, and the most fertile part of our law was the land law. The Common Law relating to land was highly technical, beautifully logical and led to inconvenient results. In this it was typically mediaeval. Equity remedied some of the abuses, various statutes others, at the expense of the Common Law symmetry. In recent years, vast changes have been made by Town Planning Statutes, and the Rent Restrictions Acts have come upon us thick and fast, each one adding to the confusion of the law. At the bottom of it all remains the Common Law framework, which even today must be clearly understood.

Land, in strict theory, may not be owned by private persons. It must be held from the Queen, either directly or intermediately. At the time of the Conquest, for example, William I distributed tracts of land to his lords. In return for this land the lords would have to perform some service. What this was would depend on their *tenure*. Thus the tenure of grand serjeanty involved some personal service to the Sovereign, such as carrying his sword on state occasions. Socage tenure, for practical purposes the only one left today, involved the payment of a rent. Knight service meant that the holder of the land had to supply the King with a certain number of armed men. Many holders of land would grant land in their turn to others, to be held on similar tenures. This process was called subinfeudation, and as it meant a decrease of revenue and weakening of allegiance to the King it was stopped by the statute *Quia Emptores* in 1290.

Tenure was thus the method by which the land was held. The size of the interest held was called the estate. An estate could never confer complete ownership—only the King had that—but lasted for varying lengths of time. The estates were: fee simple, fee tail (or entailed interest), life and term of years. The first three were called estates of freehold, the last leasehold. For historical reasons, freehold estates are known as real property or realty, whereas leaseholds are classed as personal property or personalty.

A fee simple is the highest estate that can exist in land. For practical purposes, nowadays, it amounts to complete ownership. 'Fee' means an estate of inheritance. A fee simple was conveyed to a man 'and his heirs'. If the grantee of the land died intestate,[1] the land went to his heir, normally his eldest son; but if he had no sons or none living, it might descend not to his lineal descendants but to his great-uncle, for example, if that was his closest blood relation. A fee tail,[2] however, could not be disposed of so freely, for it could descend only to the heirs of the body of the grantee; that is, lineal descendants. Thus if the grantee's great-uncle was his only living blood relation, and the grantee died, his entailed land would revert to the grantor. Estates tail may be further restricted by being either tail male or tail female (limited to descent through sons or daughters respectively), or special tail—that is, limited to the issue[3] of a particular marriage.

Life estates end with the life of the grantee, except for a kind called estates '*pur autre vie*'.[4] This occurs when land is granted to A during the life of B. On B's death the land reverts to the grantor.

Leasehold estates are those measured by reference to a fixed, known length of time. They may be continuing, thus a tenancy from year to year or week to week; or fixed, thus a lease of 999 years.

Estates may be in possession or reversion. Thus if A has a fee simple estate and grants a life interest to B, B has the possession of the land. But A has not disposed of his whole interest, for on B's death he will once more have possession of his land. This future interest is called a reversion. If A has a fee simple and divides it up as follows: to B for life and then to C in fee simple, C is said to have a future interest, known as a remainder. (It is not a reversion since it does not revert to the grantor as in the first example.)

The dispositions of land permitted by the Common Law were strictly limited by the rule that there must be no 'gap in the seisin'. The earliest method of conveying land was by 'livery of seisin'. If A wished to transfer land to B, they would go on to the land in question and A would hand B something symbolic of the land, such as a twig or piece of earth. Thus the transfer of land was made public. The 'livery' (delivery) of the symbolic twig or earth represented the nearest that could be approached to physical delivery of possession

[1] Without leaving a valid will.
[2] Tail is from the Latin '*talliatum*', meaning cut-down.
[3] Descendants.   [4] For another life.

of the land. Seisin is a difficult conception, something between ownership and possession, not readily distinguishable in mediaeval times. Sufficient be it to say that the seisin (and, for our present purpose, any freehold estate approximates to it) must always be vested in someone. It cannot disappear and reappear. This is the Common Law rule. It will be seen that a disposition such as the following was impossible. 'A gives land to B for life and then five years after B's death to C in fee simple.' The reason this could not be was that A had divested himself of the seisin (or freehold) and it passed to B. After B's death, what became of it? It was vested in nobody. It had to wander, a disembodied spirit, for five years, and this the Common Law would not allow. Had the disposition been to B for life and on his death to C in fee simple, this would have been permissible, as the seisin would flit from B to C the very instant B died.

Equity came to the rescue with uses.[1] If A granted the land to the feoffee to uses to hold to the use of B for life and then five years after B's death to the use of C in fee simple, B and C would have the enjoyment of the land in the way A intended, and meanwhile the seisin rested undisturbed with the feoffee.

The use deprived the King of various feudal privileges, and Henry VIII forced Parliament to pass the Statute of Uses in 1535. The effect of this was to transfer the legal estate of the feoffee to uses to the *cestui que use*. Whereas if, before the Statute, X conveyed land to A to the use of B, A received the legal estate and B took the equitable, under such a conveyance[2] *after* the Statute A took nothing, his legal estate passing on to B, who thus had both estates—legal and equitable. But the use was too popular an institution to be thus disposed of by the Statute, and only a hundred years later legal ingenuity found a way out. It was held that, though the Statute converted the first use into a legal estate (executed it), a second use would not be affected. The second use was given the modern name of 'trust'. If land was given to A to the use of B in trust for C, A took nothing, B took the legal estate and C took the equitable estate. So if a conveyancer wished to create an equitable estate, the land would be conveyed 'unto and to the use of' B (feoffee to uses, now called the trustee), in trust for C (the beneficiary). The Statute of Uses was abolished by the Law of Property Act, 1925, so the words 'to the use of' are no longer necessary.

Though equitable estates could be used in ways the legal estate

[1] See Chapter 1, page 10.   [2] In nearly every case.

could not, they suffered (and many types of equitable interest still suffer) from a grave disadvantage. They were not good against the whole world, as are legal estates. Only the holder of a legal estate can dispose of it. But this did not necessarily apply to equitable estates. For example, T holds the legal estate in Blackacre.[1] He holds it on trust for B, who thus has the equitable estate. Suppose T is a scoundrel and sells the land to P without telling him of the trust attached to it. If P acts in good faith and has no knowledge of B's equitable interest, then P will take Blackacre free of the trust. Such equitable interests are extinguished by sale to a *bona fide* purchaser without notice. Notice need not be express; for instance, a purchaser will be fixed with the knowledge of his agent (his solicitor, for example) and, if he shuts his eyes to facts that should put him on his guard, he will be similarly deemed to have notice. Contrast the position where a legal estate is sold. X, a fraudulent person, sells Whiteacre to P. Unknown to P, F has a legal estate in the land—the right to fish in the stream running through it. F's right will be good against P, *bona fide* purchaser without notice though he is, for F's is a *legal* right.

Certain equitable rights may be protected by registration. For example, if V contracts to sell Greenacre to P, P takes an equitable interest in the land as soon as the contract is made. This equitable interest may be protected by registration and, if so, it cannot be extinguished by sale of the land to a *bona fide* purchaser without notice (Land Charges Act, 1925, now replaced and amended by Land Charges Act, 1972). Prospective purchasers of land may inspect the Land Charges Register. As a result of the Law of Property Act, 1925,[2] it is possible to have only two legal estates in land: the fee simple absolute[3] in possession[4] and the term of years absolute. All other interests are equitable. This is important when considering strict settlements and trusts for sale.

Landowners have always been concerned to keep their land in the family and to carve such estates out of this land as will provide for the maintenance of the various members of the family. The strict settlement is a way of achieving these objects; the trust for sale is

[1] In land law pieces of land are called 'Blackacre', 'Whiteacre', etc., for the purposes of illustration.
[2] Section 1.
[3] As distinct from determinable or most conditional interests.
   As opposed to interests in reversion.

more concerned with the division of the family wealth than with keeping it in the family.

A simple example of a settlement is where A holds land in fee simple and conveys it to himself for life, then to his eldest son in tail male, subject thereto his younger son in tail male, with the fee simple reverting to himself. When A's eldest son comes of age, there is a resettlement and he takes a life interest. Otherwise he could bar[1] the entail, and the settlement's object of keeping the land in the family would be frustrated. Under this system of resettling the land, it will be seen that the head of the family was always tenant for life. He never held the fee simple in possession, and therefore he had no power of selling the land and was greatly restricted in his use of it. When the effects of the Industrial Revolution were felt, the powerlessness of tenants for life began to have serious consequences. For example, a man might be tenant for life of land with vast deposits of coal beneath it, yet in many cases he could not open mines to utilise these resources. A series of Acts, culminating in the Settled Land Act, 1925, remedied these defects.

Now, as a result, the position is as follows. The fee simple is vested in the 'estate owner', who is nearly always the tenant for life. It is vested in him by a 'vesting deed'. A separate deed, known as the trust instrument, sets out the various interests of the beneficiaries under the settlement. The vesting deed names trustees of the settlement. The advantage of having two separate instruments is that purchasers of the land are not interested in the limitations of the land under the settlement. They are concerned only with the vesting deed, which shows title in the tenant for life[2] and names the trustees to whom the purchase money is to be paid. The tenant for life[2] has, *as regards disposal of the land*, practically all the powers of an ordinary tenant in fee simple. He may sell, exchange, lease, mortgage it, etc. But when exercising any of his powers, he does so for the benefit of the beneficiaries under the settlement. For example, the tenant for life may sell the settled land. The purchaser will take the land free of all the equitable interests under the settlement. But those equitable interests then alight on the resulting purchase money, and the interests of the beneficiaries are thus protected. This dual personality of the tenant for life under a settlement is all-important. He is virtually the absolute owner to deal with the land, but as regards the beneficial ownership he is still only tenant for life and cannot deprive the

---

[1] Enlarge it into a fee simple.   [2] Or other 'estate owner'.

other beneficiaries of their interests. With such powers of the tenant for life, it can be imagined that keeping land in a family has become a secondary *rôle* of settlements.

Another way of apportioning realty or personalty to provide for the needs of a family is the trust for sale. Usually the settlor vests the property in trustees by deed. This deed orders the trustees to sell the property and hold the proceeds on the trusts set out in a second instrument. The trustees have a power to postpone the sale, and in practice the settlor's intention usually is that the trustees shall retain the specific property indefinitely, but he cannot entirely prevent the trustees from selling. As distinct from a strict settlement, under a trust for sale the trustees have the power of dealing with the property; but when they do sell, the purchaser takes free of the equitable interests, which attach themselves to the purchase money, as in the case of a strict settlement.

It has been assumed, when dealing with both strict settlements and trusts for sale, that they have been originally created by deed *inter vivos*.[1] Of course, they may be created by will. The will fulfils the function of the trust instrument.

Trusts for sale have other uses in the law; for example, with regard to concurrent interests. A concurrent interest exists when more than one person owns an interest in land. The two main ways in which this occurs are joint tenancy and tenancy in common. The most important practical difference is that of *survivorship*. If A and B are joint tenants of Blackacre, and A dies first, his share will pass to B. The survivor takes the other joint tenant's interest. But if A and B were tenants in common and A died, his share would pass to his personal representatives, to be disposed of according to A's will or to those entitled on his intestacy.

Joint tenancies are created simply by giving land 'to A and B'. 'Words of severance' are necessary to create a tenancy in common; thus 'to A and B, share and share alike'. By a rule of Equity, tenancies in common may be created even without such words, where a joint tenancy with its resulting survivorship would be inequitable. An example occurs when A and B buy land and contribute unequal amounts of the purchase money.

A joint tenancy may be 'severed' and thus converted into a tenancy in common.

The Law of Property Act, 1925, has used the trust for sale

[1] Taking effect before the settlor's death, as distinct from by will.

to simplify conveyancing of concurrent interests. Land in which concurrent interests exist must now be held on trust for sale. This means that a purchaser takes the legal estate free of the beneficial equitable interests, which attach themselves to the purchase money. Fewer titles need to be investigated, and costs are thus saved.

Remainders may be of two kinds: vested or contingent. A vested remainder exists where the person entitled to the remainder can take possession immediately the prior interest ends. A contingent remainder exists where the person entitled to the remainder may not be able to take possession immediately the prior interest ends. In other words, his power of taking possession is *contingent* or dependent on something else besides the ending of the prior estate.

For example, if A is a married man with a son of twenty-one, a limitation to A for life, remainder in fee simple to his son on reaching twenty-one would give the son a vested remainder, for he could take possession of Blackacre when his father died. But a limitation to X (the father of a ten-year-old son) for life, remainder to his son on attaining twenty-one years, would give the son a contingent remainder. If his father died, he would not be able to take immediately, as the gift to him was *contingent* on his reaching twenty-one.

Contingent remainders at Common Law were subject to the rules about seisin already discussed. We have seen how Equity has overcome these rules. Since 1925, all future interests (other than leaseholds) are equitable. Contingent remainders may, however, be frustrated by the Rule Against Perpetuities.

The idea of tying-up wealth for a long time so that, with compound interest accumulating, a modest fortune grows like a snowball to huge proportions has always appealed to testators and settlors. The law disapproves of large sums being kept in cold storage in this way and its weapon is the Rule Against Perpetuities.[1] This originally provided that a contingent interest could not be created unless it *had to* vest within the duration of a specified life or lives in being, plus twenty-one years, at the date of its creation. The Rule has been amended by the Perpetuities and Accumulations Act, 1964 (which applies to instruments taking effect after its commencement on July 16th, 1964), in two important respects. First, in addition to the traditional periods, the perpetuity period may be a specified period not exceeding eighty years. Secondly, a disposition

[1] The rule is not applicable in certain cases.

is not treated as void for remoteness until it becomes established that the interest disposed of *cannot* vest within the perpetuity period. This is the 'wait and see' rule. Examples will make this clearer. 'To A (a bachelor) for life, remainder in fee simple to his son on attaining the age of twenty-one.' The remainder is good. It is contingent on A's marrying and having a son who will reach twenty-one, but if he does and thus the remainder vests it *must* do so within the limitation period. A is the life in being, and his son cannot be born after his death. Periods of gestation are ignored for this purpose.

Supposing the gift had been: 'To A for life, remainder in fee simple to his first grandchild.' Now, if A had no grandchildren at the time of this grant,[1] the remainder would have been void under the old law. For A was the life in being, and there was no certainty that the remainder would vest within twenty-one years of A's death. Probabilities were not enough. If the remainder was not to offend against the rule, the vesting had to be certain to occur (if it occurred at all) within the perpetuity period. If the 1964 Act had been applicable, however, the gift to the grandchildren would not be avoided until an event occurred which rendered the vesting within the perpetuity period impossible. The old period may be extended by choosing several lives. Then the twenty-one years will not start to run until the last life ends. The lives chosen need not be relatives of the settlor or testator or beneficiaries; in fact, the lives of living descendants of George V were frequently chosen, as being easily ascertainable. Since the 1964 Act the period not exceeding eighty years is likely to supersede the older one.

By the Law of Property Act, 1925, as amended by the 1964 Act, income on property is not allowed to be accumulated beyond certain specified periods, notwithstanding the vesting occurs within the perpetuity period. This is the Rule Against Accumulations.

Interests in land need not be absolute. They may be determinable or conditional. An example of a determinable interest is: 'To A in fee simple, so long as he practises at the Bar.' It continues while the grantee carries out a certain requirement, and when he ceases to do so, his interest determines. Such interests created since 1925 may only be equitable. They are found in protective trusts, designed to safeguard spendthrifts and their families. The beneficiary is given a determinable life interest so long as he is solvent. On his

[1] And none had been conceived.

bankruptcy, it shifts to trustees to use in their discretion for the benefit of the bankrupt and his family.

Somewhat similar is a conditional interest. A limitation: 'To A in fee simple on condition he does not marry a Roman Catholic' is an example. If the condition is broken, the grantor may end the estate. It does not automatically end like a determinable interest. The grantor must enter and determine the interest. Not any condition which the grantor desires may be imposed. For example, a condition *completely* forbidding marriage might be void as being against public policy, though a partial restraint, as in the example above, is usually good. Another reason that may avoid a condition is that it offends against the Rule Against Perpetuities. If a condition subsequent is void for any reason, the grantee takes absolutely and free from any condition.

The law of land is concerned not merely with solid corporeal earth, the natural products of it and the buildings on it. It deals also with what are known forbiddingly as 'incorporeal hereditaments'— rights to do certain things over land or take things from it. These are rights attached to a piece of land, though not amounting to all the rights which an estate owner of the land itself would have. Incorporeal hereditaments are interests in land, and once created they pass with the land. They must not be confused with mere contractual rights, which exist only between the parties to the contract. If A, the owner of Blackacre, gives B, the owner of adjoining Whiteacre, an easement giving B the right of way over Blackacre, the easement will pass with Blackacre or Whiteacre if either is sold. A mere contract under which A gives B the right of passage over Blackacre does not confer any rights on a third party to whom A or B should sell his land. Two main types of incorporeal hereditaments exist: easements and profits *à prendre*.

An easement is a right enjoyed by the holder of a piece of land (the dominant tenement) to do something to another piece of land (the servient tenement) or to prevent the servient tenement landholder from doing something to his land. The easement must have some natural connection with the dominant tenement, and the dominant and servient tenements must be in different hands. An easement is an interest in land and, once created, passes with the land, as distinct from a mere contractual right, which exists only between the contracting parties.

Examples of easements are a right to light (the dominant tenement owner can prevent the servient tenement owner from building so as to obscure his light), a right of way over another's land or a right to discharge water over another's land.

A profit *à prendre* is the right to take something from a piece of land. In contrast to easements, there *need* not be a dominant and servient tenement;[1] a person may have the right to take something from another's land without himself owning a dominant tenement. Such a profit is known as a profit 'in gross'.

Examples of profits are the right to pasture cattle over a piece of land and the right to fish in a certain stream.

Easements and profits may be created by statute, grant (express or implied[2]) or prescription. By prescription is meant the enjoyment of an easement or profit under certain conditions for a certain length of time. In connection with express grants, s. 62 of the Law of Property Act, 1925, should be carefully noted, as it provides that where land is conveyed 'privileges, etc.' are conveyed with it. This provides a trap for the unwary, as a mere permission to walk over land or to use a coal-shed, for example, may be elevated into an easement unless the conveyance expressly excepts it. Easements and profits are ended by the dominant owner releasing them or when the dominant and servient tenements come into the same hands.

We now come to the consideration of terms of years or leaseholds. A term of years must be of certain duration or measured by relation to a fixed time. A lease must not be confused with a licence. A lease confers an interest in the land, whereas a licence is merely a right to remain on it. The test is whether the grantor retains control of the land. If he remains in exclusive possession, he obviously does retain control and a licence only is granted; it usually follows therefore that a lease is granted where the grantee is given exclusive possession. A lodger has merely a licence to remain in his room. Normally, if a licence is revoked in breach of contract by the licensor, the licensee's only remedy lies in damages. Some limited statutory protection against revocation, however, is now afforded to licensees occupying furnished premises by Part VI of the Rent Act, 1968 (see page 107). A lessee, on the other hand, enjoys a substantial security of tenure.

Do not be deceived by the expression 'term of years'. This includes both terms of fixed duration and continuing ones, and may be of any length. For example, a weekly tenancy is a 'term of years'

---

[1] There usually is, in practice.   [2] Not profits.

for this purpose. Mention must be made of two types of tenancy which, though not terms of years, are frequently converted into them. These are tenancy at will and tenancy at sufferance. A tenancy at will occurs where a person is given possession of land to hold until either he or the owner of the land chooses to end the arrangement. No notice is required to do this. Such a tenancy may arise where a person is allowed a house to live in, rent free. A tenancy at sufferance arises where a tenant who entered land lawfully remains in possession wrongfully when his term has ended. The law dislikes these uncertain tenancies. Where the person in possession of land is permitted by the owner to remain and pays rent calculated with reference to a yearly basis, the law will presume a yearly tenancy has arisen.

How are terms of years created? First, a yearly tenancy at Common Law may arise as shown above. Secondly, the term of years may be conveyed by a *lease*, which vests the legal estate in the grantee. If the term is for more than three years, it must be conveyed by deed. If for three years or less, it may be created by writing or orally.[1]

Thirdly, there may be an agreement for a lease. This does not convey the legal estate to the tenant but merely the equitable estate. He has, however, the right to call upon the landlord to convey the legal estate to him. For most purposes, an agreement is as good as a lease. Such agreements must be evidenced in writing (s. 40, Law of Property Act, 1925). As we have seen before, however,[2] part-performance may supply the want of writing.

It can be seen that where X purports to grant a lease of Blackacre to Y for five years by a document in writing signed by him but not under seal, no legal estate is conveyed. But Y will take an equitable term of years and, having this, he can call upon X to complete the transaction by transferring the legal estate to him. Supposing the purported lease to be by word of mouth only, if Y could prove part performance, he would still take an equitable term. Finally, if even that had not occurred, if Y had taken possession with X's consent and paid him a yearly rent, a yearly tenancy at Common Law would arise.

A term of years may end by being surrendered to the landlord or

[1] Provided the lease is in possession at the best rent which can be reasonably obtained without taking a fine (premium).

[2] See Chapter 4, page 72.

by both term and reversion becoming merged in one person, as where a tenant purchases the freehold of his house. Terms of years certain expire of their own accord when they have run their appointed length,[1] but periodic tenancies, such as yearly or monthly tenancies, need to be ended by notice to quit. Such notice may be given by either party. It must be unequivocal and must correctly specify the notice due. How long notice is necessary depends on the terms of the lease or agreement. If unspecified, six months' notice is usually necessary to end a yearly tenancy,[2] a month to end a monthly and a week to end a weekly tenancy. The day on which the notice expires must be the anniversary of the creation of the tenancy.[3] Thus if a weekly tenancy was created on a Tuesday, the notice to quit must take effect on a Tuesday. The Landlord and Tenant Act, 1954, provides that certain long tenancies and tenancies of business premises can only be determined in ways set out in the Act.

Yet another way in which a term may end is by forfeiture. In every tenancy there are certain conditions or covenants, express or implied,[4] the breach of which gives rise to legal liability. The difference between a condition and a covenant is that a breach of condition automatically gives the landlord a right to re-enter the land and end the term, whereas for breach of covenant there is no right of entry unless it has expressly been reserved. Note that mere breach of condition or covenant does not end the term. The landlord must enter on the land first.[5] This is called effecting a forfeiture. Considerable limitation has been placed on this right by various Statutes. Thus the Common Law Procedure Act of 1852 provides that a tenant who has not paid his rent, and has thereby incurred liability to foreiture, may avoid it by paying all rent, arrears and costs. Even after judgment has been given in an action for possession by the landlord in such a case, the tenant may still apply to the Court for relief up to six months after judgment, though such relief is purely discretionary. A hard case may arise where a tenant does not pay his rent but *his* tenant—the head landlord's sub-tenant—does, for if the tenant's term is forfeited the sub-tenant's term, being created out of the original term, must be forfeited too. The law has provided for

---

[1] Except agricultural leases of two years or longer.
[2] One year is *always* necessary for yearly agricultural tenancies.
[3] Unless agreed otherwise by the parties.
[4] The various types are discussed later.
[5] Bringing an action for possession is an 'entry'.

this in s. 146(4) of the Law of Property Act, 1925. A sub-tenant may ask for relief in such a case, and the Court may, in its discretion, vest the remainder of the tenant's term in him on such conditions as may be just.

Breaches of covenant other than that to pay rent are dealt with by s. 146 of the Law of Property Act, 1925. This provides that a landlord proceeding to enforce a forfeiture for such a breach must serve a notice[1] specifying the breach and requiring it to be remedied, if possible, and demanding compensation in money. The tenant has a reasonable time (usually three months) to comply with the notice, and if he does not the landlord may enforce a forfeiture. The tenant may apply to the Court for relief up to the date of re-entry. Sub-tenants are protected by sub-section 4 of s. 146.

In the case of covenants to repair, if the tenancy satisfies certain conditions, the Leasehold Property (Repairs) Act, 1938, may apply. Under this Act, leave of the County Court may be necessary before an action may be brought for damages or forfeiture. The Landlord and Tenant Act, 1927, limits the damages a landlord may recover for such a breach.

The other remedies for breach of covenant are damages or, if the breach is merely anticipated, an injunction to prevent it. The remedy of distress is available to recover arrears of rent. This is the right of the landlord to seize the tenant's goods on the premises[2] and sell them. The proceeds from the sale are used to pay the rent due; any excess must be returned to the tenant. The tenant's clothes, bedding and tools of his trade up to £50 may not be distrained. Distress may be levied only by a certificated bailiff or the landlord in person.[3]

Where a lease or agreement for a lease is drawn up by a solicitor, he is careful to regulate the relations of the parties by express covenants. But, in any case, certain obligations will be implied by law. The landlord must give the tenant quiet enjoyment of the premises; for example, he must not work mines in such a way that the tenant's house is damaged through earth subsidence.[4] If the subject of the tenancy is a furnished house, there is an implied term that the house is fit for human habitation at the beginning of the tenancy. There is no such term in the case of unfurnished houses, except for lettings

---

[1] Except in certain cases.   [2] Or off the premises, in some cases.
[3] Distress in respect of rent of rent-controlled premises may be levied only by leave of the Court.
[4] *Markham* v. *Paget*, [1908] Ch. 697.

where the rent is within certain limits laid down in the Housing Act, 1957, when the landlord must maintain[1] the house in a condition fit for human habitation. There is no implied term, apart from these exceptions, that the landlord will do any repairs. The landlord is also subject to an implied term not to derogate from his grant, i.e. a promise is implied on his part not to prevent the use of the land by the tenant for the purposes for which it was let.

On the tenant's side, he must refrain from waste—that is, damage to property which injures the reversion. This may be voluntary, such as opening mines; or permissive, for instance letting the property fall into disrepair. Tenants from year to year are not liable for permissive waste, and tenants at will are not liable for either permissive or voluntary waste.

Quite apart from waste, there is an implied covenant that the tenant will keep the premises in 'a tenantlike manner'.

The tenant has certain implied rights at Common Law, such as the right to take wood from the land for fuel and repairs, known as the right to estovers. More important are the statutory rights conferred by the Rent Act.[2] The Landlord and Tenant Act, 1927, as amended by the Landlord and Tenant Act, 1954, gives the tenants of trade or business premises the right, when their tenancy comes to an end, to compensation for improvements made during the tenancy.

In a lease of a dwelling-house for a term of less than seven years granted after the passing of the Act, a covenant by the leasor is implied:

(a) to keep in repair the structure and exterior of the house, and
(b) to keep in repair and proper working order certain installations, viz. for the supply of water, gas and electricity, and for sanitation and for space heating and water heating (Housing Act, 1961, s. 32(1)).

An example of an express covenant is that to pay rent. At Common Law, rent is payable in arrear, so that if the landlord wishes his rent to be paid in advance he must make it an express term of the agreement. It is the duty of the tenant to seek out his landlord and pay him, unless it is agreed between them to the contrary. Likewise, unless otherwise agreed, the tenant remains liable to pay the rent if the premises are damaged or destroyed.

[1] In most cases (see Housing Act, 1957, s. 6).
[2] See page 107 below.

It is usual for the parties to insert an express covenant about repairs into their lease or agreement. A party who has covenanted to repair must, after making due allowance for the locality, character and age of the premises at the time of the lease, keep them in the condition in which they would be kept by a reasonably minded tenant of the class who would be likely to take them.[1] If a person covenants to keep property in repair, and the premises are not in good condition at the beginning of the tenancy, he must put them into repair.

Frequently landlord and tenant divide the repairing obligations between them; for example, the landlord may covenant to repair the exterior, the tenant the interior of the premises. Also found frequently is the 'fair wear and tear excepted' clause in covenants to repair. This relieves the repairing party from the responsibility to make good damage resulting from the ordinary, reasonable use of the premises and the normal action of the elements.[2]

The tenant will usually covenant not to assign or sub-let the premises without the landlord's permission. An assignment occurs where the tenant parts with his whole interest in the premises to a third party, as, for example, where X, being tenant to Y for a term of five years, grants Z the whole of the term remaining. A sub-letting occurs when the tenant parts with the whole or part of the premises to a third party but retains a reversion. An example would be where A, having taken a lease of Blackacre for three years from B, grants C a lease of Blackacre for one year. In the above examples, Z would become the tenant of Y in place of X under the assignment, but in the case of the sub-letting, C would be A's tenant but A would still remain B's tenant.

If there is no covenant against sub-letting, etc., the tenant may sub-let. If there is a covenant, it may be absolute or qualified, providing that there is to be no sub-letting without the landlord's consent. An absolute covenant forbids any sub-letting, etc. Where there is a qualified covenant, the tenant must ask the landlord's permission, and the Landlord and Tenant Act, 1927, provides that in all such cases the landlord must not unreasonably withhold consent. Grounds for reasonably refusing consent would be, for example,

[1] *Proudfoot* v. *Hart* (1890), 25 Q.B.D. 42.
[2] He is, however, liable for damage consequential upon that caused by fair wear and tear, e.g. damages to floor boards caused by rain coming through the roof due to a missing tile.

that the proposed sub-tenant or assignee was a bankrupt or a prostitute. Unless previously agreed in the lease, the landlord may not demand a sum of money for such consent.[1]

Of immense importance in the law of landlord and tenant are the provisions of the Rent Act, 1968, which consolidates earlier legislation. The object of the Act is to give the tenant of protected unfurnished premises security of tenure. Protected tenancies may be divided into two types: controlled tenancies and regulated tenancies. Controlled tenancies have their historical roots in the period after the First World War when there was an acute housing shortage. Legislation was therefore passed, and subsequently added to and amended, to prevent profiteering in letting unfurnished houses. This was achieved by restricting the rent to a low level. The Rent Act of 1957 excluded from control any dwelling house the rateable value of which in Greater London exceeded £40, elsewhere in England and Wales £30, and in Scotland £40. Even so, many premises were still outside these provisions and remained controlled. The Housing Finance Act, 1972, however, provides for decontrol either by the issue by Local Authorities of a qualification certificate showing that the dwelling house is provided with all the standard amenities, is in good repair and fit for habitation, or by the general decontrol of controlled property, the date of which depends upon the area and the rateable value as at March 31st, 1972. According to the table, all property should be decontrolled by July 1st, 1975.

The second class, known as regulated tenancies, are all those protected tenancies which are not controlled.

What, then, are protected tenancies? A protected tenancy is defined in s. 1 of the Rent Act, 1968, as a tenancy 'under which a dwelling house (which may be a house or part of a house) is let as a separate dwelling'. A flat, being part of a dwelling house, is protected. The tenancy remains protected if living accommodation is shared with another tenant, but if shared with the landlord, the tenant is given the protection afforded to tenants of furnished premises. A protected tenancy, which is used partly for business and partly for living purposes, is only subject to the Act if it is controlled. If it is regulated, the tenancy is subject to the provisions governing business tenancies.

There are many exceptions taking certain premises outside the

---

[1] Law of Property Act, 1925, s. 144.

Act. Houses let by Local Authorities and housing associations are outside it. Furnished lettings are not protected, for they have a different scheme of control. Premises are 'furnished' for this purpose where a substantial part of the rent is for attendance or services, or for the use of furniture. Tenancies where the rent is less than two-thirds the rateable value are excluded (except a converted tenancy, as defined in the Housing Finance Act, after a conversion), and houses with a rateable value exceeding £1500 in Greater London and £750 elsewhere are also excluded.[1]

What sort of tenancy has a tenant of a protected house? Take the example of a weekly tenant holding a protected house. There are various covenants in the agreement. Suppose his landlord gives him notice to quit.[2] The contractual tenancy agreed between landlord and tenant ends and the tenant becomes a *statutory tenant*. He will hold his tenancy on the same terms as the contractual agreement, except for terms inconsistent with a statutory tenancy; for example, a statutory tenant may not assign the whole of the premises even if he is permitted by the terms of the old contractual tenancy. It is important to notice that a statutory tenancy is not an interest in land like other tenancies but merely a personal status. Therefore, it cannot be devised by will. A statutory tenancy may be lost if the statutory tenant goes away, abandoning possession of the premises.

A statutory tenant cannot be evicted without an order of the County Court. To obtain such an order the landlord must prove circumstances set out in the Acts, and also the Court must be satisfied that it is reasonable in all the circumstances of the case to make the order. Common examples of grounds for possession are that suitable alternative accommodation is available for the tenant, that the tenant has broken a covenant in the lease, or is in arrears with his rent, or has caused nuisance and annoyance to adjoining occupiers, or has sub-let the whole of the premises without the landlord's consent, or that the landlord reasonably requires the premises for himself or certain specified persons. This last is very common, and is known as 'the greater hardship' ground, as the tenant can stop

---

[1] Protection is afforded to certain long tenancies by the Landlord and Tenant Act, 1954, and by the Leasehold Reform Act, 1967, which gives the tenant satisfying its conditions the right to acquire the freehold.

[2] So far as dwelling-houses are concerned (whether controlled by the Rent Act or not), a four weeks' notice to quit must be given, even in the case of a weekly tenancy.

the landlord from gaining possession if he can show that greater hardship would result by the Court's making an order for possession than by refusing it.

Though statutory tenancy is a matter of personal status, it may pass, in some circumstances, to another. For example, if a statutory tenant dies, leaving a widow who had been living with him at his death, she will take over the statutory tenancy.

The maximum rent which can be recovered for a regulated tenancy is normally fixed by an independent official called the Rent Officer. The rent is then registered as the 'fair rent' for the premises. An appeal lies from the Officer's decision to the Rent Assessment Committee. An application can be made to vary a 'fair rent', but usually three years must have elapsed since the date of registration. If certain conditions are satisfied, a landlord and tenant jointly may apply to cancel the registration, and may agree to increase the rent. The Housing Finance Act, 1972, provides for the assessment of fair rents for Local Authority dwellings and also introduces registration of fair rents for housing association dwellings.

It is illegal in most cases to demand a premium for granting, renewing or assigning a lease. And if the purchase of furniture and fittings is made the condition of such a grant and the price asked exceeds the reasonable price of the furniture, etc., the tenant can recover the excess.

Furnished premises are dealt with by the Rent Act, 1968, Part VI. The Act applies both to tenants and to licensees, as long as they have exclusive occupation of some part of the premises. A lodger may have exclusive occupation of his room for the purpose of Part VI, although he does not have the exclusive possession of the premises necessary to create a tenancy. Note that the standard of furnishing necessary to bring premises under Part VI is less than that required to take them out of the class of protected unfurnished tenancies. Thus a tenant may be able to claim protection both as a section 1 protected tenant and under Part VI.

Either party may apply to the Rent Tribunal to determine the appropriate rent. The Tribunal fixes the rent, and it is an offence for the landlord to charge more. A reference to the Rent Tribunal confers an automatic security of tenure for six months unless it dismisses the reference altogether. In the latter case, a notice to quit can take effect seven days after the decision.

A grantee of furnished premises, who has been served with a

notice to quit, may apply to the Rent Tribunal, before the expiry of the notice, to have its operation deferred. The deferment may be for a period of up to six months and further extensions may be granted. If, however, the contract is for a fixed term, which expires automatically without the necessity for a notice to quit, Part VI cannot provide any security of tenure.

At the beginning of this chapter it was stated that for practical purposes the fee simple is equivalent to complete ownership. However, there are statutory controls on the use that may be made of land, and successive planning statutes have given the Government power over both public and private planning. The most recent statutes are the Town and Country Planning Act, 1971, and the Town and Country Planning (Amendment) Act, 1972.

The administration of planning control is in the hands of the Local Authorities, the central authority being the Department of the Environment.

In the case of private development, planning permission is required. Development is defined by the 1971 Act as the carrying on of building, engineering, mining or other operations in, on, over or under land, or the making of any material change in the use of any buildings or other land. Permission must be sought from the Local Planning Authority. An appeal lies from the refusal of planning permission to the Secretary of State for the Environment. The High Court has the power to suspend or quash the Secretary's decision if it is not within the powers conferred by the Statute, or if any of the relevant requirements in relation to it have not been complied with. In certain circumstances, if the Local Planning Authority refuse permission to develop, they may be compelled to purchase the land.

The Local Planning Authority may serve an enforcement notice upon a landowner who has neglected to obtain planning permission. This may require the landowner to restore the land to its original condition. If he fails to comply with the notice, he is liable to a fine and the Local Planning Authority may do the work themselves, recovering the cost from the landowner.

Some kinds of development need no planning permission. For example, a landowner may alter the interior of a building so long as its exterior is not materially affected, or he may erect a toolshed of a certain size in his garden. An instance of what he may not do without permission is to turn a dwelling-house into separate flats.

6 Wills and Trusts

A will is possibly the most solemn, and sometimes the most dramatic, document a solicitor has to draft. By its aid the testator may, in a sense, prolong his brief stay on earth; he may provoke bitter quarrels, arouse gratitude or, if there has been faulty drafting, cause his estate to shrink with litigation. Is it for these reasons that intestacy is regarded by so many as a disgrace?

Anyone of eighteen or more, of sound mind, may make a will. Even mental patients may, in a lucid interval. Wills, however, may be avoided if they have been procured by fraud or coercion.

As a safeguard against fraud, the Wills Act, 1837, provides that no will or codicil shall be admitted to probate[1] unless it is in a certain form. A will is the main document by which the testator disposes of his property. A codicil is a supplementary document executed in the same way, which varies or adds to a will. There may be any number of codicils attached to a will, and they must all be read as one with the will.

The requirements as to form are these. The will[2] must be in writing and signed by the testator or by someone by his direction and in his presence. The signature must be at the end,[3] but it may be by rubber stamp, for example, and an illiterate person may make his mark. The testator must sign or acknowledge the will in the presence of two witnesses. The witnesses must both sign the will in the testator's presence. This is to show they have witnessed the testator's signing or acknowledgment and is known as attestation. The witnesses need not know the contents of the will. No witness may benefit under a will. If the will purports to give a legacy to a witness, the attestation is good but the gift to the witness will fail.

Servicemen and women in actual military service and mariners at sea are excused from these strict requirements. They may make valid wills in any form; for example, an unattested letter or even orally. Neither do testators in these classes have to be eighteen.

A testator may leave by will what he pleases of his own property. Of course, life interests and joint interests die with the testator, so

[1] See below.   [2] Or codicil.   [3] As judicially interpreted.

they may not be devised.[1] Until the Inheritance (Family Provision) Act, 1938, a testator was absolutely unfettered as to whom he could leave his property. His wife and children could be cut off without even the proverbial shilling. The 1938 Act, as amended by the Intestates Estates Act, 1952, and by the Family Provisions Act, 1966, provides that dependants of the testator may apply to the Court for provision to be made for them out of the will, either by payments of income or capital. The class of 'dependants' is strictly limited and includes a surviving spouse, unmarried daughter, infant son, or son or daughter incapable of maintaining himself or herself by reason of mental or physical infirmity and an illegitimate child.[2] Before deciding whether to interfere with the will, the Court must have regard to the dependant's financial position, the past relations between the dependant and the testator, the testator's reasons for making his dispositions, and any other material circumstance. Wills will not lightly be upset. Thus in Re *Joslin*[3] a husband left nothing to his wife by will but left all his property to his mistress and his illegitimate children. His wife had an income, the mistress had none. The testator had been estranged from his wife but had had two children by the mistress. The Court refused to interfere with the will.

Under the Matrimonial Causes Act, 1965, s. 26,[4] a former spouse who has not remarried may apply to the Court for reasonable provision to be made for him or her out of the deceased's estate, on the lines of the 1938 Act.

Legacies may be of three kinds. A specific legacy indicates a particular object; thus, 'my gold watch'. A general legacy is a gift of something of a kind and not distinguished from others of the same kind, e.g. '£100'. A demonstrative legacy exists where a sum of money is directed to be paid out of a particular fund, e.g. '£100 out of my War Loan'. The differences are important. For example, if the debts paid out of the testator's estate do not leave enough assets for all the legacies to be paid, the general legacies will 'abate' before the specific legacies are utilised. On the other hand, a specific legacy may be 'adeemed'. For example, the testator may have sold his gold watch before he died, and the beneficiary will receive nothing. A

---

[1] To devise is to leave realty by will; to bequeath is to leave personalty by will.
[2] Family Law Reform Act, 1969 (s. 5).   [3] [1941] Ch. 200.
[4] As amended in 1966 and by the Matrimonial Proceedings and Property Act, 1970.

demonstrative legacy cannot be adeemed as, if the fund from which it is directed to be paid is exhausted, it must be paid from the general estate. On the other hand, while the fund from which it is to be paid remains, it does not abate like a general legacy.

Wills are said to be 'ambulatory', or, literally, they 'walk about' until death. This means that they can be revoked by the testator, and he cannot deprive himself of this power. There are three ways of revoking a will.

The first way is by executing another will or codicil revoking the previous one. If the later instrument does not clearly revoke the earlier, however, they will be read together as far as possible. Where disagreement is inevitable, the later dispositions prevail. To avoid such difficulties a will usually contains the phrase 'I hereby revoke all previous testamentary dispositions'.

The second method is destruction *'animo revocandi'* (with the intent to revoke). Both elements must be present.

In the famous case of *Sugden* v. *St. Leonards*,[1] Lord St. Leonards, a former Lord Chancellor, had made a will which had been lost. His daughter had seen it many times, and it was proved that Lord St. Leonards had had no intention to revoke it. Held, no revocation. Contrast the case of *Cheese* v. *Lovejoy*.[2] The testator wished to revoke his will, and threw it into a pile of waste paper. It was rescued and preserved by a maidservant. Held, no revocation.

Marriage revokes a previous will unless it is expressed to be made in contemplation of that marriage.

It may be that a will is to be revoked on a condition; for example, the making of a new will. If so, the old will will not be revoked until the condition is fulfilled.

In construing a will, the Court adheres to certain rules of interpretation. The most important is that the Court must give expression to the intention of the testator. But, as a will must be in writing, the Court cannot go behind that. The testator's intention must be gathered from the words of the will itself, not from outside sources. He is assumed to use words in their ordinary meanings, and if he uses terms with a technical legal meaning, then they will be given their proper legal effect.

'A will speaks from death.' This maxim means that the dispositions of the will must be considered with regard to the state of affairs obtaining at the testator's death, not at the time he made the

[1] (1876) 1 P.D. 154.   [2] (1877), 2 P.D. 251.

will, unless the testator directs otherwise in his will. An example would be where a testator makes a will leaving 'my house property to my wife'. At the time of the will he has two houses. If he were to acquire a third before he died, all three would pass to his wife.

But a word of warning must be added. As to persons named in the will, it does not usually speak from death. A testator left a silver cup to Lord Sherborne. The person who was Lord Sherborne at the date the will was made died before the testator. It was held that the will meant the person who was Lord Sherborne at the time of the making of the will, not at the testator's death,[1] so the gift lapsed.

Conditions may be attached to gifts by will. They may be conditions precedent, in which case the condition must be performed before the donee may take the gift; or conditions subsequent, in which case the donee will lose the gift if the condition is not observed. Conditions are subject to various restrictions. For example, they must not be against public policy. A condition completely forbidding marriage is *prima facie* void. Partial restraints on marriage, e.g. to a Roman Catholic, are usually good, however. A condition must not be uncertain. A condition forbidding marriage to a person not of Jewish parentage and of the Jewish faith was held void for this reason.[2] If a condition fails for any reason, the effect is different, according to whether it is precedent or subsequent. In the former case, the condition, and usually the gift fail; in the latter, the donee takes the gift free of condition.

What happens when a beneficiary under a will dies before the testator? The answer is that the gift lapses. There are two exceptions to this rule: gifts of entailed interests and gifts to the testator's issue, who have issue living at the testator's death. In both cases, the gifts take effect as if the donee had died immediately after the testator.[3] In the case of an entailed interest, there must be issue of the donee capable of taking. In the second case, for example, William, a testator, made a will in 1970 leaving £1000 to his son John, who has two children. John has made a will leaving all his property in equal shares to his two children. If John should die in 1974 and William in 1975, the two children would take £500 each.

If a gift lapses for any reason, such as the beneficiary pre-deceasing the testator, the gift falls into residue. The residue is that property

---

[1] Re *Whorwood* (1887), 34 Ch. D. 446.
[2] *Clayton* v. *Ramsden*, [1943] A.C. 320.
[3] Unless a contrary intention shall appear by the will.

which has not already been specifically disposed of by the will. Normally, there is a gift of the residue under the will. If there is not, the undisposed-of property goes as on intestacy,[1] as the testator has given no directions as to its destination. If part of the residue lapses, it goes as on intestacy.

When a testator dies, someone must take his place to carry out his legal obligations, wind up the estate and distribute his remaining property. Such person (or persons) is known as his personal representative. There are two classes of personal representatives: executors and administrators.

An executor is appointed by the testator in his will. The executor must decide whether he wishes to act or not, for the responsibility is onerous and, unless the will makes provision, the executor is unpaid.[2] A minor or person of unsound mind may not be an executor. Trust corporations, such as banks, may be executors and are frequently appointed, as they cannot die and are unlikely to make away with the assets. If he is unwilling to become executor, the person named in the will may renounce office. He must accept or renounce with regard to the whole will, unless settled land is part of the testator's estate, in which case a separate grant of probate is made.

If a person meddles with the estate of a deceased person, though he is not an executor or an administrator, he becomes an 'executor *de son tort*'.[3] This is an unenviable situation, for he is answerable for the executor's liabilities yet has few of his rights.

The executor's first duty is to prove the will (obtain probate). He must apply to the Principal Registry[4] of the Family Division and hand in the will; executor's oath, sworn before a commissioner for oaths, undertaking to wind up the estate according to law and stating belief that the will is the last testament of the deceased and the schedule is correct; a schedule of the testator's property; and an affidavit for the purposes of estate duty. When the duty is paid, and provided that the documents are in order, a certificate of probate will be granted. This is known as 'probate in common form'.

If anyone interested in the will desires, he may 'enter a caveat'. Or the executor may believe that the will will be contested. In either

---

[1] See page 117.

[2] Subject to exceptions. See page 127.

[3] By his wrong.

[4] Either the Principal Registry or District Registry or County Court in small estates.

of these cases the will may be proved in 'solemn form'. This takes the form of an action in the Chancery Division.

If there is no will, an administrator must be appointed to wind up the deceased's estate, as there is no executor. Similarly, if an executor refuses to act or is incapable through infancy, mental incapacity, etc., or if the testator has failed to appoint an executor, an administrator is appointed. In these last cases he is appointed 'with the will annexed' to carry out its terms.

The right of a person to administer an estate in the above circumstances is conferred by the grant of letters of administration. An application must be made to the Court for the purpose. Various classes of persons have the right to a grant; their priority is regulated by statute. An infant may not be appointed and a trust corporation may. Then the applicant for letters of administration must lodge the same documents at the Registry as a person applying for probate, the difference being that if there is no will it cannot, of course, be lodged, and the oath is to administer the estate according to law. In certain circumstances the administrator may be required to have one or more sureties to guarantee the due performance of his duties.

Once he has obtained probate or letters of administration the personal representative will proceed to administer the estate. He now stands in the shoes of the deceased. All[1] the deceased's property vests in him. He assumes the testator's rights and obligations, subject to certain exceptions. Thus rights of action for contract and tort,[2] which the deceased had before his death, survive. Conversely, rights of others to sue him survive. Contracts of a purely personal nature are ended by death. It must be remembered that these rights and liabilities attach to the personal representative only in his *capacity as such* and not in his personal capacity. An executor of an insolvent estate, for example, does not have to pay the testator's debts out of his own pocket.

The personal representative should compile an inventory of all the testator's assets and then 'get in' the assets. This entails calling for repayment of money due, realising unsafe investments, instituting and defending actions necessary to preserve the testator's property, etc. If there is a will, regard must be had to any directions in it about getting in the estate. The deceased may have been carrying on a business. The personal representative must wind it up as

---

[1] Subject to certain exceptions.   [2] Not actions for defamation.

soon as this may advantageously be done, unless the will (if any) directs otherwise or the creditors agree.

Debts of the deceased must then be paid. Funeral expenses rank first, then expenses of administering the estate. After that, the ordinary creditors are paid. Where the death occurred before January 1st, 1972, if the estate was insolvent, these creditors were divided into three degrees of priority.[1] A personal representative could exercise a 'right of preference'. This meant he might pay one creditor in preference to another, if there were not sufficient assets to satisfy the claims of both, provided the creditors were of equal degree. A personal representative who was himself a creditor of the deceased had a right to pay himself before he paid any other creditor of equal degree. This was known as his right of retainer. These rights have been abolished for deaths after January 1972 by the Administration of Estates Act, 1971.

When all just claims against the estate have been satisfied, the personal representative may distribute the remaining estate. If, however, he omits to pay a debt, the creditor may make him personally liable for it. The personal representative may safeguard himself from this unpleasant possibility by advertising in the *London Gazette* and a local newspaper, fixing a period (not less than two months) during which notice must be given to him of any claims and stating that the estate will be distributed at the end of it. Anyone wishing to claim against the estate must do so within the time stated, and if they do not they may not proceed against the personal representative.

The personal representative must then carry out the terms of the will. He must have regard to the rules regarding ademption and abatement of legacies set out before.

If there is no will, however, the estate will be distributed according to the Administration of Estates Act, 1925, as modified by the Intestates' Estates Act, 1952, and the Family Provision Act, 1966,[2] as follows: The administrator must hold the estate on trust for sale. First, the debts must be paid, in the order set out above. The residuary estate is then dealt with in this way: the surviving spouse receives the 'personal chattels' of the deceased. These are widely defined to include not only the personal effects of the intestate but also his domestic animals, garden effects, household furniture, wines

---

[1] According to the law of bankruptcy.
[2] In a very few cases the pre-1926 law applies.

etc.[1] Money and securities are excluded. The destination of the remaining estate depends upon whether the intestate leaves issue or not. If not, and no parent, brother or sister[2] or issue[2] of them survive, then the intestate's spouse takes the remaining estate absolutely. If there is issue, then the surviving spouse takes (besides the personal chattels) a charge of £15 000 on the remaining estate *and* a life interest in half the remainder. The other half goes to the issue on the statutory trusts. The issue take the first half on the statutory trusts, when the life estate of the surviving spouse ends.

In the third case, where the intestate leaves a spouse, no issue, but parents, or brothers or sisters[2] or their issue,[2] after taking the personal chattels, the surviving spouse is entitled to a charge of £40 000 and half any remaining estate absolutely. The other half goes absolutely to the parents, or, if there are none, to the brothers and sisters[2] on the statutory trusts.

If there is no surviving spouse, the issue or, if none, the other persons entitled take, in this order: parents, brothers and sisters of the whole blood on the statutory trusts, ditto of the half blood, grandparents, uncles and aunts of the whole blood on the statutory trusts, ditto of the half blood, and, finally, the Crown. 'On the statutory trusts'[3] means (briefly) in trust in equal shares for all the children of the intestate who are living or conceived at his death and who attain eighteen or marry. Children of a deceased child take their parents' share in equal shares.

Albert Jones dies intestate in 1973 leaving, after payment of all debts, expenses and duty, £40 000. He is mourned by a widow and two children—John aged sixteen and Mary aged seventeen who has married young. The estate will be divided as follows:[4]

To Mrs. Jones, his widow, the personal chattels (valued at £5000), a charge of £15 000 and half the remainder, i.e. £10 000 for life. The son will take £5000 when he attains eighteen, and the daughter takes £5000 immediately. On their mother's death, her life interest will be divided between them absolutely, making £5000 for them both.

Take a further example. Mrs. Jane Smith has died intestate, leaving £110 000 after payment of all debts, expenses and duty. Her

[1] A.E.A., 1925, s. 55.   [2] Of the whole blood.

[3] See A.E.A., 1925, s. 47.

[4] Interest payable on the charge has been ignored for purposes of simplicity.

husband survives her, but they have no children. Neither are her parents living. Her two sisters and her dead brother's children will benefit.

The estate is distributed as follows: Her husband, John Smith, takes the personal chattels valued at £10 000, his charge of £40 000 and half the remainder, i.e. £30 000. He retires from the scene richer by £80 000 and the remaining £30 000 is distributed as follows: each sister takes £10 000. The brother is represented by his five children, so his share is divided among them. They receive £2000 as they are all above eighteen or married.

When a personal representative has assented to a disposition, he becomes a trustee for the beneficiary. It is usual to appoint the personal representatives to be trustees as well. The difference between personal representatives and trustees may be important. For example, where there are more than one, the consent of *all* trustees is necessary to transfer personalty forming part of the deceased's estate. However, if there are more than one personal representative, any one of them may validly transfer personalty belonging to the deceased's estate.

Now is the moment to study trusts and trustees briefly. An outline of the history and development of the trust was given in Chapters 1 and 5.

A trust exists where a person (the trustee) holds property (the trust property) for the benefit of another (the *cestui que trust*). The trustee is bound to hold and dispose of the trust property in the way directed by the deed or will creating the trust, or according to law if the trust is not express, subject to the direction of the Court in certain cases. The beneficiaries have a right to enforce the trust. Sometimes it happens that a trustee may be a beneficiary, as, for example, where the trustees of a members' club hold the club property on trust for the members' benefit and the trustees are members themselves.

Trusts may be classified in several different ways. An express trust is one that the parties intend to result, as distinct from trusts which the law decrees shall arise automatically in certain circumstances.

If an *express* trust is created respecting land or any interest therein, it must be proved by writing, signed by some person able to declare such trust or by his will.[1] But Equity does not allow the statute to be used as a means of fraud. Where a trustee is holding land on trust,

[1] L.P.A., 1925, s. 53(1)(b).

parol evidence may be admitted to prove this if the absence of writing would result in a fraud on the *cestui que trust*.

A disposition of an equitable interest or trust must be in writing (not merely evidenced by writing) signed by the person disposing of it or by his agent lawfully authorised in writing or by will.[1] This sub-section must be carefully distinguished from the earlier one. It applies to disposition—not creation—of all trusts, not merely those of land, and it requires that the transaction shall actually be in writing, not merely evidenced thereby.

Trusts created by operation of law, even when the parties do not expressly create them, may be resulting or constructive. A resulting trust occurs where the settlor is presumed to have intended a trust to be set up. For example, if X supplies purchase money for Black-acre and the property is conveyed to Y, there arises a resulting trust. Y is the legal owner of Blackacre but must hold it in trust for X. But various circumstances may prevent a resulting trust arising. For example, X might have intended that Y should take Blackacre as an outright gift. Where the relationship of father and son or husband and wife exists between the person finding the money and the person taking the conveyance, it will be presumed that there is a gift out-right and no trust in favour of the settlor will arise. This is what is known as a 'presumption of advancement'.

When a person clothed in a fiduciary character—for example, a trustee—gains some personal advantage through such fiduciary character, he must hold such advantage in trust for his beneficiary. This is a constructive trust. It arises irrespective of the wishes (express or presumed) of the parties but is imposed on them by Equity in the interests of good faith and fair dealing. *Keech* v. *Sandford*[2] is an example. A trustee applied for the renewal of a lease held by him on trust for his *cestui que. trust*. As the *cestui que trust* was a minor, the lessor refused to grant it to the trustee to hold in trust but purported to grant it to the trustee for his own use. It was held that the trustee must assign the lease to the minor.

A private trust exists for the benefit of certain ascertained indivi-duals, whereas a charitable[3] trust exists for the benefit of the public generally or for a class of the public. Charitable trusts differ from ordinary trusts in many ways. First, as will be seen, their objects

---

[1] L.P.A., 1925, s. 53(1)(c).   [2] Sel. Cas. Ch. 61.
[3] The expression 'charitable trust' is used as being the same as 'public trust'.

need not be certain;[1] secondly, they are not liable to income tax; thirdly, they are exempt from the rule against perpetuities;[2] fourthly, their trustees may act by a majority, whereas private trustees must be unanimous; and, fifthly, the *cy près* rule applies to them.[3]

When is a trust charitable? The first guide is the Statute 43 Eliz. c. 4. It sets out the following objects as charitable:

The relief of aged, impotent and poor people; the maintenance of sick and maimed soldiers and mariners, schools of learning, free schools and scholars in universities; the repair of bridges, ports, havens, causeways, churches, sea-banks and highways; the education and preferment of orphans; the relief, stock or maintenance of houses of correction; the marriage of poor maids; the supportation, aid and help of young tradesmen, handicraftsmen and persons decayed; the relief or redemption of prisoners or captives; the aid or ease of any poor inhabitants concerning payment of taxes.

Fortunately, the list is not exhausted by these somewhat archaic examples. In *Income Tax Commissioners* v. *Pemsel*[4] it was laid down that there were four main divisions of charitable trusts; trusts for the relief of poverty, trusts for the advancement of education, trusts for the advancement of religion and trusts for other purposes beneficial to the community not falling under any of the preceding heads. The last class is difficult to define. Where possible, in determining whether a trust is charitable, the Court will act by analogy with the statute. For example, a gift to the Royal National Lifeboat Institution has been held to be charitable. Gifts for purely political purposes are not charitable. A gift to the National Anti-Vivisection Society was thus held not charitable, as the Society's objects were to bring about a change in the law and stop vivisection.

For a trust to be completely constituted, the trust property must be vested in the trustees, either by will or by deed. If the property is not vested and something remains to be done before this is so, the trust is incompletely constituted. A trust may be constituted either by the settlor transferring completely all his interest in the subject-matter to the trustees, or by the settlor making a declaration that in future he will hold certain property, already vested in him, on trust.

The importance of the distinction is that the beneficiaries cannot enforce an incompletely constituted trust unless consideration has

---

[1] See below, 'the three certainties'.   [2] See Chapter 5.
[3] See below.   [4] [1891] A.C. 531.

passed. Consideration may be either the valuable consideration that is necessary in contract or the consideration of marriage. Thus H agrees in writing to transfer certain property to trustees in consideration of his marriage to W. H dies before the property can be transferred. Equity will carry out the transaction at the behest of W and complete the vesting necessary for an enforceable trust, as there is good consideration.

A completely constituted trust may be executed or executory. In the first type, the settlor has set out the terms of the trust fully and completely; in the second, the settlor has set out his general intentions and, in effect, told the trustees to carry those intentions out in the best way they can. In executed trusts legal expressions are given their strict technical meaning, whereas in executory trusts the intention of the settlor is looked to.

To create an express trust 'three certainties' must be present. First, the words creating the trust must be imperative. Secondly, the subject-matter of the trust must be certain. Thirdly, the objects or beneficiaries must be certain.

To satisfy the first requirement no technical words are necessary; but the settlor or testator must intend a trust to be created. If the words used show that the donee of the property is to have a discretion as to how it is to be used, no trust exists. On the other hand, if the words used show that the donee must use the property for the benefit of certain objects, there will be a trust. Where a testator gave property to his wife by will 'in full confidence that she would do what was right as to the disposal thereof between his children, either in her lifetime or by will after her decease', it was held that these words did not constitute a trust. The testator's widow therefore took absolutely, as the gift was valid but the trust—or equitable obligation—did not arise.

The property over which the trust is to have effect must be defined with precision and certainty, otherwise the trust will have no effect and, again, the donee will take absolutely. An example of words being uncertain occurred where a testator left 'the bulk of her residuary estate' on trust. Obviously there can be no trust where it is not certain *what* is to be held on trust.

The 'third certainty' required for a valid trust is that the beneficiaries must be indicated with certainty. A gift to 'relations' is thus too vague, for the expression has no legal meaning. Note that this third requirement does not extend to charitable trusts, where the beneficiaries need not necessarily be certain, though, of course, the charitable intent must.

If a settlor wishes to benefit a class of people, he may do so by the use of the more flexible discretionary trust. This differs from a trust where each beneficiary takes a defined share, in that the trustees have a discretion as to which of the beneficiaries should benefit. An example of a discretionary trust would be a trust to distribute the net income of the trust fund at the trustees' absolute discretion among the nephews and nieces of the settlor. The trustees would be under an obligation to make a distribution, but they could choose which of the nephews and nieces should benefit. The test of certainty for a discretionary trust differs from that for a fixed trust. A discretionary trust is sufficiently certain if the trustees can say that any given individual is or is not a member of the class to be benefited.[1] For example, although a fixed trust for 'relatives' would fail for uncertainty, a discretionary trust in favour of 'relatives' or 'dependants' would be valid. The trustees could assess with certainty whether a particular person fell within that class.[2]

In a private trust, if the first two certainties are present but the beneficiaries are uncertain, what happens? There is a clear intention that the property be held on trust, and the property is clearly defined for a trust to act on. It would be unjust for the donee of the property to take it absolutely, so he must hold it on trust for the settlor, if it is a settlement *inter vivos*.[3] If it occurs in a will, the donee must hold it on trust for the person taking the residue or, if there is no gift of residue, for the person entitled on an intestacy.

If—and only if—the trust is *charitable*, the *cy près* doctrine comes into operation. Thus it may be that the objects of a trust are impossible or a surplus of income remains after the carrying out of the settlor's intentions. Furthermore, the Charities Act, 1960, s. 13, has enlarged the scope of this doctrine, so that, having regard to the spirit of a charitable gift, more effective use can be made of the trust property in view of changed circumstances since the gift was made. In such cases, the funds available will be used *cy près*; that is, in a manner as near as possible to that which the settlor intended, provided in certain cases that a general charitable intent is present. These cases are where the trust was impossible from the beginning,

---

[1] *Macphail* v. *Doulton*, [1970] 2 W.L.R. 1110.
[2] Re *Baden's Trusts* (No. 2), [1972] Ch. 607.
[3] See Chapter 5, page 97.

unless the donor cannot be identified or found, or has disclaimed.[1]

In Re *King*[2] a testatrix left residue to provide for the installation of a stained-glass window to her memory in the parish church. The residue was more than sufficient to provide a window of the best possible character and maintain it. It was held that the surplus must be used to provide a further stained-glass window or windows in the same church.

A trust may satisfy the test of the three certainties but be void or voidable for various reasons. These reasons—illegality, fraud, undue influence, duress or mistake—have been treated under the heading of contract.[3] A settlement for the benefit of future illegitimate children will be void for illegality. The reason is that such a trust conduces to future sexual immorality and is thus against public policy. A trust will be void if it offends against the rules relating to perpetuities and accumulations, discussed in Chapter 5.

A trust may be valid but unenforceable. This arises where the three certainties are present but the 'beneficiary' is an animal, so cannot set the machinery of the Court in motion to compel the trustees to enforce the trust. Another example is a trust to maintain the settlor's tomb in good condition. In neither case is there a *cestui que trust* who can enforce the trust, nor are they charitable. Various schemes have been worked out, however, to enable such gifts to have effect.

Where a settlor transfers property in order to defraud creditors, anyone prejudiced may avoid the transaction.[4] A baker purchased a grocery business and, as a precaution against his possible losses in his new venture, settled property on trust for his wife and children. Later, he discontinued the grocery business and failed in his bakery business. It was held that the trusts were void as against the creditors and they were entitled to the property settled, as the baker had in mind the object of defrauding his creditors.[5]

The section does not apply to any property conveyed for valuable or good consideration, in good faith, to any person not having at the time of the conveyance notice of the intent to defraud creditors.

Bankruptcy of the settlor will make certain trusts voidable; that is, the trustee in bankruptcy[6] may apply to the Court to set them

---

[1] Charities Act, 1960, s. 14.   [2] [1923] 1 Ch. 243.   [3] See Chapter 4.
[4] L.P.A., 1925, s. 172.   [5] Re *Butterworth* (1882), 19 Ch. D. 588.
[6] When a person is made bankrupt, his property—with exceptions—vests in a 'trustee in bankruptcy', who deals with the bankrupt's estate.

aside. The trusts affected are voluntary settlements (i.e. not made for value and in good faith or marriage settlements) made within two years before bankruptcy, whether or not the settlor was solvent at the time of making, and certain settlements made within from two to ten years before bankruptcy. These latter will be valid only if the parties claiming under the settlement can show:

(1) that the bankrupt was solvent at the time of the settlement, excluding the property settled; and
(2) that the settlor's interest passed to the settlement trustees when the settlement was executed.[1] This sub-section is subject to exceptions.

The office of trustee may be held by an ordinary person of eighteen or over, or by a corporation.[2] An ordinary person may be appointed as 'Judicial Trustee'. He acts under the directions of the Court, his books are audited yearly by an officer of the Court and he may be paid if the Court directs. This degree of supervision makes for greater efficiency and honesty than might be the case with an ordinary trustee.

Trust corporations may be corporations aggregate, conforming to certain requirements—such as banks, or corporations sole, of which the most important is the Public Trustee. Corporations aggregate may act alone in cases where normally two trustees are required, and, of course, they cannot die. The advantages of appointing a corporation such as a bank are obvious: its specialised experience and its vast resources. A trust corporation may not charge for its services unless provision is made by the trust instrument, beneficiaries or Court.

The Public Trustee is a salaried official. He may be appointed in the same way as an ordinary trustee (though he may decline to take office). He cannot be a trustee of certain trusts, notably charitable trusts. As he is a corporation sole, he does not die and may also act alone. His charges are regulated by Order. The great advantages of appointing the Public Trustee are that the knowledge and experience of the Public Trustee's office will normally prevent mistakes being made in the administration of the trust; but if any breaches of trust are committed, the State will make good any loss the beneficiaries have suffered. The Public Trustee's Office is now, most regrettably, to be abolished.

[1] Bankruptcy Act, 1914, s. 42(1).   [2] In most cases.

As will be seen, the office of trustee is an onerous one, and no one may be compelled to undertake it. Any person who is named as a trustee and does not wish to act may disclaim the office. He must disclaim as to the whole estate and must not carry out any of the trustee's functions or the disclaimer will be ineffective and he will be a trustee will-he-nil-he. Acceptance of the office may be by conduct or by express assent.

Normally the settlor appoints the trustees when the trust is created, and normally the trust instrument will provide for the appointment of new trustees. In some cases, the beneficiaries may appoint new trustees, and there is a power to appoint new trustees under certain conditions in the Trustee Act, 1925, s. 36. The Court has power to appoint new trustees.

A trustee may retire if he has consent from all his beneficiaries, provided that they are all *sui juris* and absolutely entitled.[1] The trust instrument usually provides for trustees who wish to retire. Retirement is also possible under s. 36 and s. 39 of the Trustee Act. The Court has power to allow a trustee to retire.

If a trustee is unfit to administer the trust, through illness, dishonesty, etc., he may be removed in any way provided by the trust instrument. If no such way exists, then he may be removed under the statutory power (s. 36, Trustee Act, 1925) or by the Court.

When a trustee dies, the estate and the office pass to his personal representatives. If there are more than one trustee, the estate and office pass to the survivors.

When a trustee takes office, and the property is vested in him, it is his duty to take control of it by gaining possession of title deeds, calling in loans, etc. If there are more than one, all trustees should have control of the property. Bearer bonds should be lodged at a bank in the joint names of the trustees.

The trustee must safeguard the trust property by careful investment. If the trust instrument gives him directions as to its disposal and investment, he must observe them strictly. Where any discretion is allowed him, he must exercise it with greater prudence than a careful man conducting his own affairs. Hazardous investments must be sold and the proceeds invested in authorised securities. The class of authorised investments (in the absence of specific directions in the trust instrument) has been greatly widened by the

---

[1] i.e. they are all of full capacity (not minors, mental patients, etc.) and between them are entitled to the whole of the trust assets.

Trustee Investments Act, 1961. A trustee may lend money on the security of land, subject to safeguards.

The trustee must make payments of the *corpus*[1] and interest on the trust property in accordance with the terms of the trust.

It is the duty of the trustee to act impartially between the beneficiaries, not favouring one more than another. In the interest of fairness to both those entitled to income and *corpus*, adjustments may have to be made by the trustee. For example, the law directs that, in certain cases, wasting investments yielding a high rate of interest must be sold and the proceeds invested in authorised securities. This ensures fair play between the beneficiary entitled to the income and the remaindermen. It would not be right for the first beneficiary to receive an abnormally high rate of interest if the second, when his turn comes, finds his share wasted into nothing.[2]

A trustee must keep accounts of the trust and allow the beneficiaries to inspect them. If the beneficiaries desire information about the trust and trust property, he must furnish it.

The trustee must not be in a position where his own interests and his duty as a trustee conflict. For this reason, he must not make a profit out of the trust. A trustee holding office must not purchase from himself at all or from his *cestui que trust*, except where the transaction is scrupulously open and fair. If a testator directs his trustee to carry on a business, the trustee may not compete with it by carrying on a similar business.

A trustee may not charge for his service unless authorised by the trust instrument, beneficiaries or the Court. This does not apply to the Public Trustee or Judicial Trustees.[3]

A trustee is allowed all necessary expenses in carrying out the trust. To secure these he has an indemnity against the trust property and sometimes against the beneficiary personally.

A trustee, being himself delegated by the settlor, cannot delegate his duties or powers to another.[4] He may, however, use agents such as solicitors, valuers and bankers when a prudent man would do so, acting on his own behalf. The expenses of employing such agents are recoverable by the trustee. Section 23 of the Trustee Act, 1925, provides that trustees shall not be responsible for the default of any

---

[1] Capital.   [2] *Howe* v. *Earl of Dartmouth* (1802), 7 Ves. 137a.
[3] See above.
[4] An application of the maxim '*delegatus non potest delegare*'. Delegation may be permitted by the trust instrument.

agent required in the carrying out of the trust, if employed in good faith. The trustee is not relieved of all responsibility; for example, he must not allow trust money to remain in an agent's hands for any longer time than necessary. A trustee who intends to remain out of the United Kingdom for longer than a month may delegate his office.

A trustee has all the powers necessary for the efficient carrying out of the trust. Thus he may sell property in such ways as he thinks best. He must take care not to sell under depreciatory conditions. He has power to give receipts. Two trustees or a trust corporation are necessary for this purpose when land subject to a trust for sale or strict settlement has been sold. A trustee may insure but is under no duty to do so.

In certain circumstances, a trustee may allow payments of income or capital to minors who will be entitled under the trust for purposes of maintenance and education. Likewise, sums of capital may be advanced to a minor not yet entitled to receive them.

Trustees may carry on such litigation as becomes necessary to carry out the trust. In cases of doubt, it is wise to apply to the Court for leave. If the action is one proper to be brought or defended, the costs will come out of the trust estate; if not, the trustees may have to pay them themselves.

If ever in doubt as to the proper course to adopt, a trustee may seek the advice of the Court. His duties may be summed up, however, in the following sentence: He must use the same standard of care in relation to the administration of the trust as a prudent man of business would employ in dealing with his own affairs.[1]

Any improper or neglectful act, or omission in relation to the trust property, committed by a trustee, is a breach of trust, and he will be liable for the damage suffered by the beneficiaries. The breach of trust may be wilful or reckless, or not. Fraudulent mis-appropriation by a trustee is a criminal offence. Examples of breaches of trust are investing trust money in the trustee's own business, overpaying certain beneficiaries and the like. A trustee, however, is liable only for his *own* breaches of trust. If a co-trustee commits a breach of trust, he will not be liable *unless* his own neglect or default conduced to it. An example of this would occur where a trustee unnecessarily left bearer securities in the sole control of a

[1] See page 126—Investment.

co-trustee, who sold them and absconded with the proceeds. Both trustees would then be liable.

A trustee is responsible only for breaches committed during his trusteeship. If, on taking office, he discovers a breach of trust to have been committed by a previous trustee, he must bring him to book. Once a trustee retires, he is not liable for breaches of trust committed *after* his retirement unless he retired to enable them to be committed.

The measure of the damages payable by a trustee guilty of breach of trust is the damage the trust property has suffered. In addition, the trustee may have to pay interest at four per cent. Where there has been fraud, the interest may be five per cent. If the trustee has invested trust funds in his own business and it has earned more than five per cent., the actual profits must be paid to the trust, together with the sum itself. This is in accordance with the important rule that, if a breach of trust results in a profit, the trustees may not keep it but must hold it on trust for the beneficiaries. If, however, the breach results in a loss, the trustee must make it good himself.

If there are more than one trustee and they are all guilty of a breach of trust, they must make good the loss in equal shares. In some cases, a trustee must bear the whole burden himself and indemnify the others, as, for example, where a trustee is a solicitor and the breach of trust is committed as a result of his advice.

The beneficiaries may recover in two ways what has been lost by the breach of trust. They may either sue the trustee or—sometimes —follow the trust property into the hands of the person who has possession of it and reclaim it.

Trustees may be excused from the consequence of breaches of trust in several ways. The Trustee Act affords relief to trustees guilty of breaches of trust in certain circumstances. Section 61 provides that, where it appears to the Court that a trustee has acted honestly and reasonably and ought fairly to be excused, he may be relieved—either wholly or partly—of personal liability for it by the Court.

Section 62 deals with cases where a trustee has committed a breach of trust at the instigation or request of a beneficiary, or with his consent in writing. Here the Court may order the beneficiary's interest under the trust to be impounded by way of indemnity to the trustee.

If a beneficiary *sui juris* discovers that a breach of trust has been

committed, and with full knowledge of all the circumstances formally releases the trustee or confirms the breach or even acquiesces in
the breach, the trustee will be absolved from liability.

After six years from the date from which the right of action arose,
the beneficiary will not be able to proceed against a trustee for
breach of trust unless it was fraudulent. He may, however, still
recover the property or proceeds if in possession of the trustee.

If a trustee who has committed a breach of trust dies or becomes
bankrupt, a beneficiary may claim against the trustee's personal
representative or trustee in bankruptcy.

Mention should be made of the Variation of Trusts Act, 1958,
which extends the power of the Court to sanction the variation of
trusts in the interests of beneficiaries and dealings with trust property. This Act is frequently used to lighten fiscal burdens.

7 Matrimonial Causes

It has been said that every woman should be married but no man. Great as have been the changes in our matrimonial law, a way has not been found of achieving this. However, the legislature has taken steps which it was hoped might alleviate some of the bitterness engendered by the failure of a marriage. Following two reports —the later by the Law Commission—the Divorce Reform Act, 1969, was passed. The old concept of the matrimonial offence as the basis of divorce has gone, and in its place is one ground, that the marriage has broken down irretrievably. Before we consider this change, however, we must examine the coming into being of the matrimonial relationship.

Marriage was defined as the voluntary union for life of one man with one woman to the exclusion of all others.[1] For marriage to take place there are three essentials. The parties must be capable of marrying, the marriage must be celebrated in the proper form and the parties must be of different sexes.[2] If one of these essentials is not present, no marriage exists and it is said to be void. The 'essentials' must not be confused with 'formalities'. If certain 'formalities' are not complied with, the marriage is valid but other consequences may follow.

The parties must be at least sixteen years of age. This is an essential. If either party is at least sixteen but not yet eighteen, the consent of his or her parent is required. Supposing they refuse, an application for consent may be made to the High Court, appropriate County Court or Court of Summary Jurisdiction, which will give consent if the parents' refusal is unreasonable and it is in the child's best interests to marry. But recalcitrant offspring of sixteen to eighteen may marry without consent, and the marriage will be valid, as parental or judicial consent is a 'formality'.

An essential to marriage is that the parties are not within the prohibited degrees set out in the Prayer Book.[3] The degrees, with some

[1] *Hyde* v. *Hyde*, [1866] L.R. 1 P. & D. 130.

[2] Nullity of Marriage Act, 1971.

[3] Now a man may marry his deceased wife's sister and a woman her deceased husband's brother and various other degrees mentioned in the Marriage Act, 1949, as amended.

statutory alterations, include illegitimate and half-blood relations.

There must be no previous marriage of the spouses existing at the time of the second 'marriage'. If a man has already married, and his wife is still alive and not divorced from him, any second 'marriage' he may enter into is void, and he may have committed the crime of bigamy.[1] A divorced person may marry again, though some clergymen will refuse to marry them.

Since Lord Hardwicke's Act of 1753, other formalities are necessary for the formation of a marriage in England. In Scotland, until 1940, parties could marry merely by consenting to do so in each other's presence, before witnesses. This led to the establishment of a minor Scottish industry at Gretna Green, which, being just over the border, was convenient for English couples.

In England marriage ceremonies may be religious or civil. Parties who have undergone the civil ceremony may follow it up by a religious ceremony, if the clergyman will consent.

Marriage according to the rites of the Church of England must be preceded by the calling of banns, by common or special licence, or by the granting of a Superintendent Registrar's certificate. The marriage must be solemnised by a Clerk in Holy Orders in the presence of two witnesses. If a special licence has been granted (granted only in special circumstances by the Archbishop of Canterbury) the marriage may take place at any time and in any suitable and convenient place.[2] Otherwise, it may only take place between 8 a.m. and 6 p.m. at a particular church or chapel named in the licence or certificate, or where the banns were published.

Marriages may be solemnised according to the ceremonies of Roman Catholics, Nonconformists, Quakers and Jews.

A civil ceremony of marriage takes place in a Register Office. A certificate or certificate and licence must previously have been granted by the Superintendent Registrar. He officiates at the ceremony, which is performed in the presence of two witnesses. The ceremony is according to a set form and no religious service may be used.

What is the effect of non-compliance with any of these formalities? The marriage may be void in some cases if both the parties knowingly and wilfully acquiesce in a breach of the formalities; as, for

[1] See Chapter 8, page 166.
[2] In the case of other denominations, the Registrar General may grant a special licence. Marriage (Registrar General's Licence) Act, 1970.

example, a Church of England marriage service being conducted by someone not in Holy Orders. Failing to comply with formalities in some other cases, even wilfully, will not invalidate the marriage; as, for example, celebrating it in the presence of only one witness. Offences relating to the solemnisation of marriage may be punished very heavily. For example, a person who knowingly and wilfully solemnises a marriage according to the rites of the Church of England (not being a marriage by special licence) in any place other than a church or other building in which banns may be published is guilty of an offence and may be punished with fourteen years imprisonment.

In England there is no such thing as a marriage by habit and repute such as exists in Scotland.

Special provisions apply to Royal Marriages.

The parties must be a man and a woman. It was held in *Corbett* v. *Corbett*, [1970] 2 All E.R. 33, that a man who underwent a sex-change operation could not thus alter his biological sex, which was fixed at birth. This being the case, the respondent 'wife', who had been born a man, could not contract a marriage with another man.

If any of the essentials of marriage are omitted there will be no marriage; it is said to be null and void '*ab initio*' (from the beginning). Though this is not necessary, as a rule a decree that such a marriage is null and void may be obtained from the Family Division. A void 'marriage', never having existed, cannot be of any legal effect; thus any children born under it would be illegitimate. However, the child of a void marriage is treated as the legitimate child of its parents if, at the time of the act of intercourse resulting in its birth (or at the time of the celebration of the marriage if later), both or either of the parties reasonably believed that the marriage was valid. (Legitimacy Act, 1959, s. 2.)

Some marriages suffer from a defect that renders them not void but merely voidable. In such cases, the marriage exists until the Family Division pronounces a decree of nullity. The effect of this is to annul the marriage after the decree, but the marriage is regarded as having existed up to the time of the decree.[1]

The grounds for declaring a marriage voidable are laid down in the Nullity of Marriage Act, 1971. The first is a re-enactment of the old Canonical ground of impotence.

Impotence is the inability to have normal sexual intercourse. It

[1] Nullity of Marriage Act, 1971, s. 5.

must not be confused with sterility, which is not a ground for matrimonial relief. The impotence may be due to physical or psychological causes. A man or woman may be impotent. Sometimes a wife or husband may be unable to consummate the marriage but may be able to have normal sexual intercourse with a third party. In such cases, there is a ground for a decree of nullity as the impotence relates to the marriage.

The impotence must have existed at the time of the celebration of the marriage and must be incurable. If a spouse can be cured, however, and refuses to be treated, a petition for nullity will still lie.

Either the impotent spouse or the other may petition for nullity.

A petitioner on this ground is not allowed to take advantage of the marriage, such as by taking financial benefits, and then seek to annul it. It would be unfair if a spouse were to treat the marriage as existing for the purpose of deriving gain from it and afterwards try to upset it.

So much for a party who is incapable of consummating the marriage. Section 2(b) of the Act provides that where a spouse wilfully refuses to consummate a marriage the other spouse is entitled to a decree of nullity. The insistence on the use of a contraceptive does not constitute wilful refusal to consummate.[1] Nor, it seems, does insistence on *coitus interruptus*.

Further grounds are set out in s. 2(c)–(e). The parties must consent to be married. Several causes may prevent such consent from being in the mind of either party. For instance, a person who was so insane or so much under the influence of drink or drugs that he did not know he was being married could not have given his consent to the ceremony. A marriage would be voidable if John, a blind man, thinks he is marrying Joan but, in fact, is going through a ceremony of marriage with Mary. There was no true consent when a woman who had gone through a marriage ceremony thought at the time that it was merely a betrothal ceremony.

Consent must be real. If it is given under duress, it is not sufficient for a valid marriage. Thus, if one of the parties shows that his will was overborn by a genuine and reasonably held fear caused by the threat of immediate danger to life, limb or liberty, and the danger was one for which the party was not responsible, he would be entitled to a decree of nullity. In one case, the lady in question was told by her over-eager admirer that he would shoot her if she refused

[1] *Baxter* v. *Baxter*, [1948] A.C. 274.

to marry him. The duress exercised in that situation removed the element of consent. In a more recent example[1] the wife was, at the time of the marriage, in prison in Poland for alleged activities against the state. Her health was poor and even if she survived the term she was likely to be rearrested on release. The marriage was, in fact, entered into solely to enable her to leave the country. In these circumstances, the duress was held sufficient to negative consent.

The analogy with ordinary commercial contracts void for lack of proper agreement must not be pressed too far. Marriages are not voidable for fraud alone. 'She told me her age was five-and-twenty, cash in the bank of course she'd plenty' ran the words of a music-hall song. If the singer found out after the marriage that his bride was forty and overdrawn, it would give rise to disgruntlement, but the marriage would be perfectly valid and unassailable.

The other grounds of nullity are that either party at the time of the marriage was suffering from mental disorder within the Mental Health Act, 1959, of such a kind or extent as to make him unfit for marriage; that the respondent[2] was suffering from venereal disease in a communicable form; and that the respondent was pregnant by someone other than the petitioner.

There are further conditions, however, to be satisfied before a decree will be granted on grounds other than inability to consummate and wilful refusal to consummate. The petition, except in these two cases, must have been brought within three years of the marriage, and in the case of venereal disease and pregnancy by another, the petitioner must not know of the defect at the time of the marriage.

Further, the Court is given the power to withhold the decree if the petitioner, with knowledge that the marriage could have been declared a nullity, so conducted himself as to make the respondent reasonably believe that he would not seek a decree *and* it would be unjust to the respondent to grant the decree.

A far commoner kind of matrimonial relief is divorce. Three years must elapse between the celebration of the marriage and the presentation of the divorce petition. The period may be dispensed with by leave of the judge if the case is one of exceptional hardship suffered by the petitioner or of exceptional depravity on the part of

[1] *Szechter* v. *Szechter*, [1970] 3 All E.R. 905.
[2] In matrimonial cases, the person who sues is known as the petitioner and the person sued as the respondent.

the respondent. An example of exceptional depravity might be where a husband committed adultery with his wife's sister in the matrimonial home.

The ground for divorce is set out in the Divorce Reform Act, 1969, s. 1, which provides that the sole ground on which a petition may be presented to the Court is that the marriage has broken down irretrievably. To prove to the Court's satisfaction that this is the case, the petitioner has to prove one of five facts.

The first is that the respondent has committed adultery and the petitioner finds it intolerable to live with the respondent, s. 2(1)(a). Adultery is sexual intercourse with a person of the opposite sex, one or both of the parties being married but not to one another. As adultery is usually carried out clandestinely, it is unlikely that there will be direct evidence of it. When adultery was a matrimonial offence, it had to be proved beyond reasonable doubt. In the light of recent case law and the Family Law Reform Act, 1969, it seems that it now has to be proved on the balance of probabilities. This reflects the fact that adultery is no longer seen *per se* as grounds for divorce but as a symptom of the breakdown of marriage. The Court will infer adultery where the parties are disposed to commit it and they have an opportunity to do so. Proof of one act of adultery is not enough, for the petitioner has to go on to show that he finds it intolerable to live with the respondent. This is a subjective test, and the Court must ask itself whether the petitioner found it intolerable, not whether a reasonable person would have done so.

In all cases where adultery is shown, the person alleged to have committed adultery with the respondent spouse must be given the chance to intervene and refute the allegation. When the husband is petitioning, the man alleged to have committed adultery is called the co-respondent; if the wife petitions, the 'other woman' is called the second respondent.

If the petitioner lives with the respondent for a period or periods of not more than six months after discovering the adultery, the Court may disregard the cohabitation for the purposes of this ground, but if the cohabitation is for more than six months, the petitioner can no longer rely on the adultery.

The second fact which would satisfy the Court as to breakdown of the marriage is that the respondent has behaved in such a way that the petitioner cannot reasonably be expected to live with the respondent, s. 2(1)(b). Emphasis is thus on the behaviour of the respondent; the petitioner's reaction is to be assessed objectively. Is it reasonable? The Court is entitled to look at the behaviour of both parties in the context of the particular marriage and ask itself whether the particular petitioner is justified in finding it intolerable to live with the particular respondent. A violent petitioner may reasonably be expected to live with a violent respondent. If the respondent has behaved blamelessly, the fact that the petitioner, for some psychological reason, cannot bear to live with her is not sufficient.[1] There must have been some breach by the respondent of a matrimonial obligation.

The kind of behaviour envisaged by the section includes conduct which would have constituted the former matrimonial offence of cruelty, and conduct so intolerable that it drives the petitioner away from the matrimonial home—the former matrimonial offence of constructive desertion. To establish cruelty under the old law actual physical or mental injury had to result from the conduct complained of, or had at least to be reasonably apprehended. The new Act does not require this. The respondent's conduct might be such that the petitioner, although not having suffered in health, could reasonably say that the marriage was at an end and he could no longer be expected to cohabit. However, injury to health would be of strong evidential value as showing that the respondent's actions constituted more than merely trivial annoyance.

The sort of acts that might be a basis for divorce under this section are physical violence, prolonged nagging, unnatural sexual practices, complete neglect of the family and excessive sexual demands. Less serious conduct carried on over many years might also be sufficient when regarded as a whole.

It will usually be necessary to take the respondent's intentions into account when assessing the reasonableness of the petitioner's reaction to his conduct. If, for example, both spouses adored cats, the presence of twenty in the house might be quite natural and reasonable. If, however, the wife knew that the husband loathed animals and was allergic to fur and yet introduced them, realising fully what her husband would suffer, he might claim that he could not reasonably be expected to live with her.

The fact that the respondent did not intend to harm the petitioner does not, however, prevent the behaviour from being sufficiently serious for the purpose of divorce. In one case, the husband's

[1] *Pheasant* v. *Pheasant*, [1972] 2 W.L.R. 353.

laziness and complete failure to help his wife in running their guest-house reduced her to a state of ill-health and depression. He knew the damage he was doing, though he did not wish or intend to injure her; he merely closed his mind to the consequences. The House of Lords held that his conduct was grounds for divorce (at that time cruelty) since the presence of an intention to injure, or proof that the conduct is 'aimed at' the other spouse, is not essential.[1] This was carried further in *Williams* v. *Williams*,[2] where the husband was actually insane. His conduct regarded objectively was intolerable, and the fact that he was not responsible for his action was not a defence.

To bring proceedings under the above head the petitioner must not have cohabited with the respondent for a period or periods of more than six months after the last incident on which the petitioner relies.

The third fact, s. 2(1)(c), is that the respondent has deserted the petitioner for a continuous period of two years preceding the presentation of the petition.[3] For desertion, there must be both an ending of cohabitation and a wish that cohabitation should end. For instance, a husband who left his wife for two years because he was a soldier and was posted overseas would not, for that reason alone, be in desertion.

The fact that the party responsible for the breakdown is not the one to leave does not mean that he cannot be the deserter, for by his conduct he has driven the other party out. Under the old law of divorce, as has been mentioned, this was called constructive desertion. If such a situation arose now, however, it would be more likely that the petitioner would seek a divorce relying on s. 2(1)(b) (see above). The advantage would be that two years would not have had to elapse before the presentation of the petition.

If one spouse left the other in the reasonable belief that the other had committed adultery, the party leaving would not be in desertion. This is because there was just cause for leaving and this would be a defence to desertion.

There are several ways in which desertion can be terminated. If the parties have consented to live separately, there is no desertion.

[1] *Gollins* v. *Gollins*, [1969] A.C. 644.   [2] [1964] A.C. 698.
[3] No account is taken of any one or more periods not exceeding six months during which the parties resume cohabitation. Divorce Reform Act, s. 3(5).

Similarly, a judicial separation, a separation order or separation agreement will, in most circumstances, prevent desertion. If a deserting spouse makes a reasonable and genuine offer to return, and the deserted spouse refuses, their rôles may be reversed, because it is then the formerly deserted spouse who is preventing the parties from cohabiting. However, the deserted spouse may have real grounds for refusing such an offer—if the deserting spouse has formerly behaved badly, for example, and there are no grounds for thinking he has improved. A refusal in a case of this sort would not turn the deserted party into the deserting party.

If the parties resume cohabitation with the intention of living together, desertion will be ended, subject to the statutory exception mentioned in footnote 3 on page 138. If a deserting husband visits his wife and they have sexual intercourse together, that alone will not suffice to end the desertion. They must both intend to resume their married life.

If the deserting party becomes insane, so that he can no longer be said to have the intention to desert, the Court will infer such intention if it is satisfied that the intention would have continued but for the insanity.

The fourth and fifth heads of fact are entirely new. The fourth, s. 2(1)(d), is that the parties to the marriage have lived apart for a continuous period of at least two years immediately preceding the presentation of the petition, and that the respondent consents to the decree being granted. The respondent must really agree, however, with full knowledge of the consequences. Up to the grant of the decree nisi, the agreement may be withdrawn at any time. After decree nisi, if two years' separation is the only fact relied on by the petitioner, the respondent may apply to the Court to consider the respondent's financial position. The Court must then take into account all the factors of the case, and it may refuse to make the decree absolute unless it is satisfied that the petitioner should not make financial provision for the respondent or that such provisions as have been made are satisfactory. If the respondent can show that the consent was only given because the petitioner misled him as to some matter the respondent took into account in giving consent, the Court may rescind the decree nisi altogether. Thus if a wife agreed to a divorce under this head on the understanding that she was to have the matrimonial home and surrounding property and subsequently discovered, after decree nisi, that the husband had transferred most of the property to his mistress, she could apply to have the decree nisi set aside.

Husband and wife are considered as 'living apart' under the Act unless they live in the same household. Household, however, means more than living together in the same house. If therefore a married couple lived under the same roof but never communicated, ate and slept apart, and considered the marriage as at an end, they could be living apart for the purposes of the Act.

The fifth head, s. 2(1)(e), has been the most controversial. It is that the parties to the marriage have lived apart for a continuous period of five years immediately preceding the presentation of the petition. This means that a divorce can be granted against the wishes of the respondent.

There are, however, provisions to protect the respondent in such a situation. Under s. 4(1) the respondent may oppose the petition on the grounds that the dissolution of the marriage would result in grave financial or other hardship *and* it would be wrong in the circumstances to dissolve the marriage. This has but limited application. The hardship has to arise from the divorce itself. In most cases, the hardship will have already arisen from the breakdown, and the respondent will not be able to show any additional grave hardship from the formal divorce. The respondent may also apply, in the same way as with two years' separation, for the Court to consider his financial position. Of course, after the divorce, the respondent can apply for financial provision in proceedings for ancillary relief.

There is one further ground of divorce, independent of the Act. If one spouse has reasonable grounds for believing the other to be dead, he may apply to the Court to pronounce a decree of presumption of death and a decree of divorce. If it is later found that the missing spouse is alive the decree still holds good. The procedure enables a spouse to remarry without disastrous consequences if it should turn out that the other were alive after all.

When a party has proved grounds for either nullity or divorce, the Court grants a decree nisi. This means a decree 'unless'. It does not end the marriage. This ends when the decree is made 'absolute', which happens in nearly every case six weeks after the decree nisi. During the interim period an official known as the Queen's Proctor may intervene if the decree had been obtained irregularly. If he intervenes, the case is reopened and the decree nisi is set aside.

The Court, except in exceptional cases, may not make a decree absolute unless it has declared by order that it is satisfied that arrangements have been made for the welfare of specified children of the family or that no such children exist.[1] A child of the family is a child of both the parties to the petition or one that has been treated by both the parties as one of the family, provided that it is not a foster child. To be included in the order the child must be under sixteen, or under eighteen and receiving education or training. In special circumstances, an older child can be included.

Another matrimonial remedy is judicial separation. A decree of judicial separation may be awarded on any of the five facts specified to prove breakdown of marriage for the purpose of divorce.[2] The effect of judicial separation is to end the duty of the spouses to live together, though they still remain married. The Court has power to make an order relating to the custody and welfare of the children, and to financial provisions. As regards property belonging to a spouse, after the decree it devolves, should the spouse die intestate, as though the other spouse were dead.

If a man or woman falsely gives out that he or she is married to a certain person, that person, if he objects, may have recourse to a rarely used procedure. He or she may petition for a decree of jactitation of marriage, which will enjoin the person asserting the marriage 'to keep perpetual silence' on that subject.

A new form of relief was introduced by s. 23 of the Matrimonial Causes Act, 1950 (as amended by section 6 of the Matrimonial Proceedings and Property Act, 1970). If a spouse wilfully neglects to provide reasonable maintenance for the other or a minor child of the family for whom it is reasonable to expect the spouse to provide, or to contribute towards, the other may petition for relief. The Court will then make such order as it thinks fit.

Having considered the main forms of matrimonial relief, let us now examine the procedure to be followed.

First, a petition is prepared. This gives the full name of the husband and wife (including her maiden name), the date and place of marriage, and the last address of cohabitation.

Next, the petitioner must state that both parties are domiciled in England, and give their occupation and address. If they are not,

---

[1] Matrimonial Proceedings and Property Act, 1970, s. 17.
[2] Divorce Reform Act, 1969, s. 8.

the Court has no jurisdiction,[1] subject to an exception in the case of a married woman who has been resident in England for three years immediately preceding the commencement of proceedings, or whose husband has left her or been deported and who was immediately before that domiciled in England. To be domiciled in England means (very roughly) that England is the country where the husband wishes to live permanently. His wife's domicile is automatically the same as his.[2]

The names and dates of birth of the children of the family must be stated and whether there is any dispute as to their being children of the family. Thus might arise where the husband disputed paternity. Also it must be stated whether there have been any previous proceedings in any Court relating to the marriage or children, or to property. The petitioner then states if he proposes to make any arrangement or agreement as to the support of the children and the respondent, and, if so, gives details.

The petitioner must then state that the marriage has broken down irretrievably and set out the facts on which the divorce is claimed. If the petitioner alleges the respondent's adultery, the petitioner mentions the name of the other adulterous party.

The prayer is the part of the petition setting out the relief required. In the case of a wife's adultery, the petitioner finding it intolerable to live with her, the prayer might be for the dissolution of the marriage, custody of the children and that the co-respondent be ordered to pay the costs.

The petition is signed by the petitioner's counsel, solicitor, or the petitioner himself.[3]

In the case where the petition discloses the existence of a child of the family under sixteen or over sixteen and receiving full-time educational instruction or training, a separate written statement must accompany the petition stating the arrangements proposed for the child if the decree is granted.

---

[1] When the Domicile and Matrimonial Proceedings Act, 1973, comes into force on January 1st, 1974, the Court will share jurisdiction when either party has been habitually resident throughout the period of one year immediately preceding the petition.

[2] After January 1st, 1974, a wife may have a separate domicile. Domicile and Matrimonial Proceedings Act, 1973.

[3] A petition may be drafted by counsel, solicitor or the petitioner himself.

When the petitioner relies on five years' separation and has set out the proposed financial arrangements for the respondent without the respondent agreeing to them, an affidavit must be included giving brief particulars of the petitioner's financial situation.

The petition must then be filed in the appropriate Registry and copies served on the respondent (and co-respondent if adultery is alleged). Service may be by post or personally, or in certain cases an advertisement may be placed in a newspaper, as substituted service.

If the respondent wishes to defend the petition or be heard in Court as to any relief claimed, he must enter an appearance. Appearance may be general, where he intends to deny the charge, or limited, to a matter of the relief claimed, e.g. costs or custody of the children.[1]

The respondent, among other forms, will receive a notice of proceedings telling him to complete the attached acknowledgment of service and return it within eight days. In the acknowledgment, the respondent is asked whether he intends to defend. In the case of a petition based on two years' separation and consent, the respondent must say whether he consents, and in the case of a petition based on five years' separation, whether he intends to oppose on the grounds of grave financial or other hardship.

If the appearance is general, the respondent, having stated in the acknowledgment that he intends to defend, must later file an answer giving a defence to the charges in the petition. The answer may contain cross-allegations and claim relief in its turn. Thus it may be both a shield and a sword against the petitioner.

The petitioner may in return file a reply to this but is not obliged to do so. If the petitioner does not reply, this is taken as a denial of the respondent's allegations.

These documents—the petition, answer and reply (if any)—together with any further and better particulars, form the pleadings. The pleadings set out the differences between the parties.

In due course, the petitioner's solicitor attends before a Registrar, who certifies that the cause is ready to be set down for trial, i.e. that the petition has been duly served and the time for entry of appearance has expired. In due course it will come for hearing by a judge in a Divorce County Court if it is undefended, or by a judge in the High Court if defended.

[1] One who disputes the jurisdiction of the Court may enter an appearance 'under protest'.

If an undefended cause goes ahead, it will usually be disposed of in a very short time. Nevertheless, the Court must be satisfied that all the requirements of the law have been satisfied.

Let us take a hypothetical case. Mr. Black is seeking to divorce his wife on the grounds that she has committed adultery and he finds it intolerable to live with her. There are no children of the marriage and the petition is undefended. The evidence in the case might be as follows: Mr. Black is called by his counsel and gives evidence that his marriage was happy in its early stages but then deteriorated owing to his wife's behaviour. He describes the increasing friendship of the co-respondent with his wife. Because of this relationship he finds it intolerable to live with her. He has not actually seen the adultery, however, so the next witness is Mr. Green the enquiry agent. He tells the Court how he visited an address and found Mrs. Black and the co-respondent living together as man and wife. He produces statements by Mrs. Black and the co-respondent admitting the adultery to corroborate his evidence. They were both given, so he informs the Court, after he had cautioned both parties that they were not obliged to give them, and were signed by them in his presence. How does the enquiry agent recognise the wife? He produces a photograph which the husband identifies as his wife's and which the enquiry agent identifies as a photograph of the woman he saw. Previously, in his evidence, the husband had identified the wife's signature on the acknowledgment of service and the confession of adultery.[1]

The husband's counsel now asks for a decree nisi of divorce and the relief prayed for. The judge considers whether the evidence shows that the marriage has broken down irretrievably and, if satisfied that this is the case, grants a decree nisi and says that there will be a declaration that there are no children of the family for the purposes of s. 17 of the Matrimonial Proceedings and Property Act, 1970.

It is obvious that the Court's work is not finished merely by pronouncing a decree in a matrimonial case. First, who is to have the custody of the children? The court has jurisdiction to make orders for the custody of children up to eighteen but does not usually make

---

[1] A practice direction issued in July 1973 provides that, in undefended proceedings based on adultery, the enquiry agent need no longer be called to give evidence where there is an admission statement signed by the respondent. If his evidence is necessary, it may be given on affidavit.

an order for custody of a child of sixteen or over. When considering the question of custody, the paramount consideration is the welfare of the child. This custody might be given to the party substantially to blame for the breakdown of the marriage or to a third party, if this course is in the child's best interests. The Court may make an order for access permitting the former spouse, who has not been awarded custody of the children, to visit them. Orders as to custody forbid the children to be taken out of the jurisdiction of the Court except by its leave, otherwise it would have no control over them. Disobedience to such an order is a contempt of court. In some cases, children, especially those entitled to property, may be made wards of court. This means that until eighteen they are under the supervision of the Family Division. For instance, a ward of court who wants to marry must first obtain the Court's consent.

Disputes as to the custody of the children are heard not in open court but in the privacy of the judge's chambers.

After the decree has been pronounced, the question of the financial situations of the parties must be settled. Who is to pay how much and to whom? This is known as ancillary relief. The parties, if they can come to an agreement, may refer their arrangement to the Court either before or after the petition for divorce. The Court may express its opinion as to the reasonableness of the agreement and give such directions as it thinks fit. This provision is to enable the parties to agree among themselves and obtain the Court's advice in doing so.

If the parties cannot come to a satisfactory agreement, the Court must decide for them. The points it must bear in mind in doing so are set out in the Matrimonial Proceedings and Property Act, 1970. These include the health, income and age of the parties, their financial needs and the standard of living enjoyed before the breakdown of the marriage. Also the contribution made by each to the welfare of the family and any benefit, such as a pension, that one party will lose the chance of acquiring by reason of the dissolution will be considered. There is finally an overall provision that the Court should, as far as possible, place the parties in the same financial position that they would have been if the marriage had not broken down.

In deciding what financial provisions are to be made after divorce, the Court will normally disregard the conduct of the parties, except in the rare case where one party has wilfully persisted in

conduct calculated to destroy the marriage, in circumstances where
the other party is substantially blameless. In such circumstances, the
Court might refuse to order the blameless party to support the
other or might reduce the amount of the support. Such financial
penalties for misconduct will, however, seldom find a place in the
working of the new legislation. Either a husband or a wife may
apply for financial provision. If later on their financial circumstances
alter, either may apply to the court for an order to increase or decrease the payments. If the spouse who is being paid maintenance
remarries, the liability to maintain that spouse ends automatically,
although liability for the children of the family does not.

The Court has wide powers of suiting the financial provisions to
the situation. It may order secured or unsecured periodical payments or a lump sum, or both. It may order that property be transferred by one party to the other, or that a settlement of property
be made, or that a previous settlement be varied. Thus, for example,
a husband deserts his wife and emigrates. She obtains a divorce on
the grounds of desertion, but her husband is at the other end of the
world and she has no means of getting maintenance from him.
Supposing the matrimonial home to be in his name, the Court
might consider it just to transfer it to her and extinguish the husband's interest.

Before a matrimonial cause is tried, the Court may order either
party to make periodic payments to the other.

Mention should be made of the Matrimonial Homes Act, 1967,
which protects the right of a deserted spouse (usually the wife) to
occupy the matrimonial home when it is held in the name of the
other spouse. For example: Mrs. A is deserted by her husband, who
owns the matrimonial home. She fears that he will sell or mortgage
it to a third party, who, having no notice of her occupation, will be
able to evict her. The Act enables her to register her right to occupy
the home as a Class F land charge so that the third party will have
notice of her right and cannot evict her. She must act quickly, however, for the third party must be put upon notice of her occupation
before the sale or mortgage, otherwise he can take free of it.

Matrimonial relief may be obtained in the Courts of Summary
Jurisdiction as well as in the Divorce County Courts and the Family
Division of the High Court. The forms of relief, however, in
Magistrates' Courts are unaffected by the Divorce Reform Act and
are more limited. Under the Matrimonial Proceedings (Magistrates

Courts) Act, 1960 (as amended by the Maintenance Order Act, 1968), various orders may be made. In general the relief available to a husband is substantially the same as that available to a wife. The Court may make an order corresponding to a decree of judicial separation under which the parties are not bound to cohabit. Maintenance may be awarded to a wife or husband, in the case of the latter where it is reasonable to do so an account of impairment of his earning capacity through age, illness or disability. Custody of children under sixteen may be awarded to either party and access by either party may be granted. Maintenance may also be awarded for the children when under sixteen or, exceptionally, under eighteen.

The grounds on which either party may apply for relief under the Act are as follows: certain assaults, persistent cruelty to him, her or the children; desertion; adultery; wilful neglect of him, her or the children; habitual drunkenness; that either party, knowing he or she had venereal disease, compelled him or her to have sexual intercourse. A wife may apply on the ground that her husband compelled her to submit to prostitution.

Domestic proceedings before magistrates must be heard apart from other cases. The public are not permitted to attend.[1]

When proceedings are pending in the High Court, proceedings should not be taken before a magistrate. Orders for maintenance and custody made by a Court of Summary Jurisdiction are not automatically affected by subsequent High Court proceedings.

[1] Magistrates Courts Act, 1952.

8 Criminal Law

If a man breaks his contract or trespasses on another's land, the person who is aggrieved has his remedy in the civil courts. This is all that is necessary. The public at large has not been injured. But some wrongful acts are of such a nature that the welfare of the State requires that their redress should not be left to private individuals. Such acts are crimes, and they vary from treason and murder to pulling a railway communication cord without proper cause.

Prosecutions for crime are always in the name of the Queen; the case being styled *Regina* or R.[1] v. (*the accused*). It lies on the prosecution to prove the guilt of the accused. Though the prosecution may be discontinued in various ways, a criminal case may not be settled in the way a civil case can. Many differences in evidence and procedure exist between civil and criminal trials, owing to the fundamental distinction between a dispute between individuals and an infringement of law affecting the community as a whole.

What are the essential ingredients of a crime? At Common Law, two things are nearly always necessary: an act and a state of mind. A wrongful act (*actus reus*) is not a crime unless the person committing it does so with a guilty mind (*mens rea*). If I take away your fountain-pen, that act alone is not a crime (though it is tortious). If, however, I intend, when I take it, permanently and dishonestly to deprive you of it and I have no claim of right made in good faith, I commit the crime of theft. This intent is the *mens rea*.

Not only deliberate intention but also recklessness may constitute *mens rea*. The motorist who drives so heedlessly that he kills a pedestrian may be guilty of manslaughter. In such a case, there is no intention to kill but a degree of recklessness that incurs criminal liability. Such conduct must not be confused with negligence *in tort*. A very much greater degree of lack of care is needed to establish criminal liability.

Statutes creating offences may or may not require *mens rea* for the offence to be committed. It depends on the statute. The Legislature regards it as so desirable that certain acts should be prohibited that

[1] In speech always refer to 'The Queen and (or against) X'.

the act itself without *mens rea* is made a crime. Or the necessary intention may be so difficult to prove that only the act need be proved.

Types of offences not requiring *mens rea* are less serious, as a rule, than those of which it is an essential part. For instance, in *Hobbs* v. *Winchester Corporation*[1] a butcher was convicted of exposing unsound meat for human consumption even though he did not know it was unsound.

But in *R.* v. *Prince*[2] a man was convicted of abducting a girl under sixteen contrary to s. 55 of the Offences against the Person Act, 1861. It was held that his honest belief on reasonable grounds that the girl was over sixteen was no defence; in other words, absence of *mens rea* in this case was no excuse.

Mens rea means intention to do the criminal act. If I voluntarily commit a certain criminal act, it is no defence that I did not know that offence *was* a criminal act. Ignorance of the law is no excuse.

It is an offence for a publican to serve drink to a police officer on duty. If a publican thinks a policeman who is actually on duty is not, because he is not wearing an armlet, and serves him, it is a defence to the charge. There is no *mens rea* present.[3]

If, however, the publican did know the policeman was on duty, it would be no defence for him to say he did not know of the law's existence, as he had deliberately done the forbidden act.

Nor should *mens rea* be confused with the motive for doing an act. Though it may serve to reduce punishment, an honest or good motive is never by itself a defence to a criminal charge. If I steal from my rich neighbour (himself a criminal) that I may give the proceeds to the Church, it is still a crime.

Crimes are divided into two classes: indictable offences and summary offences. Indictable offences are more serious and may be tried by judge and jury. Summary offences are tried by the Courts of Summary Jurisdiction.[4] This distinction is somewhat blurred in practice, as some indictable offences may be tried summarily, in certain circumstances, if the accused is seventeen or over and consents. Moreover, any person of seventeen and above charged with a summary offence[5] which is punishable with three months' imprisonment has a right to jury trial, subject to certain conditions.

[1] [1910] 2 K.B. 471.   [2] (1875), L.R. 2 C.C.R. 154.
[3] *Sherras* v. *De Rutzen*, [1895] 1 Q.B. 918.   [4] See page 173.
[5] Not assaults or sections 30–32 of the Sexual Offences Act, 1956 (living on immoral earnings, etc.).

Certain offences are both indictable and summary.

Indictable offences were originally divided into treason, felonies and misdemeanours. The distinction between felonies and misdemeanours was originally very real as all felonies, except petty larceny and mayhem, were punishable with death. Now, by s. 1 of the Criminal Justice Act, 1967, the distinction has been abolished, and crimes are divided into arrestable and non-arrestable offences.

An arrestable offence is one for which the sentence is fixed by law, e.g. murder, or for which a person, without a previous conviction, could be sentenced under any enactment to at least five years imprisonment, e.g. theft. An attempt to commit such a crime is also an arrestable offence.

The distinction between serious and less serious offences, which was the reason for dividing crimes into felonies and misdemeanours, has thus been preserved. The distinction is now between those offences for which a warrant would be necessary before the perpetrator could be arrested and those serious offences for which he could be arrested without a warrant.

A person who does not himself commit an offence, whether arrestable or non-arrestable, but either aids, abets, counsels or procures the commission of it is an accomplice of, and liable to the same extent as, the person who actually carries out the crime.

For someone to be an accomplice in a crime, there must be a common purpose between him and the party actually committing it. If A and B set out to steal, and while B takes the money from a drawer in a room B stands at the door and keeps watch, A and B are both guilty of theft. Suppose, however, that they have agreed to use no violence in their crime. Unknown to B, A has secreted a weapon on his person. They are surprised while A is stealing the money and A wounds their discoverer with his weapon. A is guilty of wounding, but B is not, as there was no common purpose to use violence.

Merely standing by and watching while an offence is committed does not make the onlooker an accomplice.

A person who actively persuades or induces the commission, or assists in the preparation, of a particular offence is an accomplice, even though he is not present when the crime is actually committed. Not only is he answerable for the crime he urges the other to commit, but he is also answerable for other consequences resulting from it. Thus if A urged B to beat up C, and C died as a result, B would be guilty of murder and so equally would A. He would not be liable, however, if B committed an entirely different crime. For example, if X persuaded Y to snatch Miss Z's handbag and he raped her instead, X would not be liable.

When a person has committed an arrestable offence, anyone who, knowing or believing him to be guilty of that offence or any other arrestable offence, does any act, with the intention of impeding his apprehension or prosecution, is guilty himself of an offence.[1] For instance, a man who hides his friend in his house to enable him to escape the attention of the police, as he knows his friend has committed burglary, would be guilty of this offence.

It is also a crime to accept, or agree to accept, any consideration in return for not revealing information that would assist in the conviction or arrest of a person who has committed an arrestable offence.[2] Consideration does not include reparation or reasonable compensation for the loss or injury caused by the offence. It is therefore not a crime for an employer to agree not to prosecute an employee if he makes good the loss caused by stealing the employer's property. It would be a crime, however, if a person surprised someone in the act of stealing a third party's property and agreed to say nothing in return for a share in the proceeds.

Inchoate Offences

An inchoate offence is one in which the criminal purpose contemplated has not been carried out.

An attempt is an act done with the intent to commit an offence and forming part of a series of acts which would constitute its actual commission if it were not interrupted. The act must be a proximate cause of the intended offence, not a mere preparation. In R. v. *Robinson*[3] a jeweller hid his stock and tied himself up. His object was to obtain money from his insurance company by fraudulently representing that his shop had been raided. His plan was discovered. As he had not yet claimed insurance, however, it was held that his acts were merely preparation and that he was not guilty of an attempt to obtain money by false pretences.

A person may be guilty of an attempt to commit an impossible crime, such as attempting to pick an empty pocket.

[1] Criminal Law Act, 1967, s. 4.
[2] Criminal Law Act, 1967, s. 5(1).
[3] [1915] 2 K.B. 342.

Inciting or soliciting the commission of an indictable offence is a crime in itself.

When two or more agree to commit an unlawful act or to do a lawful act by unlawful means, they commit the crime of conspiracy. Mere intention is not enough; but once the parties agree together, that is all that is necessary. An unlawful act for this purpose need not be a crime. A tort or breach of contract or act generally injurious to the public may be sufficient. The last category is vague. It was held that to combine to hiss and boo an actor in order to harm him was a conspiracy (*Gregory* v. *Duke of Brunswick*).[1]

Husband and wife cannot conspire together.

Defences

There are many defences to criminal liability. Several arise from the lack of necessary intention.

Insanity is thus a defence. The legal definition of insanity is contained in the 'MacNaghten Rules', named after the case after which they were laid down.[2] To escape criminal liability it must be proved by the defence that the accused, at the time he committed the act, was labouring under such a defect of reason from disease of the mind as not to know the nature or quality of the act he was doing, or, if he did know it, that he did not know he was doing wrong.

If a man is merely suffering from insane delusions, the test of guilt is whether he knew at the time of committing an act that it was contrary to law. This leads to some rather artificial results. If a man is under the insane delusion that he is a certain millionaire and drives away the millionaire's Rolls Royce, he has a good defence to a charge of driving away the car without the owner's consent. If, however, while driving away the car he ignores traffic lights and drives on the wrong side of the road, he could not, merely because of his delusion, escape conviction for dangerous or careless driving. Millionaires must drive as carefully as anyone else. Of course, it could be that our driver was not merely suffering from delusions but was so insane as to satisfy the first part of the Rules above and so escape liability.

[1] (1843), 6 Man. & G. 205.
[2] 10 Cl. & Fin. 200. MacNaghten was a lunatic who shot dead Sir Robert Peel's secretary.

A person found by the jury to be 'not guilty by reason of insanity' is ordered to be detained during 'Her Majesty's pleasure'; in other words, he is kept in Broadmoor for as long as the Home Office thinks fit. As this is the result, pleas of insanity are usually confined to charges of murder. In passing, it may be noted that a person who was sane at the time of committing an offence may become insane before or during trial. If the jury then finds him unfit to plead, he is detained during Her Majesty's pleasure. When there is evidence of a defence to a charge as well as an issue of unfitness to plead, the judge has a discretion to postpone the issue until the end of the prosecution's case. If that is so weak that it could not justify a conviction, the judge may order an acquittal without the issue of unfitness being considered.

The MacNaghten Rules have been much criticised by the medical profession. In particular, it was urged that 'uncontrollable impulse' should be made a defence. Uncontrollable impulse occurs when a person knows he is doing wrong in committing a crime yet cannot stop himself by reason of a disease of the mind.

The Homicide Act, 1957, s. 2, has introduced the Scottish doctrine of 'diminished responsibility' into English Law and this covers the case of 'uncontrollable impulse'. If a person kills or is a party to the killing of another, he is to be guilty of manslaughter and not murder (see below) if he was suffering from such abnormality of mind as substantially impaired his responsibility for the killing. The abnormality of mind may arise from a condition of arrested or retarded development of mind, or from any inherent causes, or be induced by disease or injury.

Drunkenness may be a defence. The House of Lords laid down these principles in the case of *D.P.P.* v. *Beard*.[1] The prisoner had raped a girl while under the influence of drink. It was held that drunkenness amounting to insanity was as good a defence[2] as insanity from any other cause. Where a specific intent to commit an offence is necessary, it may be that the accused was so drunk that he could not form the necessary intent. If so, his drunkenness would be a good defence. If he was *not* so drunk, the mere fact that he was, because of intoxication, less able to control himself is not a defence.[3]

A child under ten years old cannot be guilty of a crime. A child from ten to fourteen is presumed not to have the 'mischievous

[1] [1920] A.C. 479.   [2] See above.
[3] Thus 'irresistible impulse' is no defence.

intention' necessary to commit a crime. This may be rebutted by the prosecution proving that the particular child had.

The Sovereign is, of course, exempt from the operation of the Criminal Law, though servants of the Crown are subject to it. Corporations aggregate were formerly said to be unable to commit crimes as they had 'no body to be hanged or soul to be damned'. Nowadays, a corporation may be convicted of nearly every crime. Where *mens rea* is necessary, the intention of the directors is attributed to the company. Heads and Ambassadors of foreign states are not subject to the Criminal Law of this country.

We have seen that a master is liable for torts committed by his servant in the course of his employment. If a crime requires *mens rea*, then the master is not liable for the servant's crimes committed during his employment unless the master himself has the necessary *mens rea*. Some statutes, however, impose criminal liability on the master for his servant's acts even though the master has no *mens rea*, in fact has even forbidden the act. Thus in *Allen* v. *Whitehead*[1] a refreshment-house proprietor was convicted of knowingly suffering prostitutes to meet and remain on the premises, even though he did not know they went there and had, in fact, instructed his manager that they were not to be allowed on the premises.

To say that an offence was committed under threats or coercion is no defence. There are two exceptions to this.[2] The first is apparent rather than real. If A seizes B's arm and compels him to strike C with his fist, B is not criminally liable, as the act of striking is not B's but A's. The second exception is in s. 47 of the Criminal Justice Act, 1925. Except for charges of treason and murder, it is a good defence for a wife to prove the offence charged was committed under the coercion and in the presence of her husband.

'Necessity' is no defence to a criminal charge. This is to say that a person may not committ a crime against the person or property of another in order to preserve his own life or property, unless in self-defence. The grisly case of *R.* v. *Dudley and Stephens*[3] is authority for this. The two prisoners were shipwrecked and cast adrift on a raft for many days with a cabin-boy. To save themselves from death by starvation they killed the cabin-boy and ate him. Necessity for

---

[1] [1930] 1 K.B. 211.
[2] It is doubtful whether there are certain other rare exceptions to this rule.
[3] (1884) 14 Q.B.D. 273.

preserving their own lives was no defence to a charge of murder.

In defence of one's person, such force may be used as is necessary to defend oneself, and no criminal liability will result. Even homicide is justifiable to prevent the commission of a forcible and atrocious crime such as murder or rape. If possible, however, the person attacked should retreat and not fight unless he has to in order to prevent the commission of the intended attack.

Not only the person himself but his or her husband or wife, parent or child, master or servant, or even sometimes a stranger, may defend the person attacked.

In defence of a man's house, the owner or his family may kill a trespasser who would forcibly dispossess him of it and need not retreat, as in defence of his person, for that would be giving up his house to his adversary. Hussey rented a room from Mrs. West. She tried wrongfully to dispossess him and attempted to force her way in, aided by two companions, who were armed with a hammer, spanner, poker and chisel. Through a broken panel of the barricaded door, Hussey fired at Mrs. West's helpers and wounded them. He was held not guilty of unlawful wounding, as he was acting in defence of his home.[1]

It is a good defence to a criminal charge that there was no *mens rea*, because the act was committed inadvertently, without deliberate intention or criminal negligence. But if a person voluntarily does an act resulting in harm, he is taken to intend the natural consequences of his acts. So if he acts maliciously, i.e. intending to do a wrongful act, and his malice has different results from those he intended, he *may* be criminally liable for those results and cannot put forward the defence of accident. His malice is said to be transferred to the unexpected result. For example, in R. v. *Latimer*[2] the accused had quarrelled with a man and swung his belt at him, intending to injure him. By accident the buckle struck a woman standing nearby and wounded her. The accused was held rightly convicted of malicious wounding.

In R. v. *Pembliton*,[3] however, the accused had thrown a stone at a man, intending to injure him. It missed and broke a window. He did not intend to break the window and was not reckless regarding it. He was not guilty of malicious damage to the window. Though malicious with regard to the man, he was not malicious with regard

[1] R. v. *Hussey* (1924), 18 Cr. A.R. 160.
[2] (1886), 17 Q.B.D. 359.   [3] (1874), L.R. 2 C.C.R. 119.

156 *The Law*

to the window. Such malice cannot be transferred, because the consequences are of a totally different *kind* from that intended or foreseen.

The types of treatment available for offenders are very wide-ranging. Throughout the last two centuries, there has been a gradual tendency to regard criminal punishment as a means of reforming the criminal and less as a means of punishing him and deterring others by the rigour of his punishment. The aim now is to try to enable the offender to resume his place in society as a responsible citizen, and to use imprisonment as a last resort when other methods have failed.

The death penalty can only be imposed for high treason and piracy with violence. Sentence of death may not be imposed on a pregnant woman or a person whom it appears to the Court was not eighteen when he committed the offence.

Since the Murder (Abolition of Death Penalty) Act, 1965, the punishment for murder is imprisonment for life.

Whipping, penal servitude and hard labour were abolished by the Criminal Justice Act, 1948.

Sentences of imprisonment may be imposed for many offences. The maximum terms are usually fixed by statute, and vary as the offence is tried on indictment or by a Court of Summary Jurisdiction. The maximum sentence of imprisonment a Court of Summary Jurisdiction may impose is one year. If the offender is at least seventeen, and his character and antecedents make a longer sentence more appropriate, he may be committed to the Crown Court, where he will be liable to the full punishment he could have received if his offence had been tried at the Crown Court originally.[1]

In lieu of or in addition to any other penalty, a fine may be imposed as punishment for any offence.[2] It must not be excessive. Fines for most offences are fixed by statute. Time may be allowed for payment and, in the last resort, an offender may be sentenced to imprisonment if he does not pay the fine.

Some offences carry monetary penalties similar to fines. Thus, a person knowingly, etc., in possession of goods on which customs duty has not been paid is liable, in addition to other penalties, to pay treble the value as a penalty.

[1] Of course, this provision applies to indictable offences tried summarily or offences both indictable or summary tried summarily.
[2] Not those punishable with death.

A convenient way of dealing with minor offences, such as trifling assaults, is binding over, which originated in the time of Edward III.

The offender is ordered to enter into a recognisance[1] to keep the peace and be of good behaviour. A recognisance is an agreement whereby a person agrees to be indebted to the Queen in a certain sum on condition. If the condition (such as to keep the peace and be of good behaviour) be fulfilled, he need not pay the money, but if he breaks it he must pay the stated sum. Usually he will have to find sureties as well. Binding over may be used not only to ensure that an offence is not repeated but also to prevent the commission of an offence that is apprehended.

Recognisances are used for other purposes, such as bail or compelling the attendance of witnesses. They were also the basis of the probation system before the Criminal Justice Act, 1948.

The essence of probation is the reclamation of offenders, not their punishment. When an offender is convicted of any offence,[2] if, from the character of the offender or the nature of the offence, the Court thinks it would be expedient to do so, it may make a probation order. The Court must explain the effect of the order to the convicted person and he must consent to the order being made. Seventeen is the minimum age for probation. The effect of the order is that the offender is liable to come up for the sentence for which he was originally liable if he breaks the terms of the order or commits another offence. The order places him under the care of a probation officer for a term of from one to three years. It may contain further conditions, such as residence in a hostel. The duty of the probation officer is to see that the terms of the order are observed and to be a guide, philosopher and friend to the person under his care.

If a person is convicted of an offence,[2] and the Court, having in mind the nature of the offence and the character of the offender, thinks neither punishment nor probation suitable, it may discharge the offender, conditionally or absolutely. The difference between the two is that a conditionally discharged person may be brought back and sentenced for the original offence if he commits another offence within three years of his conditional discharge.[3]

If the Court, having considered all other methods of dealing with

[1] Pronounced 'reconnaisance'.
[2] Not those punishable with death.
[3] Criminal Justice Act, 1948, as amended by the Criminal Justice Act, 1967, s. 52.

an offender, decides that a sentence of not more than two years should be imposed, it may order that the sentence shall not then take effect but be suspended. If during the period of suspension the offender commits another offence, he will be liable to serve the suspended sentence as well as any sentence for the subsequent offence. This differs from a conditional discharge in that the sentence for the original offence has been fixed by the first Court, whereas with a conditional discharge it has not.

Except for those sentenced to life imprisonment, all prisoners sentenced for a term of more than one month are eligible to be released after serving two-thirds of their sentence. This is known as remission. A prisoner who has served one-third of his sentence, or one year, whichever is the greater, can be considered for release on licence by the Parole Board. The Board is an independent body, and, in deciding, it takes into account all the facts of the case. If the prisoner is released, with certain exceptions the licence remains in force until the date when he would have been released on remission if he had not had parole.

The Court is empowered by the Criminal Justice Act, 1967, to impose an extended sentence on persistent offenders. The Act lays down the number and type of convictions necessary to bring the offender into this category. The extended sentence would be appropriate where the Court felt that the offender needed a longer period of custodial treatment (followed by supervision on licence) than it would normally impose for the crime charged, and that such a course was required for the protection of the public. Subject to limitations, the extended term may be longer than the normal maximum prescribed for the offence or less than the normal maximum sentence, but much greater than would ordinarily have been imposed in the circumstances.

The Court has power to order restitution of goods or money criminally obtained, or to order the convicted person to pay compensation.[1]

If an alien is convicted of certain offences, the Court may recommend that he be deported. It lies with the Home Secretary whether he will be deported. Commonwealth citizens may now be deported in certain circumstances.

---

[1] The Criminal Justice Act, 1972, provides for community service orders which will enable the Court to order a suitable offender to do unpaid social work. It also introduces the concept of criminal bankruptcy.

Special penalties are fixed for young offenders. In the absence of special circumstances, no offender under twenty-one should be sent to prison. No Court may imprison a person under seventeen.

The Children and Young Persons Act, 1969, provides methods of dealing with young offenders, depending on their age and criminal record. They may be sent to a detention centre or Borstal. A care or supervision order may be made committing them to the care or supervision of a Local Authority. A child or young person in care may be sent to a community home or fostered out.

The parents of a child or young person[1] may have to pay a fine imposed on their offspring and may have to enter recognisances that their child will be of good behaviour. Young offenders may be discharged, absolutely or conditionally.

Special provisions apply to the treatment of persons of unsound mind.

Now we may consider the individual crimes. For convenience, the subject will be divided into three: offences against the State, offences against the person and offences against property. Space will allow us to deal with only the main crimes in each case.

Offences against the State

The most heinous of these is treason, which may be committed in a variety of ways. The first is 'levying war against the Queen in her realm'. This is a forcible insurrection of a general character, directed not necessarily against the Queen herself but against the Government or towards changing the law by unconstitutional means. The second is compassing or imagining the death, bodily harm or restraint of the Queen, her heirs and successors. 'Compassing or imagining' is a mental process and therefore must be proved by an act, such as a conspiracy or publishing a writing.

The third is 'being adherent to the Queen's enemies in her realm, giving them aid or comfort in the realm or elsewhere'. Enemies are only foreign powers, not British subjects in rebellion. The wording of the statute was considered in *R. v. Casement*.[2] Sir Roger Casement was a British subject who had urged British troops in a prison camp in Germany during the Great War to fight for Germany. It was held that Casement was guilty of treason by giving 'aid and comfort' to

[1] Under fourteen = child; fourteen to seventeen = young person.
[2] [1917] 1 K.B. 98.

the King's enemies. The offence may thus be committed by a British subject outside the Queen's realms.

There are various other ways in which treason can be committed. Among these may be mentioned: attempting to prevent, by an overt act, the person authorised by the Act of Settlement, 1700, from succeeding to the throne, or maintaining by writing that some other person has a right to the throne.

Every British subject and every alien resident in British territory owes allegiance to the Crown and can therefore commit treason. Even an alien may commit treason outside the realm if he is under the protection of the Crown by virtue of holding a British passport and he has not renounced that protection. This was held by the House of Lords in the case of William Joyce (Lord 'Haw-Haw') (*Joyce* v. *D.P.P.*).[1]

Misprision of treason is knowing that a treason has been committed and failing to disclose it, though not participating in it. It is punishable with life imprisonment and forfeiture of property.

Incitement to mutiny or disaffection of H.M. Forces or the police is punishable under various statutes.

Such matters as unlawful assembly have been dealt with in the chapter on Constitutional Law (see page 28).

Trade unions were formerly illegal, and membership was the crime of conspiracy. Nowadays, to belong to a trade union and to participate in a strike is perfectly lawful, subject to the provisions of the Conspiracy and Protection of Property Act, 1875, as amended by the Industrial Relations Act, 1971. Though the Act is general in its phrasing, it relates to trade disputes. Section 7[2] forbids, among other practices, intimidation and picketing other than peaceable picketing. Section 5 prohibits strikes and lockouts where the person wilfully breaking the contract of employment knows or has reasonable cause to believe that the probable consequences of his doing so, either alone or in combination, will be to endanger life or cause serious bodily injury, or to expose valuable property to destruction or serious injury.

It is an offence to bribe or offer a bribe to any public officer and for any such officer to accept a bribe. Corrupt practices at elections, such as treating, are prohibited by various Acts. Bribery of agents in relation to their principal's business is an offence.

A number of offences relate to proceedings in Court. A person

[1] [1946] A.C. 347.   [2] As amended by a later Act.

sworn[1] as a witness or interpreter in any judicial proceeding who wilfully makes a material statement in that proceeding which he knows to be false, or does not believe to be true, commits the offence of perjury and is liable to seven years' imprisonment (Perjury Act, 1911, s. 1).

A material statement is one that influences the Court in coming to a decision. It need not refer to a fact directly in issue but may relate to the character of a witness, as his credibility, and thus the effect of his evidence, will be affected. When a person has been found guilty of an offence, statements as to his previous convictions are material, for they affect the sentence to be passed.

If a person unwittingly makes a false statement, he is not guilty of perjury. An intention to mislead is necessary. Indeed, a person who wilfully gives evidence which he believes to be false is guilty of perjury even if it happens to be true.

The making of various false statements other than in judicial proceedings is also punishable under the Act.

Corruptly influencing jurors is a Common Law offence known as embracery. Interference with witnesses is an offence. Interference with jurors or witnesses is also a contempt of court.

Criminal contempt of court may occur in several ways. Failing to attend as witness when subpoenaed,[2] use of abusive language to the judge and publication of matter prejudicing a fair trial are all instances. The *Daily Mirror*, while Haigh (the 'acid-bath' murderer) was awaiting trial, published sensational articles stating that he had committed other murders. The editor was committed to prison for three months, and the newspaper company was fined £10 000. Criminal contempt of court may be tried as an ordinary offence. Superior courts may, however, fine or imprison anyone guilty of contempt, summarily, there and then.

Offences against the Person

Homicide is the killing of a human being. According to the *mens rea* and other attendant circumstances, it may be murder, or a less serious crime, or no offence at all.

Murder is homicide of a person under the Queen's peace,[3] with

[1] Includes affirmation, see Chapter 9, page 186.
[2] See Chapter 9, page 184.
[3] This excludes only enemy aliens in battle.

'malice aforethought'.[1] Malice means the intention that death will result; it may be actual or implied. Thus if A without excuse, shoots B and kills him, intending to kill him, A commits murder. As we have seen before, malice may be transferred. So if, in the example, A was a bad shot and killed C instead, A would be guilty of C's murder even though he did not intend to kill him.

At one time, it seemed to be the law that when a man killed another, even when not intending to do so, circumstances might be present which would make the killing murder. The malice aforethought was implied. If an ordinary reasonable man would have foreseen that death or grievous bodily harm was the natural and probable result of the action, it was implied that the accused man must have foreseen it.

However, s. 8 of the Criminal Justice Act, 1967, now provides that this is not the law. A judge or jury must consider, as a matter of fact on the evidence before them, whether the accused intended the result of his conduct. It cannot be assumed as a matter of law that, because the result of the accused's conduct would have been contemplated by a reasonable man, it was necessarily contemplated by the accused.

Implied malice must be distinguished from constructive malice, which was abolished by the Homicide Act, 1957, s. 1.

Suicide is the intentional taking of one's own life. At one time, a suicide was buried at a crossroads, with a stake through his heart, and his goods were forfeited. It is no longer a crime to commit or attempt to commit suicide, by the Suicide Act, 1961, s. 1. But s. 2(1) of the Act makes it an offence punishable by fourteen years' imprisonment to aid, abet, counsel or procure the suicide of another, or an attempt by another to commit suicide.

It is manslaughter, not murder, for a person acting in pursuance of a suicide pact[2] between him and another person to kill the other or be a party to the other being killed by a third person.

Manslaughter is another form of homicide. It is the most elastic of all offences, for it may be just short of murder or just more than

---

[1] In murder and manslaughter, death must ensue within a year and a day. This old rule dates from the time when medicine was less advanced than today.

[2] Homicide Act, 1957, s. 4. 'Suicide pact' means a common agreement between two or more persons, having for its object the death of all of them, whether or not each is to take his own life.

excusable homicide. The maximum punishment is imprisonment for life. The offence may be committed in any of three ways. If a person *unintentionally* causes death while committing an unlawful act and does not intend to cause grievous bodily harm, he is guilty of manslaughter. For example, a schoolmaster beats a boy moderately, which the law permits. The boy has an obscure disease and the schoolmaster does not know this. As a result of the beating, the boy dies. The schoolmaster is not guilty of any crime; it is an unfortunate accident.

Another schoolmaster beats another boy with great severity. He goes beyond the limits of reasonable chastisement that the law allows. If the boy dies as a result of this unlawful act of the schoolmaster's, the schoolmaster will be guilty of manslaughter. If the schoolmaster intended to cause grievous bodily harm to the boy and the boy died, the schoolmaster would have been guilty of murder. Of course, wherever there is a positive intention to kill, the offence is murder.[1]

If a person is so negligent that he causes the death of another, he may be guilty of manslaughter. Much greater negligence is needed for manslaughter than for mere tortious negligence. It must be so gross that it amounts to criminal misconduct deserving of punishment. It is still no crime to watch a man drown in 2 feet of water when you can easily rescue him, because you owe him no duty of care. Parents owe their children a duty of care, however, and if a child dies through the negligence of its parents, they may be guilty of manslaughter. A similar duty exists where a person has undertaken the care of another.

Motorists owe a duty of care to other road users. A motorist who drives so negligently that he kills someone may be guilty of manslaughter. But the lack of care necessary for this is very great, greater than that required for a conviction for dangerous driving or driving without due care and attention, which are two offences under the Road Traffic Act, 1972.[2]

It is an offence under the Road Traffic Act, 1972, s. 1, to cause death by dangerous driving.

Provocation may reduce what would otherwise be murder to manslaughter. The provocation must be that which would overbear the reason of an ordinary man and cause him temporarily to lose

[1] Subject to exceptions of provocation, justifiable homicide, etc.

[2] *Andrews* v. *D.P.P.*, [1937] A.C. 576.

control of himself. What amounts to sufficient provocation is entirely a question for the jury. Mere words may be enough.[1] Physical violence or discovery of a spouse in the act of adultery have been held sufficient provocation. The killing must take place at the moment of provocation before the killer's passion has had time to cool. The mode of resentment must bear a reasonable relationship to the provocation if the offence is to be reduced to manslaughter. To strike with the fist when provoked is a different matter from using a double-edged sharp knife.[2] Note that provocation, though it may reduce murder to manslaughter, does not make the killing lawful.

See above as to 'diminished responsibility'.

Homicide may be justifiable or excusable, in which case it is not a crime at all. We have seen that a man may kill in certain circumstances to protect his person or property.[3]

Section 3 of the Criminal Justice Act, 1967, provides that: 'a person may use such force as is reasonable in the circumstances in the prevention of crime, or in effecting or assisting the arrest of offenders or suspected offenders, or of a person unlawfully at large.' Thus if an officer of justice or a private person is making a lawful arrest, he would be justified in killing only if it were impossible to arrest an offender or prevent his escape by less violent means.

The hangman carrying out the lawful sentence of the Court in the proper manner is justified.

Finally, if an accident resulting in death should occur during a lawful occupation and which is not due to gross negligence, no criminal liability results. To shoot at an object near a crowd of people might be so negligent that if one were killed it would be manslaughter. But if a man was shooting and exercising proper care, and a pellet ricochetted off a tree and killed a bystander, this would not be a crime.

A mother who kills her child under the age of twelve months, in such circumstances that normally her act would amount to murder, is guilty of the lesser crime of infanticide if her mind was disturbed by the birth of the child or her lactation at the time she killed it.

Child destruction is the crime of wilfully killing a child *before* it has an existence independent of its mother.[4] Any person may com-

---

[1] Homicide Act, 1957, s. 3.
[2] *Mancini* v. *D.P.P.*, [1942] A.C. 1.   [3] R. v. *Hussey*. See above.
[4] Infant Life (Preservation) Act, 1929.

mit this crime. It is a good defence to prove it was done in good faith to preserve the life of the mother.

Attempting to procure abortion is a crime.[1] It may be committed in two ways. A *pregnant* woman who, with intent to procure *her own* miscarriage, unlawfully administers poison or other noxious thing, or uses an instrument or other means, is guilty of the offence. The second part of the section makes it an offence for *anybody* unlawfully to administer poison, use an instrument, etc., with intent to procure the miscarriage of a woman, *whether she be pregnant or not.*

To be an offence, the attempt to procure abortion must be unlawful. By the Abortion Act, 1967, a pregnancy may be lawfully terminated if two registered practitioners are of the opinion, formed in good faith, that there is a danger that its continuance would involve a risk to the life or the mental or physical health of the mother or any existing child of the family, or that the child would be born seriously handicapped.

The three previous crimes are all punishable with imprisonment for life.

Sexual offences cannot be dealt with in great detail in a work of this character.

Rape is the offence of having sexual intercourse with a woman without her consent. Mere submission is not consent. The offence may be committed by force, threats or fraud. If consent is obtained by personation of the woman's husband, for example, there is no real consent and it is rape.

A husband cannot commit rape (as a principal) on his wife unless they are living apart under the terms of a separation order containing a non-cohabitation clause. Neither can a boy under the age of fourteen be guilty of rape as a principal. They may both be guilty, however, as accomplices.

To have carnal knowledge of a girl under sixteen is an offence.[2] If she is under thirteen, it is punishable with life imprisonment. In neither case is the girls' consent a defence, nor a reasonable and honest belief that she was over sixteen.[3]

Indecent assault may be committed on either sex. Unnatural offences between male persons may be sodomy (punishment— imprisonment for life) or gross indecency (punishment—imprisonment two years). An act of sodomy or gross indecency is not an

[1] Section 58, Offences Against the Person Act, 1861.
[2] Sexual Offences Act, 1956.   [3] Save in limited circumstances.

offence, provided that the act is in private and both parties are over twenty-one and consent.[1] Unnatural offences between females are not crimes.

Various other offences are set out in the Sexual Offences Act, 1956, dealing with abduction of women and girls of various ages for various purposes.

A person already validly married who goes through a ceremony of marriage while the first spouse is still alive commits the crime of bigamy (s. 57, Offences Against the Person Act, 1861). Both the first marriage and the second 'marriage' may have been celebrated anywhere, not necessarily in England, but if the second 'marriage' was outside England or Northern Ireland there is no offence if the person going through the ceremony was not a British subject.

This branch of the law is complicated by the varying requirements for a valid marriage or divorce by the different countries of the world. For present purposes, this aspect will be ignored.

If the first marriage is void[2] or dissolved, no offence is committed by marrying again. For example, A goes through a ceremony of marriage with B. They are under sixteen. No marriage has been formed, so if A then marries C, he will not have committed bigamy.

If a married person marries again, it is a defence to a charge of bigamy that the original spouse has been absent from the accused for the seven years continuously preceding the second 'marriage' and has not been known by the accused to be living within that time.

An honest belief on reasonable grounds that the first spouse is dead, even though seven years of absence have not elapsed, is a defence.[3] So is an honest belief that the first marriage was void.[4] An honest belief that the accused has been divorced, when he is still married is a defence, provided that the belief is reasonable.[5]

It must be remembered, of course, that if the first marriage is valid the second 'marriage' will have no legal effect, even though there may be a defence to a charge of bigamy.

We have considered the tort of assault already.[6] It is also a crime. Besides the general defences mentioned before, a parent or school-

---

[1] Sexual Offences Act, 1967, s. 1.
[2] See Chapter 7, page 131. Void means void, whether annulled by the Court or not. It does not mean merely voidable.
[3] R. v. *Tolson* (1889), 23 Q.B.D. 168.   [4] R. v. *King*, [1963] 3 W.L.R. 892.
[5] R. v. *Gould*, [1968] 1 All E.R. 849.   [6] Chapter 3, page 47.

master is permitted moderately to chastise a child. Consent is a defence, if the assault takes place as a part of a lawful activity. It is no defence if it takes place as a part of an unlawful activity, such as a prize fight. Thus the consent of a girl who was caned by a man for purposes of sexual gratification was no defence to a charge of assault against him.[1] Provocation is not a defence but may reduce the punishment.

A simple assault is known as a common assault. Various other types of assault are punishable more severely, such as an assault occasioning actual bodily harm (s. 47).[2] This phrase means the victim must have suffered hurt or injury calculated to interfere with his health or comfort, though not necessarily permanently. Of course, it must be more than merely transient and trifling.

Wounding occurs whenever the victim's skin is broken. It may be unlawful wounding (s. 20),[2] or the more serious offences of wounding with intent to cause grievous bodily harm (s. 18)[2] or wounding with intent to murder (s. 11).[2]

Various offences relating to poisoning exist, of which it will be sufficient to mention two. Unlawfully and maliciously administering or causing to be administered any poison or other noxious thing so as to endanger life is a crime, punishable with ten years' imprisonment. If the poison, etc., is administered, etc., with intent to injure, aggrieve or annoy, the offence carries five years' imprisonment.

Offences against Property

The Criminal Damage Act, 1971, deals with offences relating to damage to property. A person is guilty of an offence if without lawful excuse he destroys or damages *another*'s property, either intending to do so or being reckless as to the consequences of his actions. Further, if he damages or destroys another's property *or his own*, intending thereby to endanger the life of another, or being reckless as to the danger to another's life, this is an offence. Threatening to destroy or damage property, or possessing anything with the intent to use it to destroy or damage property is an offence.

If the damage or destruction is caused by fire, the offence is called arson. Arson is punishable with life imprisonment, while the other offences are punishable with up to ten years' imprisonment.

[1] R. v. *Donovan*, [1934] 2 K.B. 498.
[2] Offences Against the Person Act, 1861.

A person has 'lawful excuse' if he believes honestly that the owner of the property consents, or would have consented, to his actions if he had known the circumstances, or if he acts believing that the damage or destruction is the only reasonable way of protecting other property which is in immediate need of protection. It might be reasonable to pull down a building belonging to one person to prevent fire spreading and destroying a whole street.

Theft is defined by s. 1 of the Theft Act, 1968. This states that a person is guilty of theft if he dishonestly appropriates property belonging to another with the intention of permanently depriving the other of it.

This definition should be considered in detail. First, what is meant by 'dishonestly'? The Act provides that a person is not dishonest, when he appropriates another's property, in any of three circumstances: first, when he does so in the belief that he has the right in law to deprive the other of it; secondly, if he believes that he would have the other's consent if the other knew of the appropriation and the circumstances; and, thirdly, when the owner of the property cannot be discovered by taking reasonable steps.[1]

A person may be dishonest even though he is willing to pay for the property he has appropriated. One may still steal a diamond necklace even though one leaves the money to pay for it.

For there to be theft, the property must be 'appropriated'. This is defined by s. 3 as the assumption by a person of the rights of the owner, and it covers the case where a person acquires property innocently and later dishonestly decides to treat it as his own. However, the Act protects someone who acquires property in good faith and for value, and subsequently discovers that the seller had no right to the property. In this situation, the buyer does not become a thief himself if he deals with the property or keeps it.

A person would assume the rights of an owner if he did any act that showed he was treating the property as if it belonged to him. This would cover taking the property, destroying it or using it in an unauthorised way.

All property, real or personal, may be stolen, with exceptions relating to land, wild plants and wild creatures. Examples of things that are nobody's property are human corpses (unless, for example,

[1] The state of the accused's mind is a question of fact for the jury to decide. *R.* v. *Feely*, [1973] 1 E.R. 341.

owned by hospitals for dissection) and things which have been abandoned by their owners.

A person cannot steal land or things forming part of it except in three cases. A trustee or personal representative may be guilty of theft if he deals with the land in breach of the confidence imposed in him. Of course, all the elements of theft would have to be present; merely an unauthorised sale would not be enough. If a person who does not own the land severs something from the land, this is theft. Also, a tenant may be a thief if he appropriates a fixture that is meant to remain part of the land.

Someone who picks wild flowers or fruit might technically be guilty of theft. However, the Act provides that this is not the case unless he intends to sell them for gain. Wild creatures tame or untame are property, but neither a wild creature nor its carcase can be stolen unless it has been reduced into possession, which possession has not been subsequently lost or abandoned. Thus if a landowner kills a wild animal on his land it becomes his property, and if, while he is approaching to collect the carcase, someone runs off with it, that person is guilty of theft. If, however, the landowner abandons the carcase, the fact that someone then carries it off does not constitute theft, since the landowner has abandoned possession.

'Belonging to another' covers the situation where someone possesses or controls property, or has any proprietary right or interest in it.

A bailee can steal though he is lawfully in possession of the goods. So can a part-owner. Bailment exists where A (the bailor) gives B (the bailee) possession of a thing in order that the bailee may keep it, carry it or do some other thing with it. If your boot-repairer steals your shoes, he is guilty of theft even though he is lawfully in possession of them as bailee.

The Act speaks of 'any proprietary right or interest', and therefore it would be possible for the owner of the property to steal it from his bailee. Consider *R. v. Turner*.[1] In that case, a man took his car to be repaired. The garage proprietor left it outside the garage after he had finished work on it, and the owner dishonestly removed it without paying. He was guilty of theft since he had deprived the garage proprietor of his security for the unpaid money, namely the car that was in the proprietor's actual possession and control.

A person may be guilty of theft even though legal ownership has

[1] [1971] 1 W.L.R. 903.

passed to him. The Act provides that, where a person obtains property by another's mistake in such a way that he is under an obligation to return the property or its value, he is guilty of theft if he dishonestly fails to do so, since the property is to be regarded as belonging to the person entitled to restoration. Thus if an employee was overpaid in error and, having discovered the mistake, dishonestly failed to return the excess, he would be guilty of theft.

In some cases, a person might get legal ownership of property from another but be under an obligation to deal with that property in a certain way. For example, A is the treasurer of a loan club and is under an obligation to deal with the money to benefit the members. Instead of doing so, he misapplies it for his own use. He has the legal ownership of the money, but he is still guilty of theft, for s. 5(3) provides that in such a situation the property is regarded as 'belonging to' the members.

The final ingredient of theft is that there should be an intention permanently to deprive. Thus if someone removed an object meaning to return it in a short while, that would not be theft. This even covers the case where someone deprives the owner of his property to see if it is worth taking and, finding it is not, returns it.

A person convicted of theft on indictment may be imprisoned for a term not exceeding ten years.

If a person in the course of stealing uses force on someone or seeks to put them in fear of being then and there subjected to force, he is guilty of robbery. Thus where a man snatched an earring from a woman, thereby injuring her ear, it was held to be robbery.[1] The force must be used or threatened immediately before or at the time of the theft, and must be in order to carry out the theft.

Robbery, or an assault with intent to rob, is punishable with life imprisonment.

Section 9(1)(a) of the Theft Act provides that a person is guilty of burglary if he enters any building or part of a building as a trespasser with the intent to commit specified offences. These are theft, the infliction of grievous bodily harm and rape. Section 9(1)(b) provides that it shall also be burglary to enter a building or part of a building as a trespasser and steal or attempt to steal therein, or inflict or attempt to inflict grievous bodily harm on any person.

A person enters a building as a trespasser when he has not the consent of the owner of occupier to enter.

[1] R. v. *Lapier* (1784), 1 Leach 320.

When a man puts any part of his person in a building, even his little finger, he is said to have entered it. Entry may result if an instrument is inserted in a building without any part of the body of the wielder entering, provided that the instrument is used to commit the offence itself and not the mere entering. Thus if a burglar stands outside a house and puts a jemmy through the window in order that he may get in, there is no entering. If he puts it through the window to strike a person inside, however, there is an entering.

Burglary is punishable with fourteen years' imprisonment. A person who commits burglary and has with him at the time any firearm, explosive or offensive weapon is guilty of aggravated burglary and is liable to life imprisonment.

It is also an offence if a person, while not at his place of abode, has with him any article for use in the course of, or in connection with, any burglary, theft or cheat. If a person is proved to have such an article on him, for example a jemmy, it is evidence that he has it with him for the purpose of committing such an offence.

The Act defines various offences constituting fraud. By s. 15(1) a person is liable to imprisonment for ten years if he by any deception dishonestly obtains property belonging to another with the intention of permanently depriving that other of it.

The deception could be express or by conduct, as when a man walked into a shop in a university town wearing a gown, thereby falsely making himself out to be a member of the university. The deception must, however, be made dishonestly, or at least recklessly. If a person erroneously supposed from his dealings with a business man that he was a person of substance and therefore gave him goods on credit, the business man would not have obtained the property by deception if he had done nothing to give rise to the belief in his solvency.

To constitute an offence under s. 15, *property* belonging to another must be obtained. There are situations, however, where a person does not obtain specific property but nevertheless obtains a pecuniary advantage by deception, to which he is not entitled. Section 16 provides for such a case, which is punishable with five years' imprisonment.

A person obtains a pecuniary advantage for the purposes of the section when a debt for which he makes himself liable is, or may become, liable is evaded or deferred; when he is allowed to borrow on an overdraft etc.; and when he is given the opportunity to earn remuneration or greater remuneration in an office or employment, or to win money by betting.

Thus if a man obtained a reduction at the cinema by falsely pretending to be an old-age pensioner, he would have dishonestly reduced a debt for which he was liable. Similarly, if a secretary obtained increased pay by dishonestly pretending to have a degree, she would have obtained a pecuniary advantage by deception, namely greater remuneration.

Blackmail is committed when someone makes an unwarranted demand with menaces with the intent to cause loss to another or with a view to gain. A menace has been judicially defined as 'any action detrimental to or unpleasant to the person addressed'.[1] The gain or loss must be an economic one.

It will be seen that the legal net to catch thieves and fraudulent persons is of close mesh. Punishing these offenders is not very effective, however, if they may easily dispose of their ill-gotten gains. Handling stolen goods is therefore an offence by s. 22 of the Theft Act. A person is guilty of handling if (otherwise than in the course of the stealing), knowing or believing goods to be stolen, he dishonestly receives them, or undertakes or assists in their retention, removal, disposal or realisation by or for the benefit of another person, or if he arranges so to do. The scope of the section is therefore very wide. The person must know or believe them to be stolen, however. Evidence of this knowledge may be, for example, the extreme cheapness of the goods, or the fact that they were stolen very recently.

Forgery is the making of a false document that it may be used as genuine. In general, a mere intent to deceive is necessary for forgery of documents of a public character, such as a marriage register, whereas forgery of a private document needs an intention to defraud. It seems that an intent to deceive is merely meant to induce a state of mind, whereas an intent to defraud is meant to induce a course of action or inaction.

The presence of a false statement in a document will not suffice alone to make it a forgery. The very document itself must masquerade as something it is not.

The alteration of a genuine document with intent to defraud may be forgery, as where an 'o' was added to '£8' on a bill of exchange to make it '£80'.

[1] *Thorne* v. *Motor Trade Association*, [1937] A.C. 797.

The Criminal Courts

Having very briefly examined some of the main crimes, we must consider the courts in which they may be tried.

The humblest of criminal tribunals are the Courts of Summary Jurisdiction or Magistrates' Courts. These are usually staffed by lay magistrates, in which case at least two[1] must be present to try offenders.[2] Many towns, notably the Metropolis, have stipendiary magistrates, who can try cases sitting alone. They receive a salary and are legally qualified.

Besides trying small offences, magistrates[3] have the duty of conducting a preliminary investigation into indictable offences. If they decide a *prima facie* case has been made out by the prosecution, they commit the accused for trial at the Crown Court. If not, the accused is discharged. This is not an acquittal; if more evidence comes to light, the prosecution may try again.

Juvenile offenders under seventeen are in most cases tried by specially constituted Juvenile Courts which sit at different times or places from the ordinary Magistrates' Courts.

Persons committed for trial for indictable offences are tried by jury at the Crown Court.

The Crown Court is a very new concept. The Courts Act of 1971 swept away the old system of Assizes and Quarter Sessions, and in their place put one Court—the Crown Court—which, together with the High Court and the Court of Appeal, constitutes the Supreme Court. It is a single Court which sits at various places in England and Wales. The country is divided into six areas for legal administrative purposes known as circuits. Two High Court judges are appointed to serve each circuit (three in the South-east) and there are also circuit judges.

The Crown Court's jurisdiction may be exercised by a High Court judge, a circuit judge or a recorder. A recorder is a part-time judge and must be a barrister or solicitor of at least ten years' standing. Between two and four lay justices are to sit in the Crown Court with the judge or recorder when an appeal from a Magistrates' Court is being heard or when a person is committed for sentence.

The Crown Court is organised into a tier structure. The first tier

---

[1] One is sufficient in the City of London.
[2] Except for certain offences.
[3] For this purpose a lay magistrate may sit alone.

is for both criminal and civil cases and is presided over by High
Court and circuit judges. The second tier hears criminal cases only
and is served by High Court and circuit judges. The third tier also
hears criminal cases only and is served by circuit judges. Thus, for
example, on the South-eastern Circuit, Norwich and Greater London are the first tier, the second tier includes Lewes and Ipswich,
and the third includes Brighton and Kings Lynn.

The nature of the offence decides which judge shall hear it. Murder and some other crimes are tried by a High Court judge. Other
serious indictable offences such as manslaughter and rape are tried
by a High Court judge unless he releases the case to a circuit judge
or recorder. Offences triable summarily or on indictment such as
theft and certain specific offences such as causing death by dangerous
driving and burglary would usually be tried by a circuit judge or
recorder unless there were aggravating factors which made the
committing magistrate feel that it should be tried before a High
Court judge.

The Central Criminal Court, known as the Old Bailey, is the
sitting of the Crown Court in the City of London. The judges include the Lord Mayor and Alderman. These, however, do not try
cases in practice.

The Queen's Bench Division has power to try certain criminal
cases at first instance, but the power is virtually obsolete.

An appeal lies by way of case stated from a Magistrates' Court to
a Divisional Court of the Queen's Bench Division, purely on a point
of law. An appeal lies to the Crown Court on a question of law, fact
or sentence. An appeal lies from the Crown Court, on law alone, to
the Divisional Court in cases not on indictment.

Note that only a convicted accused may appeal to the Crown
Court, but the prosecution may appeal, as well as the accused, to the
Divisional Court.

A person convicted on indictment at the Crown Court may appeal
against either his conviction or his sentence to the Criminal Division of the Court of Appeal. This sits at the Royal Courts of Justice
and consists of the Lord Chief Justice and the other Judges of the
Queen's Bench Division. Normally, three are present, which is the
minimum number. For very important appeals there may be more,
but the number must be uneven.

The final court of appeal is the House of Lords. Either the prosecution or the accused may appeal to the Lords from a decision of the

Criminal Division of the Court of Appeal (or the Divisional Court), with the consent of either court. The Criminal Division (or the Divisional Court) must certify that a point of law of general public importance is involved.[1]

[1] Criminal Appeal Act, 1968, s. 1.

9   Evidence and Civil Procedure

A lawyer asked by a layman to elucidate a point of law is only too likely to have his explanation greeted with: 'But how do you prove it?' What is meant, of course, is: How are the facts proved? A whole branch of the law is devoted to the topic, what facts must not or need not, what facts need to be proved and how they are to be proved. This is the law of evidence, which is closely related to the law of procedure.

In every case that comes before a court of law, there exists what is known as the burden of proof. This expression is, confusingly, used in two senses. First, it means the facts that have to be proved to establish a good cause of action, or a defence in civil cases or a verdict of guilty in criminal cases.[1] This is a burden imposed by law and does not shift. For example, a seller sues a buyer for the price of goods sold and delivered. The burden of proof on the seller is to prove the contract of sale and the delivery of the goods. It may be that the buyer has a defence; for instance, that the goods were not up to sample. To succeed with this the burden of proof is on him to show the sale was by sample and that the goods were not up to sample.

In criminal cases, the burden of proof is always on the prosecution, except for insanity and where provided otherwise by statute.

'Burden of proof' is used in a second sense. In this context, it may be compared with a pair of scales. The side that wins is the one which can produce the weightiest evidence and tip its end down. Though, as has been said, the burden of proof in the first sense does not shift, it plainly does in the second. For instance, A is charged with a crime. X, the prosecution witness, gives evidence, tipping the scales down on the prosecution side. Adroit cross-examination by A's counsel lightens the weight. A gives evidence for the defence and brings the scales down once more on the side of the defence. A is entitled then to an acquittal.

Not only evidence in its proper sense may tip the scales of the burden of proof but also such matters as presumptions, to be dealt with later.

[1] Or such defences as insanity in criminal matters.

Burden of proof must be distinguished from weight of evidence. In civil cases, the victory lies with the side with a preponderance of evidence, be it ever so slight. In criminal cases, it is up to the prosecution to prove a case to the reasonable satisfaction of the jury or bench or, as used to be said, beyond reasonable doubt.

The first question is, what is evidence? In its wider sense it means the facts that each party seeks to prove in an action between them. In a narrower sense it means those facts which the law allows each party to adduce in order to prove their case. Thus counsel for one side may ask a witness a question which will be objected to as its answer is 'not evidence', i.e. the laws of evidence exclude it for some reason. To be admissible, evidence must be relevant, but not all relevant facts are admissible; for example, evidence of a prisoner's previous convictions is not permitted when he is charged with a criminal offence. Some facts are privileged from disclosure, e.g. State secrets.

Some evidence is admissible which is not directly logically relevant to the fact in issue. It is admissible because it is legally relevant. For instance, the occupation of a witness is relevant, as it may affect the weight of his evidence. Again, facts not directly connected with the issues to be proved may be admissible, as in deciding whether other evidence is admissible. An example frequently occurring in criminal cases is evidence of the circumstances in which an accused person made a confession, because, if the confession were extorted by threats, for example, it would be inadmissible.

Evidence may be direct or circumstantial. Where a witness has direct personal knowledge of a fact, his evidence of it is direct; where a witness has direct personal knowledge of circumstances from which that fact can be logically inferred, his evidence of the fact is circumstantial.

For instance, A is charged with shooting B. C is present and sees it happen; D does not see or hear a shot but comes into the room just afterwards and sees B lying dead and A standing nearby with a gun in his hand. C's evidence of the shooting is direct, D's is circumstantial. Note that they must both have personal knowledge of the facts to which they depose. Neither C nor D could give evidence if they had been told of the facts by E. This is discussed later. It must be emphasised that circumstantial evidence is hardly less weighty than direct evidence, and in many cases direct evidence cannot be produced.

Evidence may be oral, documentary or real. Thus A sells B some goods and B pays him. A gives B a receipt but later sues him for the price. B can give oral evidence of the payment and he may produce the receipt as documentary evidence. An object produced to prove a fact of itself, and not merely by what is recorded on it, is known as real evidence. Thus in the shooting example above, the revolver would be real evidence. When documents and real evidence are produced in Court they are termed 'exhibits' and are numbered.

To return to the question of admissibility, the position is that all relevant facts are admissible, provided they are not hearsay or otherwise excluded by the laws of evidence.

It is impossible to lay down a hard-and-fast rule as to what is relevant. In every case, there will be a main fact or facts in issue, and surrounding the fact in issue will be a number of facts relevant to that main fact. Evidence of the fact in issue is admissible; facts relevant to the fact in issue may or may not be admissible.

Where facts form part of the main 'transaction' to be proved (known in law as the *res gestae*)[1] they are admissible. Statements accompanying the main act are admissible, provided that they are made at the time. An example is *The Schwalbe*.[2] A steamer collided with a brig. As the steamer backed, its pilot stamped his foot and said: 'The damned helm is still astarboard.' This was admitted, as it accompanied and explained the collision.

Statements by a person as to his own health at the time are admissible, but statements as to the *cause* of ill health are not. Thus in *R. v. Gloster*[3] statements by a sick woman that her illness was brought on by an abortion were held not admissible.

The motive, opportunity or subsequent conduct of a person may well be relevant when considering whether or not he has done a certain act. Thus in *Moriarty* v. *L. C. & D.R.*[4] the plaintiff sued the defendant railway for negligence. Evidence was tendered by the defendants that the plaintiff had attempted to persuade someone to give false evidence. It was held this was admissible as showing the plaintiff had a bad case.

An oral statement made in the presence of a party may be admitted in evidence in two ways. First, it may to prove knowledge. Thus

---

[1] Literally, 'the things done'. The expression is vague and best avoided; it has only been used for completeness.

[2] (1859), Swa. 521.   [3] (1888), 16 Cox 471.

[4] (1870), L.R. 5 Q.B. 314.

if A accuses B of a crime in his presence, evidence of A's words is admissible to prove B knew he had been accused. Secondly, if the statement is such that a reply would reasonably be expected and if the person to whom the statement is made is capable of replying, his silence may be evidence of the truth of what has been said. Silence is no admission, of course, where a prisoner is accused of a crime and has previously been cautioned, as the caution warns him he need say nothing if he wishes.

Statements made in the absence of a party are not evidence as to his acts, for he has no opportunity of confirming or contradicting them. There are two exceptions to this rule. First, the fact that a woman or boy sexually assaulted complained of it at the first opportunity is evidence that there was no consent and the complainant's story is consistent. It is *not* evidence of the truth of the complaint— that would be hearsay and obviously unfair to the prisoner. Secondly, statements made by a person with an 'identity of interest' with another are evidence for or against that other. Thus the statements of one conspirator regarding the conspiracy are evidence for or against any other conspirator as well as himself.

Merely that facts are similar to the fact in issue does not make them admissible. They must be relevant as well. Thus a publican asserts that a brewer has sold him bad beer. The fact of the quality of beer sold by the brewer to other publicans is not admissible, *unless* the beer sold to the others was of the *same* brewing as that sold to the first publican.

It is not competent for the prosecution in a criminal case to adduce evidence tending to show the accused has been guilty of criminal acts other than those with which he is charged, for the purpose of showing from his criminal conduct or character that he is likely to have committed the offence with which he is charged. It may, however, be open to the prosecution to adduce such evidence to rebut a defence of accident, for example. In the famous 'Brides in the Bath' case, the prisoner was convicted of murdering his 'wife' by drowning her in a bath. Evidence that two other women were drowned in similar circumstances was admitted to show system and rebut the defence of accident.[1]

Hearsay evidence, whether oral or documentary, is, subject to exceptions, not admissible in criminal cases. It is admissible in civil cases, subject to the conditions of the Civil Evidence Act, 1968. In the

[1] R. v. *Smith* (1915), 11 Cr. A.R. 229.

trial of *Bardell* v. *Pickwick* in the *Pickwick Papers*, Sam Weller answered 'Oh, quite enough to get, sir, as the soldier said ven they
ordered him three hundred and fifty lashes,' and the judge told him
he must not say what the soldier or any other man said as it was not
evidence. Witnesses in criminal cases must depose to what is in their
own personal knowledge and may not retail at second-hand what
others have told them. What the soldier or any other man said was
hearsay to Sam Weller. The principal objection to hearsay is its unfairness, as the person who made the statement is not there to be
cross-examined. If his evidence is to be admitted, he must be
brought to Court so that the judge and counsel for the other side
may have an opportunity of testing his evidence. What has been said
applies to the admission of evidence as regards the truth of what is
contained in the statements. Sometimes the statements may be
admitted for other purposes. For example, A tells B that C, who is
not present, has stolen his (A's) watch. C is tried for theft of the
watch. A or B may not give evidence of the conversation. A may
give evidence only of facts of which he has personal knowledge, and
his evidence may be tested and given its proper weight in Court.
Suppose the allegation was untrue and C sued A for slander. B could
then give evidence that A said those words. It would not be evidence of their truth, however—that would be for A to deal with—
but would be evidence that A had used the words complained of.

In *civil* cases the Civil Evidence Act, 1968, provides that first-
hand hearsay evidence is admissible by virtue of the provisions of
the Act and by agreement of the parties. Thus the Act would allow
Sam Weller to give evidence of what *he* heard the soldier say, as this
is first-hand hearsay, but not what a *third party* told him the soldier
said, as this would be second-hand hearsay. A party wishing to
introduce hearsay evidence must serve a notice on the other party to
the proceedings giving particulars of the evidence. The other party
can serve a counter-notice requiring the maker of the statement to
be called, unless he is dead, unfit to appear, unobtainable, etc. Even
if the required notice has not been given, the Court has discretion
to allow hearsay evidence.

The Act provides that, where direct oral evidence of a fact would
be admissible, a statement in a document tending to establish that
fact shall be evidence of that fact in certain cases and provided that
certain conditions are satisfied.

Statements in public documents are admissible in civil and

criminal cases even if hearsay. Public documents comprise a wide class. Examples are registers of births, marriages and deaths, the public books of corporations and recognised maps and almanacs.

At Common Law there are exceptions to the hearsay rule. These now apply mainly to criminal cases as civil cases are governed by Statute. Some Common Law exceptions, however, are expressly preserved in the Civil Evidence Act.

Statements by deceased persons are excepted from the hearsay rule at Common Law if they fall into one of six categories and satisfy certain conditions. A statement by a deceased person in the course of his duty may be admissible. An example occurred in *Price* v. *Earl of Torrington*.[1] To prove that beer had been delivered, entries in his employer's book which the drayman had to make as part of his duties were held admissible in an action by the employer for the price of the beer. At the time of the action the drayman was dead, so could not give evidence himself.

The law assumes a man will not make untrue statements against his own interests. So, statements by deceased persons against pecuniary or proprietary interest are admissible. An example is an entry by a creditor in his ledger that a debt owed to him has been paid.

The third category is statements as to public rights, thus the boundary of a borough, as distinct from the boundary of private land.

In criminal trials for homicide, where the dying man is in 'settled hopeless expectation of death' his words may be given in evidence by anyone who heard them. Thus A strikes B a mortal blow. B, knowing his last hour has come, tells C that A has murdered him. B then died. C may give evidence of B's last words at A's trial for murder.

Declarations as to pedigree and certain declarations by testators form the fifth and sixth categories of this exception to the rule.

An admission was an exception to the hearsay rule at Common Law, and this exception is retained by the Civil Evidence Act. Thus if A is sued by B for a debt and he admits to a third party that he owes the debt, the third party may give evidence of this to prove that A did owe the debt. But 'admissions' may not be manufactured to serve one's own advantage. If A had told a third party he did *not* owe the debt, such a statement would not be admissible to prove he did not owe the debt.

Confessions are of enormous importance in criminal cases and

[1] 1 Salk. 285.

frequently are the most damaging evidence against the accused. No confession is admissible, however, if it has been induced by threats or promises of favour emanating from some person in authority, such as a police officer interviewing the accused. A police officer formally charging a person should, before doing so, administer a caution in these terms:'Do you wish to say anything? You are not obliged to say anything unless you wish to do so, but whatever you say will be taken down in writing and may be given in evidence.'[1] This is the procedure laid down by the judges and included in the 'Judges' Rules'. If they have not been observed, a subsequent confession is still admissible[2] but is not adduced in evidence in practice.

Hearsay evidence is sometimes permitted[3] in affidavits.[4] Thus a witness may swear: 'I am informed by my solicitors and verily believe that . . .' This is an oath of information and belief, and the source of information must be set out.

In criminal cases an ordinary witness should depose only as to facts and should not give opinions.[5] There are exceptions to this rule; an ordinary witness may give opinion evidence as to the speed of a motor vehicle or as to the age of a person, for example, but his opinion will not be admissible on any specialised subject. Where technical matters, such as medicine, foreign[6] (not English) law or building practice arise in a case, a witness experienced in the particular topic may give his opinion in evidence. Such a witness is known as an expert witness. A doctor may be asked in divorce procedure, for example, whether certain treatment of a wife by her husband would result in injury to her health if continued.

Certain classes of evidence are privileged by the law from disclosure in court unless the witness, or party on whose behalf he is called, waives the privilege.

[1] Much recent discussions has been provided by the Law Reform Committee's recommendations on evidence in criminal trials.
[2] Unless, of course, it has been obtained by threats, etc.
[3] By the Rules of the Supreme Court.
[4] See below, page 186.
[5] But see the Civil Evidence Act, 1972, which relaxes some of the rules on opinion evidence in civil cases. The opinion of an ordinary witness concerning any relevant matter is admissible if made as a way of conveying relevant facts personally perceived by him.
[6] Foreign law (which includes Scots Law) is treated as fact.

It is for the judge to decide whether evidence falls in one of the privileged classes. Perhaps the most important class of evidence which is privileged is that which relates to affairs of State. Even so, it was held in *Conway* v. *Rimmer*[1] that the Court may order production of documents, even when the Crown privilege is claimed, if the public interest, in the administration of justice, demands it.

Another privilege is designed to encourage the settlement of actions. Parties between whom there is a dispute have freedom to negotiate, because all *bona fide* efforts to agree on a settlement are privileged. Thus if negotiations break down, they will not prejudice the trial of the action. For this reason, all such letters, conversations, etc., are styled 'without prejudice'.

It is the privilege of a client who has consulted a lawyer about a legal problem to withhold what passed between them. Probation officers are nowadays frequently consulted in matrimonial matters and they may not disclose what any spouse has told them unless he or she consents.

No such privilege exists for communications, however confidential, between clergymen and their charges, or doctors or other professional men and their clients.

A party may swear an affidavit claiming privilege on the ground that documents in his possession relate solely to his own case and do not assist his opponent.

Communications between husband and wife during marriage are privileged in criminal cases. However, the privilege can only be claimed by the party *receiving* the communication. If a husband wrote to his wife confessing a crime and the letter was intercepted by the police, it could be produced in evidence against him.[2]

Questions as to the bad character of a witness may be put in cross-examination. Usually this is 'cross-examination as to credit' and the intention is to show that his character is such that the witness's evidence is not worthy of belief. Cross-examination as to character may relate, however, not merely to credit but directly to the matter in dispute. For instance, a man is charged with theft. The chief witness for the prosecution is a prostitute. Her character may be attacked by the defence to show that any evidence she has given is unreliable. In another case, a man is charged with the rape of a prostitute. She gives evidence for the prosecution and the defence may reveal her bad character in evidence, not only for purposes of

[1] [1968] A.C. 91.　　　　[2] *Rumping* v. *D.P.P.*, [1964] A.C. 814.

credit but also to show such a woman was less likely to refuse consent to sexual intercourse.

In criminal cases, an accused has certain privileges. He may give evidence of his own good character, but the prosecution may not lead evidence or cross-examine an accused to show that he is of bad character or has committed or been convicted of any offence other than that with which he is charged.[1] If an accused is so unwise as to give evidence of his 'good' character when it is in fact bad, the prosecution may rebut his evidence by evidence in chief or cross-examination.[2] Similarly, the prosecution may cross-examine the accused as to his own bad character if the defence has attacked the character of a witness for the prosecution in evidence in chief or by cross-examination. This does not stop the defence from being vigorous and vehement. A suggestion by the defence that a police officer had concocted a confession was held an attack on the officer's character in R. v. *Clark*.[3]

Evidence of bad character is usually by proof of previous convictions. In no case may evidence be adduced by the prosecution, merely that the accused has been tried previously for a similar offence and acquitted.[4]

Evidence of the accused's character, including his previous convictions, is always given by the detective in charge of the case, *after* a conviction, to assist the judge in deciding the appropriate treatment of the offender.

Privilege should not be confused with competence and compellability. The law does not permit some persons to give evidence. Some persons are competent to be witnesses, but no one can compel them to give evidence if they do not wish to.

Normally, any person who can give evidence in a case may be summoned by a subpoena,[5] so called because if he does not appear he commits a contempt of court and is liable to punishment. The subpoena may be *'ad testificandum'* (to give oral evidence) or *'duces tecum'* (to bring a document).

Very young persons and persons of unsound mind are not competent witnesses. Young children are asked questions by the judge to ascertain whether they know what an oath is and whether they realise they must tell the truth. Young children who are capable of

---

[1] Subject to exceptions.   [2] See below.
[3] [1955] 2 Q.B. 469.   [4] *Maxwell* v. *D.P.P.*, [1935] A.C. 309.
[5] 'Under penalty.'

telling the truth and understand their duty to do so but do not understand the implications of an oath may, if the Court permits, give unsworn evidence in criminal cases. It must be corroborated.

In criminal trials the accused is not competent to give evidence for the prosecution. As a rule, neither is the spouse of the accused. There are exceptions to this, however. At Common Law a spouse is a competent *and* compellable witness in cases of personal violence,[1] and by statute spouses are made competent witnesses for various offences. The most important statutory exceptions are certain sexual offences, certain offences against children and offences by one spouse against the property of the other. In these instances, the spouse is a competent but not compellable witness. If, therefore, Mr. X is charged with theft from Mrs. X, she can give evidence for the prosecution. Such proceedings must be instituted by the Director of Public Prosecutions. If Mr. X is charged with child destruction, his wife is again competent but not compellable. If, however, Mr. X is charged with the attempted murder of his wife, she may be called as a witness whether she likes it or not.

A person accused jointly with another (or his spouse) may not give evidence for the prosecution while they are being tried together, as a rule.

Until the Criminal Evidence Act, 1898, an accused person or his spouse could not give evidence for the defence. The removal of this bar has proved more of disadvantage than otherwise to the guilty accused, as his story may be tested by cross-examination. Furthermore, although counsel for the prosecution may not comment on any failure to give evidence on the part of one who should know most about the case, the judge is at liberty to do so and such failure is very damaging in the eyes of the jury. An accused may make an unsworn statement from the dock, and this is not liable to cross-examination, as it is not, strictly speaking, evidence; this carries little weight, however.

The spouse of an accused is not compellable as a witness for the defence except in cases of personal violence.

Judges and jurymen cannot give evidence in a case before them.

In most cases, the evidence of a witness or document will by itself be sufficient to prove a fact, though corroboration will give the evidence more weight. Sometimes, however, evidence must be corroborated as a matter of law. Thus in cases of perjury, evidence

[1] Against him or her.

as to the falsity of the statement must be corroborated or there can be no conviction.

Sometimes corroboration is required as a matter of practice. For instance, in a criminal trial evidence of accomplices may be accepted even if uncorroborated, but the jury must first be warned that it is dangerous to accept such evidence.[1]

In nearly every case, a witness who gives oral evidence must first take an oath or affirm that he will give truthful evidence. The normal method by which a Christian witness makes oath is by taking the New Testament in his right hand and speaking the words: 'I swear by Almighty God that the evidence I shall give shall be the truth, the whole truth and nothing but the truth.' Jews take the oath on the Old Testament and with head covered. Adherents to other religions take the oath in different ways. Only Quakers and atheists may affirm—that is, promise to tell the truth without swearing by Almighty God.

In some circumstances, evidence is taken on oath and used on a later occasion. Thus some civil cases are tried on affidavit instead of by oral evidence. This procedure is found most frequently in the Chancery Division. An affidavit is a written statement of evidence sworn before a commissioner for oaths.

In the trial of indictable offences, the evidence at the preliminary hearing is given on oath, taken down in writing and read over and signed by the witness. The examining justice then signs the statement; it is known as a deposition. When the evidence is of formal character, the witness's presence may not be required, after committal, at the trial, and his deposition is then read by the Clerk. Witnesses whose evidence is likely to be contested, however, give oral evidence at the trial and may be cross-examined on discrepancies between their depositions and their oral evidence at the trial.

Provision for taking evidence out of Court for the trial of indictable offences is given by the Criminal Law Amendment Act, 1867. Where a witness is dangerously ill and unlikely to recover, a justice may take his evidence, which may be used in subsequent proceedings if the witness is dead or unlikely ever to be able to travel or give evidence. Notice must be given to the other side, who must have an opportunity of cross-examination. When the justice has signed the evidence it becomes a deposition.

A procedure which is widely used is a committal under s. 1 of the

[1] *Davies* v. *D.P.P.*, [1954] 1 All E.R. 507.

Criminal Justice Act, 1967. When a magistrates' court is inquiring into an offence with a view to committal, if they are satisfied that all the evidence consists of written statements, they may commit without considering the evidence themselves. In these circumstances, the defendant must be represented and must admit that there is a *prima facie* case to answer and not wish to challenge any of the prosecution's evidence at that stage. Committal proceedings may not be reported in the Press unless the accused requires it.

The normal method of taking evidence in English Courts is by the oral testimony in open Court of witnesses, who are liable to cross-examination. This unquestionably affords the best way of testing the accuracy of their evidence. Their demeanour in Court is of great assistance to the Court in weighing their testimony.

After the witness has taken the oath or affirmed, he will be examined by the counsel[1] appearing for the side which has called him as a witness. This is called examination in chief. The object of counsel is to extract his witness's evidence in the shortest, simplest and most telling way. Counsel may not put evidence into his own witness's mouth by asking leading questions. A leading question is one which suggests its own answer; for instance, 'You were in Blank Street that evening were you not?' The proper form is 'Where were you that evening?'

To this rule there are exceptions. Counsel may lead his witness in introductory matters, such as name and address, and on matters over which there is no dispute, provided that the other side consents. Counsel may refresh his witness's memory on matters of which he has given evidence before. If a witness proves hostile, the Court may give his counsel leave to cross-examine him and ask leading questions. It must first be shown, however, that the witness has made a previous inconsistent statement. For example, a witness for the prosecution has deposed in the Magistrates' Court that the prisoner wounded X. The case is committed for trial at the Crown Court. Counsel for the prosecution there calls the witness, who gives evidence that he has never seen the prisoner or X. Counsel for the prosecution then produces the deposition (the previous inconsistent statement) and must specify the occasion on which it was made, asking the witness if he made it. The judge may then give

[1] Unless he appears by solicitor (in the lower Courts) or in person. In Magistrates' Courts the clerk examines the witnesses of parties who are not represented.

leave for the witness to be treated as hostile and cross-examined.

Cross-examination is directed to destroying the effect of an opponent's witness. It may be either as to the substance of his evidence or as to credit.[1] Leading questions are permitted. The cross-examination is not confined to the matters raised in examination in chief, though, of course, it must be relevant. Cross-examination is a great art, and a good cross-examiner is profoundly fascinating to listen to. Cross-examination, it has been said, does not mean examining crossly. Counsel who is bullying or abusive will not only be rebuked by the judge but will also lose the sympathy of the Court or jury. *Suaviter in modo fortiter in re*[2] is the best principle for the cross-examiner to adopt.

When counsel for the other side has finished questioning a witness, it is open to the witness's counsel to re-examine him. Again, he must not ask leading questions, and the scope of the questions is restricted to the matters raised in examination in chief and cross-examination. The purpose of re-examination is to clear up (if possible) points raised in cross-examination. It may be that no re-examination is needed.

At all stages of the trial, the judge may ask questions of the witnesses. He must not do so too frequently, however, or he will be said to have 'descended into the arena and become blinded by the dust of the conflict', in which case a new trial may be necessary.

In passing, it may be noted that in a civil case the judge has no power to call witnesses. In a criminal trial, however, where the interests of the community are more directly affected, he has.

Documents may be of many kinds; thus: letters, photographs, legal documents such as wills and agreements, accounts, invoices, etc. Private documents must usually be proved. For example, a witness producing a signed letter he wrote must give evidence that it is his letter and signature. If the document is 'ancient'—that is, at least twenty years old—it need not be proved, however, provided that it comes from proper custody. 'Proper custody' is custody in which the document, if genuine, would reasonably be expected to be found. Usually, public documents do not have to be proved in this way. They are said to 'prove themselves' by mere production.

Whenever possible, original documents must be produced. Sometimes, however, contents of documents may be proved by 'secondary evidence'—that is, by a copy of the original or by oral evidence.

[1] See page 183 above.   [2] 'Courteous but firm', very roughly.

Thus public documents are usually provable by copies. To prevent the dislocation of banking by the removal of books of accounts, entries in bankers' books are provable by copies (subject to conditions) in most cases.[1] Secondary evidence is admissible where the original has been destroyed or would be highly inconvenient to adduce; for example, writing on a wall.

If a party to an action wishes to put in evidence a document in the possession of the other side, he should give his opponent a 'notice to produce' it. If his opponent fails to produce the document at the trial, he may give secondary evidence of its contents.

In civil proceedings only, certain documents will not be admissible unless properly stamped;[2] thus a deed bears duty of 50p and must be impressed with a 50p stamp.

Where the terms of a transaction have been formally set down in a document, either because the law requires it or because the parties have agreed that it should be so, no evidence outside the document itself[3] can be adduced to vary or contradict the contents of the document. This rule, which does not apply to public documents, is subject to exceptions. Thus an oral agreement, made at the same time as the one reduced to writing and not inconsistent with it may be proved. For example, a document is produced showing that A agreed to hire B as an employee, the notice to terminate the hiring being a week. Neither party can vary this by stating an oral agreement was made at the same time that notice should be one month. On the other hand, collateral terms of the agreement not included in the written document may be proved by either party, if not inconsistent with it; for example, that B would not solicit A's customers on leaving his employment.

Extrinsic evidence may be adduced to show a transaction is not what it seems, e.g. what purports to be an outright sale is a mortgage or that a transaction is fraudulent.

If the parties desire, they may later, by agreement, vary orally an agreement in writing, provided that it is not one *required by law* to be in writing. In such a case, the parties may orally end the agreement completely but may not orally vary it.[4] A deed may be discharged by writing or orally but can be varied only by another deed.

[1] Bankers' Books Evidence Act, 1879.
[2] Stamp Act, 1891.
[3] Known as extrinsic evidence.
[4] *Morris* v. *Baron*, [1918] A.C. 1.

At the beginning of the chapter it was remarked that the burden of proof may be affected by means of proof other than evidence pure and simple. These are presumptions, judicial notice and estoppels.

The only presumptions relevant to the law of evidence, in the author's opinion, are rebuttable presumptions of law. These exist to prove facts for which proof would otherwise be very difficult or impossible or inconvenient. Actual evidence to the contrary will rebut them. An example occurs in the Matrimonial Causes Act, 1965, s. 15. If Mrs. X is petitioning for divorce on the ground of her husband's presumed death, the fact that Mr. X has been continually absent from her for a period of seven years, and she has no reason to believe that he has been living within that time, will be evidence of his death, *until the contrary is proved*. Thus the presumption of death would be dramatically and perhaps inconveniently rebutted were Mr. X to walk into Court during the hearing. Many other rebuttable presumptions exist, a prominent example being the presumption of innocence.[1]

The Court will take judicial notice of certain matters—that is to say, they need not be proved by evidence. Public statutes and the unwritten law are judicially noticed, for example. Usually, facts judicially noticed are those so commonly known that formal proof of them would be a waste of time—for instance, the number of days in a month. When a judge asks 'Who is X?', naming a well-known person of the day, he is not displaying a lamentable ignorance but merely indicating he cannot take judicial notice of their existence or occupation and that it must be proved by evidence.

In civil cases, the parties may dispense with the proof of certain facts by formally admitting them.[2] In criminal cases, the only formal admission permitted is the plea of guilty.

Before leaving the law of evidence, the doctrine of estoppel must be mentioned. Estoppel arises when a party is not permitted to deny a certain fact or facts, whether or not they are true. It arises in three cases. The first is estoppel by record. Where a fact has been determined by a court of law, the Court's findings may, *in appropriate*

---

[1] A student once gave this as an example of an *irrebuttable* presumption. Our large prison population would be the first to disagree.

[2] Formal admissions are made for the purposes of the trial and must not be confused with the informal admissions adduced as part of the evidence. See above.

circumstances, be binding on the parties to a later action in which the same fact is in dispute. The second is estoppel by deed. Parties who assert material facts in a deed, the most solemn of documents, may not afterwards deny them. The third is estoppel by conduct.

If a person, either expressly or by his conduct, represents to another the existence of a certain state of facts which he apparently intends to be acted upon in a certain way and it be acted upon in that way in the belief of the existence of such a state of facts, to the prejudice of him who so believes and acts, the first person is estopped from denying the existence of such a state of facts in a subsequent action between them. Thus P was the owner of goods in possession of M. The goods were seized by a creditor of M. P knew of the seizure and that the creditor intended to sell the goods, yet he stood by and did not assert his title. It was held that P's own conduct estopped him from asserting his ownership of the goods against the creditor later.[1] Estoppel by conduct may arise from a particular relationship; thus a landlord who has granted a lease of land to a tenant is estopped from denying his own title to the land.

The practising lawyer must not only know the substantive law and the law of evidence, he must also be intimately familiar with the machinery of the Courts—the law of procedure. The Supreme Court Practice (known as the 'White Book') is over 3000 pages long, so it will be realised how vast is the law of procedure and practice. Let us, therefore, take a specimen case in the Queen's Bench Division of the High Court, from cradle to grave, and observe not only the procedure at the trial itself but also the ground work that precedes it and its consequences.

The story starts when Mr. A, while driving his motor car in London, knocks down and severely injures Miss B. She is consequently away from work for many weeks and has to spend a long period in hospital. She claims that Mr. A came round the corner at speed when the lights were against him, while he says that the lights were still in his favour and Miss B rushed into his path without looking to see if anything was coming.

Miss B consults her solicitor, and after a short sharp correspondence between her solicitor and Mr. A's she decides to sue Mr. A for negligence.

The first step in the litigation is the issue and service of a writ. Service must be effected on the defendant personally, unless his

[1] *Pickard* v. *Sears* (1837), 6 Ad. & E. 469.

solicitors accept service on his behalf, which is usually the case.[1] The writ is an alarming document calling on the defendant in the name of the Queen to enter an appearance within fourteen days[2] or judgment will be given against him. It is 'generally indorsed'—that is, it contains a brief statement of the nature of the plaintiff's case.

The defendant enters an appearance and the next step is for the plaintiff to deliver a Statement of Claim. This is a document drafted and signed by Miss B's counsel. It sets out the facts which the plaintiff intends to prove in order to establish her claim. It concludes with a prayer for damages. Two kinds of damages are claimed. There are the items of special damages, such as the cost of her damaged clothing, her loss of wages while in hospital, etc., and the general damages for pain and suffering, etc. The general damages are unliquidated, at large, for the judge to decide. No amount is specified.

If there had been criminal proceedings against Mr. A arising from the accident, and he had been found guilty of careless or dangerous driving, Miss B could rely upon this finding as evidence to support her case. The burden of proof would then be on Mr. A to disprove want of care, for the finding of the criminal court would be *prima facie* evidence of it. Miss B would state in her Statement of Claim that she intended to rely on the conviction as evidence.[3]

Shortly afterwards, the defendant delivers a Defence. This deals with the allegations in the Statement of Claim. Every fact alleged in the Statement of Claim not specifically denied in the Defence is presumed to be admitted. In this case, all the facts alleged are denied.

Such a denial is known as a traverse. In passing, it may be noted that a traverse is not the only way of dealing with the allegations in a Statement of Claim. The defendant may 'confess and avoid' the plaintiff's allegations. By this he admits the plaintiff's statement of the facts but alleges other circumstances destroying his cause of action. For example, in an action for assault the defendant might confess the assault but plead self-defence to avoid the legal consequences of his conduct. It might have been that no cause of action was disclosed in the Statement of Claim. In such a case the defendant could 'object in point of law'.

---

[1] If the defendant cannot be found, the Court may order 'substituted service'.

[2] In all cases the various time limits specified in the rules of the Supreme Court may be extended by the Court or by agreement of the parties.

[3] Civil Evidence Act, 1969, s. 11.

Sometimes a case may call for an answer to the Defence; this is known as a Reply.[1] This is not such a case. If there is no Reply, all the statements of fact in the Defence are taken to be denied by the plaintiff.

If either party is unsure of the case his opponent is to present at the trial, he may ask him for further and better particulars of his pleadings hitherto delivered. The object of particulars is to narrow the issues to be tried so as to save expense and prevent parties from being taken by surprise at the trial. For instance, had Mr. A's counsel alleged contributory negligence on the part of Miss B without giving sufficient particulars, she would be entitled to particulars to enable her to meet the allegation at the trial. If a party refuses to give particulars, his opponent may take out a summons.[2] The parties then appear before an official of the Supreme Court, known as a Master,[3] who determines whether the particulars are proper to be given. For example, the particulars desired may be of an immaterial averment and will not be ordered.

In our case, the pleadings consist of Statement of Claim and Defence, as there have been no particulars. These set out concisely the issues between the parties. As a party is usually not allowed to prove at the trial what is not in his pleadings, they must be drafted with great care. Pleading is a great art, as nothing essential must be omitted and it is undesirable that anything superfluous should be included.

Where it will assist a fair trial or save costs, the Master may order discovery of documents. The party or parties against whom the order is made must disclose material documents[4] in their possession, so that their opponents may inspect and take copies of the documents if necessary. Usually, discovery is made automatically without the necessity for an order.

Another type of discovery is obtained by interrogatories. Interrogatories are questions prepared by a party with a view to maintaining his own case or attacking that of his opponent. The master will

---

[1] Even further pleadings are possible if the Court orders.

[2] All the proceedings before a case is actually tried in Court are known as interlocutory proceedings.

[3] The Rules of the Supreme Court provide for certain matters being heard by 'the Court'. Usually this means a Master (in the Q.B.D.), and appeal usually lies from him to a Judge in Chambers.

[4] Unless they are privileged.

decide whether they are to be allowed, and those he allows must be answered on oath by the opponent. Interrogatories must be relevant and must not be 'fishing'. A 'fishing' interrogatory is one which is not directed to the present dispute but seeks to uncover a fresh cause of action. Privilege, as with evidence in open Court and discovery of documents, is a ground for refusing to answer an interrogatory.

To return to our own example. Fourteen days after delivery of Defence, the pleadings are 'closed'. No more may be delivered; the plaintiff must then take out a 'summons for directions'. The parties[1] appear before the Master, who gives the directions necessary for the trial of the action. For instance, the mode of trial is decided. Our case is not tried by a jury, as it is not one of the types of action in which the parties are entitled as of right to a jury.[2] Such matters as discovery will be dealt with on the summons for directions.

The plaintiff's solicitor sets down the action for trial, and in due course it comes up for trial at the Royal Courts of Justice.

The trial proceeds as follows. Counsel for the plaintiff opens the case, setting out the facts briefly for the benefit of the judge. If this had been a jury trial, the jury would have first been sworn by the associate. The associate is an official of the Court and sits, robed, at a table beneath the judge. His duties are administrative, and, though he must have knowledge of procedure, he is not usually a lawyer.

Counsel for the plaintiff, after opening, calls his witnesses, who are sworn by the associate before they give evidence. Our first witness is the plaintiff. She gives all the evidence necessary to prove the allegations in her Statement of Claim. This includes how she waited until the lights were in her favour and then crossed the road. As she did so, Mr. A came round the corner against the lights and knocked her down. After her examination comes the cross-examination by the defendant's counsel and any re-examination necessary. The judge will probably ask questions.

The plaintiff then calls a second witness, Mr. C, another driver. He gives evidence that as he came up to the traffic lights they were at amber and he stopped as they turned red. As he did so, Mr. A overtook him at great speed in his Jaguar and turned right, hitting the plaintiff who was crossing the side road. Mr. C is cross-examined

---

[1] By solicitors' clerks as a rule. If a difficult point is involved, counsel are employed.

[2] See Chapter 10, page 198.

and re-examined. The plaintiff puts in a medical report prepared for the trial to show the result of her injuries. If it was challenged by the other side, the doctor who made it would be called to give evidence.

Counsel for the defendant opens the case for the defendant briefly, then calls his witnesses, who give their account of the facts in dispute and are cross-examined and re-examined if necessary. Counsel for the defendant then makes his final speech to the Court, presenting his case as favourably as possible to them on the evidence that has been given. The 'last word' is had by the plaintiff's counsel, who similarly addresses the Court. Had the defendant called no evidence, the defendant's counsel would have been entitled to the last speech. The judge then gives judgment stating his reasons. If this had been a trial with a jury, the judge would have summed up to the jury explaining the law and reviewing the evidence. Whenever a judge sits with a jury, all questions of law are for the judge to decide; all questions of fact, with exceptions, must be decided by the jury. These exceptions are questions of fact relating to admissibility of evidence—for example, whether threats were made which induced a confession—questions of foreign law and certain questions as to reasonableness.

When a submission as to admissibility of evidence is made, the jury retire, while the judge hears argument, lest their minds be prejudiced by evidence which may be ruled inadmissible.

In our case the judge finds for the plaintiff and awards damages[1] of £2000. If the judge found that Miss B had contributed to the accident by her own negligence, he would proportionally reduce the award to take this into account.

The judge then decides who shall bear the costs of the action. He has a discretion which he must use judicially. This means that normally the unsuccessful party will bear the costs of his successful opponent as well as his own. Misconduct by a successful party may deprive him of costs.[2] If the judge makes no order as to costs, each party must bear his own.

A party may not saddle his opponent with excessive costs. A party will only have to pay his opponent's 'taxed' costs. The bill of costs is 'taxed' before an official of the Court known as a Taxing

[1] See Chapter 3, page 63.
[2] A successful *defendant* may never be made to bear the whole of the *plaintiff's* costs.

Master, who disallows unnecessary expenditure. What remain are 'taxed costs'.

In our example, the unsuccessful defendant might appeal against the verdict and judgment to the Court of Appeal. Appeal is possible on questions of law or fact, or both, without leave. The Court of Appeal is reluctant to disturb findings of fact, as the Court below had the advantage of observing the demeanour of the witnesses and assessing the weight of their evidence at first hand, whereas the Court of Appeal has only a transcript of the evidence taken by the shorthand-writer. The verdict of a jury is even more difficult to upset than a finding of fact by a judge sitting alone.

The Court of Appeal may allow the appeal, reversing the decision of the Court below, allow the appeal and order a new trial, or dismiss the appeal.

Appeal from a decision of the Court of Appeal lies to the House of Lords, provided that the House or the Court of Appeal gives leave. Such an appeal is a very expensive matter and is thus undertaken by few litigants.

If, in our example, the defendant did not pay the £2000 damages and the plaintiff's taxed costs, the plaintiff would have to take steps to enforce the judgment. This can be done in five ways.

The first is execution. The sheriff is commanded by writ to take various steps to enforce the judgment. The best-known writ is that of *fi. fa.*,[1] which orders the sheriff to seize the defendant's chattels and sell them, applying the proceeds to discharge the judgment debt.

The second is the judgment summons. The judgment debtor is summoned before the Court (Chancery Division or County Court)[2] and examined on oath as to his means. Usually he is permitted to pay by instalments if he cannot pay the whole debt at once. If he can pay and refuses to do so, he is imprisoned for a period of up to six weeks. He may obtain his release by paying the debt. Perpetual imprisonment for debt was abolished by the Debtors Act, 1869.

The third method is to threaten to make the judgment debtor bankrupt.

The fourth is an attachment of earnings order, which requires the judgment debtors' employer to deduct part of his wages to pay the

---

[1] *Fieri-facias* (cause to be made).
[2] In appropriate cases judgment summonses may be heard in the Family Division and Divorce County Court.

debt. Lastly, a garnishee order may be made. This means that a debt owing to the judgment debtor is ordered to be paid to the judgment creditor instead.

The foregoing is just a brief outline of a specimen procedure in one Division of the High Court. Many different procedures exist, notably the Order XIV procedure, a summary way of collecting debts when no real defence exists. It has been said that the Supreme Court procedure is cumbrous and far too expensive. A Committee under the chairmanship of Lord Evershed, M.R., reported on the problem in 1953 and a result was an extensive rewriting of the Rules, but the complexity of modern civilisation means that Court procedure must be involved. Unfortunately, the inevitable conclusion seems to be that some sacrifice of the machinery, evolved in theory for the litigant's benefit, must be made if he is to be able to afford to litigate at all.

10 Juries, Judges, the Legal Profession, Legal Aid

In the first chapter, an outline was sketched of the history of the jury. Now is the time to examine the institution of jury trial as it stands today. No better words can be found to preface the topic than those of the great legal writer, Blackstone, writing in the eighteenth century:

'And this is a species of knowledge most absolutely necessary for every gentleman in the kingdom: as well because he may be frequently called upon to determine in this capacity the rights of others, his fellow-subjects; as because his own property, his liberty, and his life, depend upon maintaining, in its legal force, the constitutional trial by jury.'[1]

There are many types of jury, the main division being into juries of presentment and juries of assessment. Juries of presentment enquire into a matter laid before them and present a finding. Grand juries, now abolished, stood in this category; a modern example is the coroner's jury.[2] The jury of assessment tries an issue in dispute between parties. The only types necessary to consider here are the criminal and civil juries in ordinary trials.

Every criminal case tried on indictment at the Crown Court is tried by a jury. Civil juries are less common than they were; in Blackstone's time, all cases heard in the Common Law Courts were tried by jury. Nowadays, in the Queen's Bench Division, it rests with the Court[3] whether the parties shall have a jury. There is a right to a jury if the case is one of libel, slander, false imprisonment or malicious prosecution, or if a charge of fraud has been made against the party applying, unless the Court is of opinion that the trial requires a prolonged examination of documents or accounts, or any scientific or local investigation which cannot conveniently be made with a jury.[4] Juries are not used in the Chancery Division. Certain probate and divorce suits have been tried by jury, though rarely. In

---

[1] *Commentaries*, III, page 350.   [2] See below.
[3] See Chapter 9, page 194.
[4] Administration of Justice (Miscellaneous Provisions) Act, 1933, s. 6(1).

Admiralty actions there are no juries; occasionally the judge sits with nautical assessors, who are Elder Brethren of Trinity House and who are merely advisers on matters of nautical skill, not judges of fact. For some matters, a jury may be obtained in the County Court, but this is very rare.

All persons, men and women, from twenty-one to sixty, of a certain property qualification,[1] may be placed on the register unless they claim exemption or are disqualified.[2] Once they are on the register, they are liable to serve[3] unless excused by the Court. Disobedience to summons to serve on a jury, which must give six days' notice at least, is punishable by fine.

There is a long list of those entitled to exemption from jury service. Peers, Members of Parliament, judges, clergymen are a few examples. Aliens and persons convicted of certain offences are disqualified. Women have been liable for jury service since the Sex Disqualification (Removal) Act, 1919. Most juries now contain two or three women. It is no longer possible to apply for a jury of men or women only.

The jury are selected by ballot in open Court, and they take their places in the jury-box. They may be challenged, i.e. a party may object to the whole panel or individually and have them replaced. This last type of challenge may be peremptory (no cause need be stated) or for cause. Only persons indicted may challenge without cause, and the number of such challenges is limited to seven. Any number of challenges for cause may be made. The grounds are that a juror is a peer, or not qualified or biased, or has been convicted of a crime rendering him infamous and affecting his credit.

The jury are then sworn, well and truly to try the case, and a true verdict given according to the evidence.

In ordinary civil and criminal juries, the number of jurors is twelve. In criminal trials, if up to three die or become ill and are discharged, the trial proceeds unless the number is below nine. However, the judge has a discretion to discharge the whole jury if he sees fit to do so. In the case of a trial for murder or an offence punishable by death, the trial cannot continue with less than twelve unless the accused and prosecution consent in writing.

[1] See coroners below.
[2] Reform of the jury system is imminent. The property qualification will be replaced by an electoral qualification in 1974.
[3] Except nuns or unless ill.

Before the judge's summing-up has concluded, the jury may separate but should not speak of matters connected with the trial to anyone not a member of the jury. Such conduct may result in a new trial and the offending juror's punishment for contempt of court.

After the summing-up, the jurors must consider the verdict on the evidence. A juror who has personal knowledge of the case should not act as a juror but should give evidence from the witness-box. The jury may consider the case in Court or may retire to the jury-room under the care of the bailiff, who swears not to let the jury communicate with other persons. When the jury are considering their verdict, they may not separate in criminal cases. A separation after summing-up and before verdict in a civil case will not necessarily invalidate the verdict.

Juries, in fact, are extremely conscientious and spend hours discussing a verdict. Cases of misconduct are rare, but in *Lord Fitzwater's Case*[1] a new trial was ordered where the jury had arrived at a verdict by throwing dice. If the jury cannot come to a decision in a criminal trial, after having been deliberating for not less than two hours or such longer time as the Court feels that the complexity of the case warrants, they may bring in a majority verdict. If there are not less than eleven jurors, ten must agree, and when there are ten, nine of them must agree. If the verdict is 'guilty' the foreman of the jury must declare in open court the number who agree and disagree. Majority verdicts extend also to civil cases, but the two-hour mandatory deliberation is not required of a civil jury. In criminal cases, it is customary, if the jury cannot come to a decision, for the prosecution to offer no evidence at the third trial, the jury returning a formal verdict of 'not guilty'.

The verdict should be given to the judge in open court. In criminal cases, the verdict will be 'not guilty', 'guilty' or 'not guilty by reason of insanity'. The jury may add a recommendation to mercy. In civil cases, the finding may be either general—i.e. for plaintiff or defendant; or special—i.e. a finding of certain facts on which the judge can enter judgment. For instance, in an action for malicious prosecution, the jury could either find for the plaintiff or find that the defendant prosecuted the plaintiff, that the plaintiff was acquitted of the charge, that the defendant acted maliciously and without reasonable or probable cause. Where the jury find for the plaintiff, they will fix the amount of damages.

[1] Freem. K.B. 414.

What is discussed in the jury-room is secret and ought not to be disclosed.

After the verdict has been delivered, the jury, if they are not to try another case, are discharged. It is customary for the judge to exempt a jury which has tried a long case from further service for several years.

Since the Juries Act, 1949, jurors are entitled to travelling and subsistence allowances, and compensation for loss of earnings. Before this Act, special jurors were entitled to a guinea a case, common jurors sometimes to as much as the princely sum of one shilling a case.

In certain cases—for instance, where it is suspected that a deceased person has been murdered—the coroner must hold an inquest with a jury to enquire into the circumstances of death. To serve on a coroner's jury no property qualification is necessary and there are no age limits; there is no right of challenge. The numbers are from seven[1] to eleven, and the verdict may be by majority, provided that the minority is not more than two.

The verdict specifies the nature of death—e.g. suicide while the balance of the mind was disturbed—but must not be framed in such a way as to appear to determine any question of civil liability. The jury may add a rider (a recommendation or observation) to the verdict, but the coroner must not record it, unless in his opinion it is designed to prevent the recurrence of fatalities similar to that in respect of which the inquest is being held.[2]

As we began the study of juries with Blackstone, we may conclude with another quotation from his *Commentaries*: 'Upon these accounts the trial by jury ever has been, and I trust ever will be, looked upon as the glory of the English law.'[3]

This country has reason to be well-satisfied with its juries and to be proud of its judges, too. Nowhere in the world are the judges regarded with such great respect as in Great Britain. This is for several reasons. First, judges of the superior courts are not dismissible at the pleasure of the Executive but only by the Crown on an address presented by both Houses of Parliament. No English judge has ever thus been dismissed.

Secondly, judicial salaries are very much higher in this country

---

[1] Save for inquests on treasure trove.
[2] Coroners' Rules, 1953.
[3] *Commentaries*, III, page 379.

than on the Continent. A good salary is the best safeguard against corruption.

Thirdly, the judges are recruited from the Bar. In France, the judges spend the whole of their career in the judicial service, working their way up like other Civil Servants.[1] They do not have practical experience as advocates. There is the temptation to secure promotion by partiality to the State. In this country, however, judges rarely pass from the County Court to the High Court. The system of recruiting judges from practising barristers of good standing ensures a certain competence and makes for a practical approach. The judge has dealt in his time with just the same problems, legal and factual, as counsel appearing before him. The Bench and Bar meet in their Inns of Court, and a close relationship is enabled to be formed. With this similarity of outlook and training, the judge and counsel can get to grips with a case with a sureness and speed surprising to persons accustomed to other legal systems.

Judges in this country are appointed by the Crown. In some of the United States they are elected, an undignified procedure lending itself to corruption.

Let us now examine the judicial pyramid. At its apex is the Lord High Chancellor of Great Britain. He is, or should be, a lawyer of the highest eminence, and his office is the one most coveted by the ambitious at the Bar. We have seen in Chapter 2 how he presides over the House of Lords, in both its legislative and judicial capacities. He is the head of the Court of Appeal and the Chancery Division, though nowadays, he sits in these Courts only for a few moments, to open the sittings at the beginning of the legal year.

The puisne[2] judges of the High Court are appointed by the Crown on the Lord Chancellor's recommendation, and he advises the Prime Minister, who recommends the appointment of the other superior court judges. He appoints and can dismiss inferior judicial officers.

The Lord Chancellor must be a member of the Church of England. For this reason, neither Lord Russell of Killowen (a Roman Catholic) nor Lord Reading (a Jew) was appointed to the office. They were both appointed Lord Chief Justice.

---

[1] In this country, judges, though employed by the Crown, are not Civil Servants.

[2] Pronounced 'puny'. They are judges of the High Court other than heads of the Divisions.

The Lord Chancellor is invariably a peer, and receives a salary of £20 000.

The next most important judge is the Lord Chief Justice of England, who receives a salary of £18 500, and is nowadays always a peer. Unlike the Lord Chancellor, his functions are purely judicial, though he contributes to debates in the House of Lords on legal topics. He is the head of the Queen's Bench Division. In addition, he is an *ex-officio* member of the Court of Appeal.

The office, though of great dignity and importance, is descended from one of even greater consequence, that of Justiciar. The Justiciar, in Norman times, was not only a judge but virtually Prime Minister and Commander-in-Chief as well.

The Lords of Appeal in Ordinary are the usual members of the House of Lords when sitting as a court. There are ten of them, each receiving £17 250 per annum.

The Lords of Appeal are life peers but do not take part in the deliberations of the Lords as a legislative body, save when there is a legal topic under discussion. Scots and Northern Ireland Law Lords are appointed, as well as English.

Next comes the Master of the Rolls. His office was formerly of much less importance, being a subordinate one in the Court of Chancery. The Master of the Rolls sits in the Court of Appeal. In addition, he has certain powers relating to solicitors and articled clerks. His salary is £17 250.

The President of the Family Division is an *ex-officio* member of the Court of Appeal and receives a salary of £17 250.

The Lords Justices of Appeal sit in the Court of Appeal. Their salary is £15 750.

The puisne judges are appointed from barristers of at least ten years' standing. Each is appointed to one of the three Divisions, but transfers sometimes take place. Their salary is £15 750. At the time of writing, there are forty-five Queen's Bench, ten Chancery and sixteen Family Division judges.

All judges of the Supreme Court are knighted on appointment. All superior judges except puisne judges of the High Court are made Privy Counsellors. Puisne judges are styled thus: The Honourable Mr. Justice ——.

To turn to the courts below the Supreme Court. Mention has already been made of recorders and magistrates.[2] Circuit judges are

---

[1] Puisnes.   [2] See Chapter 8, page 173.

recruited from barristers of at least ten years' standing[1] and are paid £9750 per annum. A Circuit judge is styled: His Honour Judge—— and can sit in both the Crown Court and the County Courts.

Mention should be made of the robes of the superior judges, which add such dignity and impressiveness to the sittings of the highest tribunals.[2] At the opening of the Law Courts at the beginning of the Michaelmas sittings every year, the procession of judges presents a magnificent spectacle. The Lord Chancellor, preceded by his mace and the purse of the Great Seal, heads the procession. He wears a robe of black and gold. The Lord Chief Justice follows, wearing robes of scarlet trimmed with ermine. Round his neck is the symbol of his office, a gold chain. The Master of the Rolls, President and Lords Justices all wear black and gold robes. The puisne judges of all Divisions wear scarlet robes trimmed with ermine. All the judges wear full-bottomed wigs.

On ordinary working days, the judges present a less colourful spectacle. They all wear simple black gowns, except for the Lord Chief Justice and his puisnes of the Queen's Bench Division. For civil cases, these wear purple robes with a red sash. For criminal cases, they wear red robes. The scarlet and ermine robes are worn (by Queen's Bench Division judges only) on red-letter days, such as certain Saints' days. Be it noted, too, that full-bottomed wigs are worn by judges[3] only on ceremonial occasions. The normal headdress of a judge is a short wig, somewhat similar to a barrister's.

In England the leader of the Bar is the Attorney-General. He is invariably a Queen's Counsel of eminence and a Member of Parliament. He is the Government's chief legal adviser. He appears for the Crown in important civil and criminal trials. He is, of course, an important member of the Government and is often a well-known political figure. His sanction is necessary for various legal proceedings. His salary is £14 500.

His deputy is the Solicitor-General, who earns £10 000. Together they are the Law Officers of the Crown. Neither may now practise privately at the Bar while holding office. After ceasing to hold office, in due course they usually are appointed to high judicial office.

[1] Or a recorder of five years' standing. A solicitor can be appointed a recorder and thus become a judge.

[2] Oddly enough, the members of the House of Lords sitting as a court wear no robes.

[3] Except the Lord Chancellor.

In England, unlike the United States for example, the legal profession is divided into two: barristers and solicitors. There has lately been much discussion as to this dichotomy. Many say it increases costs, and would welcome fusion. This is not borne out by American experience. Fusion would mean a risk that judges would be appointed from men who had no experience of presenting a case in Court; this has happened in some Dominions with unhappy results. On the whole, both branches of the profession in this country prefer to remain distinct.

Barristers have the exclusive right of audience in the superior courts. Judges are recruited from their ranks.

All barristers belong to an Inn of Court. The four Inns are: Inner Temple, Middle Temple, Lincoln's Inn and Gray's Inn. These are autonomous bodies dating from the fourteenth century, under the control of Masters of the Bench, usually called Benchers. These are senior members of the Inn. Vacancies among them are filled by co-option of barristers of the Inn by the Benchers themselves. The Benchers of the Inn have complete and exclusive power to call or refuse to call, suspend or disbar any member of the Inn, without interference, save only that an aggrieved member of the Inn may appeal to the judges.[1]

The General Council of the Bar is the professional association charged with safeguarding the interests of barristers. It issues directions regarding professional etiquette but has no disciplinary powers; it can only refer an offender to his Benchers.

Professional etiquette at the Bar is extensive and complicated. The most important rules are these:

A barrister may not advertise. He may not accept instructions from a lay client direct but only through a solicitor.[2] He may not practise at the Bar and at the same time engage in any other profession or in business (with a few exceptions). A barrister is bound to accept a brief at a proper fee in a court in which he holds himself out as willing to practise. However much he may dislike a prospective client, he cannot, in the above circumstances, turn him away. This is a valuable safeguard of public liberties. It is sometimes misunderstood. A barrister is sometimes asked how he can defend a man

---

[1] The actual conduct of disciplinary proceedings is delegated to the Senate of the Four Inns of Court. This is a body formed to act on behalf of all the Inns in matters where a common policy is required.

[2] Except for certain cases.

accused of a crime whom he knows 'to be guilty'. To start with, it is
hardly ever possible for counsel to 'know a man to be guilty'. If the
accused confesses his guilt, his counsel should, if the accused insists
on a plea of 'not guilty', withdraw from the case. Otherwise, a man
is presumed to be innocent until he is proved guilty. Counsel may
have his private suspicions of his client's guilt, but the accused is
entitled to a hearing. Any other rule would result in the substitution
for trial by judge and jury by trial by counsel.

Barristers have certain privileges. They may give unsworn evidence regarding cases in which they have appeared. Only law
reports by a barrister may be cited in Court. A barrister may not be
sued for negligence in his professional capacity in litigation.

Barristers are of two kinds: Queen's Counsel and juniors. A
barrister is a junior, no matter how long he may have been called,
until he becomes of Queen's Counsel. If a barrister is of sufficient
eminence, he may apply to the Lord Chancellor for silk.[1] If this is
granted, he is entitled to put the letters Q.C. after his name. After
this, he may only appear in Court with a junior, who receives a fee
appropriate to his own standing. 'Silks' occupy the front row of
counsel's seats. No matter that no 'silks' are in Court and the
junior's seats are full, no junior may sit in the front row. Taking silk
is a hazardous step, as a man who was very successful as a junior
may not do so well as a 'silk'. The scope of the work is less; for
example, Queen's Counsel are not allowed to settle pleadings, and
the qualities demanded are in some ways different.

Queen Elizabeth I appointed the first Queen's Counsel. In her day
they had, in fact, to advise and appear on behalf of the Crown.
Nowadays, they are completely independent and may act for anybody.

The Bar is the most prodigal of its talents of any profession. The
competition is very great. Every call-day, numbers of aspiring
young men and women are called to the Bar. Of these, a few start in
practice. Many of them drop out after a time. Of those that remain,
most will earn a modest income. A small minority will become really
successful, becoming judges and 'fashionable silks' with large incomes. Success at the Bar calls for good luck, keen intelligence and
a robust constitution to stand the hard work and long hours.

Assuming anybody to be so rash as to wish to become a barrister

[1] The gown of Queen's Counsel is silk, as opposed to the junior's which
is of 'stuff'. Hence the colloquialisms 'silk' and 'stuff-gownsman'.

what does he do? The training is very different from that of a solicitor. He must join one of the Inns of Court as a student, usually paying a substantial deposit. Then he must keep twelve terms. This takes three years. Terms are kept by dining in Hall a certain number of times. Dining in Hall is usually accompanied by a certain amount of ceremonial, which varies with the Inns.

Besides keeping terms, the student must pass the Bar examinations, in two parts. When he passes the Final and has kept nine of his terms, the student is proposed for call by a Bencher of his Inn. He is then called to the Bar by the Benchers. If he intends to practise, he will then read in the chambers of a junior barrister, usually for twelve months. This practical experience as a pupil is indispensable, in fact, but is not required as a preliminary to being called to the Bar.[1]

The robes of barristers vary according as they are of Queen's Counsel or juniors. The full dress of a 'silk' consists of a full-bottomed wig and a silk gown (hence the name) worn over court dress of velvet coat, knee-breeches, black silk stockings and buckled shoes. This is normally worn only for the procession which opens the Law Courts and as part of the procedure of taking silk. The new 'silks' must go to every court sitting in the Law Courts, and each must make a bow to every presiding judge. For everyday wear, Queen's Counsel wear an ordinary barrister's wig (bob-wig) and a gown which is not made of silk but of different pattern from that of a junior, worn over a tail-coat of distinctive appearance.

The solicitor's branch of the profession is essentially different from the Bar. Solicitors may act as advocates in the Crown Court, County Courts and Magistrates' Courts. The bulk of the work of most solicitors is not litigation but consists of conveyancing, the drawing of wills and other documents, and other non-contentious business. The relationship between barrister and solicitor is similar, in many ways, to that between specialist and general medical practitioner. The solicitor is as much a business man as lawyer in many cases. Since the National Health Service was introduced, the family solicitor is tending to replace the family doctor as adviser on many matters outside the sphere of purely professional advice.

The professional body which controls the activities of solicitors is the Law Society. It admits solicitors and can suspend or strike

[1] Students about to be called must undertake not to practise unless they intend to read as a pupil for at least twelve months.

them off the roll for misconduct. The code of professional etiquette of solicitors is stringent, though not so restrictive as that of the Bar; for example, a solicitor may be a legal adviser to a business or association, yet remain in private practice.

Whereas barrister's fees are not regulated by statute, those of solicitors are. Solicitors' bills of costs must be drawn up in accordance with the Solicitors Act, 1957. A client who objects to a bill of costs may take it to a Taxing Master, who will disallow exorbitant items.

A solicitor may be sued for negligence in his advice or conduct of a case.

To qualify as a solicitor the aspirant must pass an intermediate and then a final examination. He must be articled to a practising solicitor for a period of, usually, five years. During that time, he must receive approved instruction in the law. When these requirements have been satisfied, the articled clerk is entitled to be admitted a solicitor. Before practising, however, he must take out a practising certificate. The Law Society may suspend or revoke this for misconduct.

A lucrative position usually filled by solicitors is that of Town Clerk. This office is of great dignity and importance in a large city. A humbler but important position occupied by many solicitors is that of clerk to lay justices. He is their legal adviser and on him rests a grave responsibility for seeing law and procedure are observed, especially in view of the enormous mass of cases that come before lay magistrates.

The word solicitor is derived from those persons who used to solicit the officials of the Court of Chancery on behalf of litigants. Those acting for litigants in the Common Law Courts were known as attorneys, those in the Courts of Probate, Divorce and Admiralty as proctors.

Certain solicitors are licensed as commissioners for oaths. They may administer oaths and take affidavits but not in any matter in which they are interested as solicitors.

The public as a whole has a distrust of lawyers. They are generally supposed to be avaricious. A carving in an Assize Court in Wales depicts two men—one pulling at the head of a cow, the other pulling on its tail in the opposite direction. A man in wig and gown meanwhile sits, milking the cow. Whilst the impression is popular, it is a misleading one, for the profession is generous with its time and learning in helping those unable to afford the normal costs of legal advice. Formerly 'poor man's lawyer' centres gave free legal advice, but the position is altered now. How does the Legal Aid system work nowadays?

Legal aid in criminal cases is governed by s. 4 of the Criminal Justice Act, 1967, and in civil cases by the Legal Aid and Advice Acts, 1949 and 1960. Legal aid extends to the House of Lords, Court of Appeal, High Court, Crown Court, Magistrates Court and County Courts.

Dealing first with civil cases, certain proceedings are exempted from the Legal Aid and Advice Acts. These are actions for defamation, relator actions,[1] election petitions and judgment summonses.

The part of the Act introducing free legal advice apart from the carrying on of proceedings was implemented in 1959. This was replaced in 1973 by the £25 scheme as recommended by the Legal Aid Advisory Committee. This new addition is the scheme for assisting those of restricted means contained in the Legal Advice and Assistance Act, 1972.

For an applicant to obtain legal aid, his 'disposable income' must not exceed £1175 per annum. 'Disposable income' is gross income less tax, rent, allowance for dependants, etc. Neither will legal aid normally be given to those whose capital, less certain deductions, exceeds £1200. However, most persons who receive legal aid will have to bear part of their costs. This contribution may be payable by instalments. Persons with a 'disposable income' of less than £375 and a 'disposable capital' of less than £250 will not be required to make any contribution.

The legal aid scheme is operated by the Law Society. A person desiring legal aid and eligible must apply to the Local Committee under the Act, giving details of his financial circumstances and cause of action. Barristers and solicitors are both on the committee, which decides whether legal aid shall be granted. If it is, the applicant is given a Civil Aid Certificate. This entitles him to counsel and solicitor of his own choosing[2]—provided they undertake legal aid work—to take all necessary proceedings.[3] Their fees and the Court fees are borne by the State through the Legal Aid Fund.

[1] Actions brought in the name of the Attorney-General.
[2] Further leave is necessary for some steps, such as employment of Queen's Counsel.
[3] Legal Aid Act, 1964, s. 1.

A legally aided person has an important privilege. His liability by virtue of an order for costs made against him with respect to the proceedings shall not exceed the amount (if any) which is a reasonable one for him to pay, having regard to all the circumstances, including the means of all the parties and their conduct in connection with the dispute. Successful unassisted opponents of legally aided persons may now be awarded costs out of the Legal Aid Fund.[1]

Costs recovered by a legally aided person with respect to the proceedings shall be paid to the Legal Aid Fund.

In criminal cases, there are provisions for legal aid under the Criminal Justice Act, 1967. Generally, representation will be by a solicitor and counsel, but in the Magistrates' Courts it will generally be by solicitor, except in the case of an indictable offence serious enough to make the presence of counsel desirable.

The Court will make a legal aid order when it appears desirable to do so in the interests of justice. It must do so when the person is committed for trial on a charge of murder, and where the prosecution appeals to the House of Lords. When considering granting legal aid the Court must be satisfied that the applicant requires assistance in meeting the costs. To assist in this the applicant must produce a written statement of his means and the Court will also request the Supplementary Benefits Commission to inquire into the applicant's means. Where a doubt arises as to whether to grant legal aid the doubt is resolved in the applicant's favour.

In some circumstances a person for whom legal aid has been ordered may be required to make a contribution towards the costs.

The Courts Act, 1971, provides that costs in criminal cases may be ordered to be paid out of central funds.

Besides legal aid, there is the famous procedure known as the Dock Brief by which an accused who is not represented may select any member of the Bar present in the Court to represent him. However, with the growth of legal aid, the procedure is now of little importance.

The extension of the legal aid scheme to criminal cases is to be welcomed, and sufficient has been done both in the civil and criminal field to take some of, if not all, the sting from Lord Darling's aphorism that the law, like the Ritz Hotel, is open to all.

A little learning is a dangerous thing. It would be foolish to pretend that a reader who has absorbed this book is thereby fit to be his

[1] Legal Aid Act, 1964, s. 1.

own solicitor. But if it has given him some idea of when he ought to consult a solicitor, that will be something. As in medicine, so in law, prevention is better than cure, from the layman's point of view at any rate.

More important than this, however, is the necessity for every citizen to know something of the law that touches him at every point, and of whose operation he is constantly reading in the newspapers. The English legal system, though we may not always realise it, is a precious thing. It belongs to all of us, not merely to the lawyers. If this book has stimulated the reader's interest in matters legal, and has lit even one small candle in a hitherto Stygian blackness, it 'will not have been written in vain'.

Index

TEACH YOURSELF BOOKS

LOGIC
A. A. Luce

Dr. Luce here presents a straightforward and fundamental introduction to that most essential of all philosophical disciplines, logic. His book clearly and concisely examines the developing structure of logical thought, from terms, propositions and syllogisms to reduction and the principles of reasoning.

The whole purpose of *Logic* is to encourage the reader to develop and acquire a knowledge of logic which will enable him to think and argue successfully within the structure established by it.

UNITED KINGDOM	75p
AUSTRALIA (recommended)	$2.45
NEW ZEALAND	$2.55
CANADA	$2.75
ISBN 0 340 18264 4	

Available wherever Teach Yourself Books are sold.

TEACH YOURSELF BOOKS

ETHICS

A. C. Ewing

In very simple terms Ethics is the systematic study of what the words 'good' and 'bad', 'right' and 'wrong' mean. As a branch of philosophy it is therefore most immediately concerned with the human character and conduct, and this becomes particularly true when one regards the problems imposed upon society by the development of modern science.

Dr. Ewing, an Honorary Fellow of Jesus College, Cambridge, and a Fellow of the British Academy, has made a study of this 'moral science' in which he discusses not only its history and development but also its importance to the individual in modern society.

Through examining and commenting on the work of the great moral philosophers in the past and relating this to the study of Ethics today, Dr. Ewing has written a book which is both humane, learned and a clear and readable introduction to this, the most relevant of philosophical studies.

UNITED KINGDOM	95P
AUSTRALIA (recommended)	$3.05
NEW ZEALAND	$3.20
ISBN 0 340 05577 4	

Available wherever Teach Yourself Books are sold.

TEACH YOURSELF BOOKS

POLITICAL THOUGHT

C. L. Wayper & C. W. Parkin

Political thought must be concerned with determining the *morality* of the State, with deciding whether its nature and purpose are justifiable in terms of the individual.

This book examines the major ideas of the State that have emerged during the history of Western Society. The Greek, in particular Platonic, concept of the State as an organism is the starting point from which the author embarks on a discussion of the history of Political Thought, ranging through the scientific rationalism of Mill and Bentham, and the subsequent Romantic reaction, typified by Rousseau, to the Marxist concept of the State as Class.

This expanded edition includes a new chapter, *The State as Permanent Revolution*, an account of Maoist China, by C. W. Parkin of Cambridge University.

UNITED KINGDOM	50p
AUSTRALIA (recommended)	$1·50
NEW ZEALAND	$1·50
CANADA	$1·95

IBSN 0 340 17887 6

Available wherever Teach Yourself Books are sold.

TEACH YOURSELF BOOKS

HISTORY OF PHILOSOPHY

J. Lewis

In providing a historical narrative of philosophy, this book sets out to describe the chief rival attitudes towards life and its meaning, as they have developed during the history of Western thought.

To cover the history of philosophy from the Pre-Socratics through to Hegel, Whitehead and Popper is an immense task; in this slim volume Dr. Lewis has only attempted to communicate some insight into these philosophers' major ideas and their historical inter-action or conflict with each other.

As such, *History of Philosophy* will be read both by the general reader seeking to understand the development of thought in the West and by the student looking for an introduction to the major philosophers and philosophical movements of Western history.

UNITED KINGDOM	50p
AUSTRALIA (recommended)	$1·50
NEW ZEALAND	$1·50
CANADA	$1·95

ISBN 0 340 05682 7

Available wherever Teach Yourself Books are sold.